A NEW THEORY ON COUPLES,
RELATIONSHIPS AND LOVE

The

Story

of

WE

DIMITRA DOUMPIOTI

First paperback edition April 2021

Cover design by Matt Davies
Interior design by David Ter-Avanesyan/Ter33Design
Illustrations by Margarita Ulrich

ISBN 978-84-09-29607-1

www.dimitradoumpioti.com

To Greg,

And our wonderful WE.

To Danae and Alex

For making it all so beautiful.

CONTENTS

INTRODUCTION

I was once told that I was in love with love. It was a long time ago; I must have been around sixteen. I did not quite understand what it meant at the time. I cannot even say I fully understand it now. It was a therapist's insight—the kind of esoteric pronouncement that we, clinicians, produce sometimes, platitudes that sound transcendent and intelligent but do not make much sense to the recipient. And it stuck with me, as it happens, for a few decades. I do not think this was the "author's" intention. Nevertheless, as a diligent client and wisdom-seeker, I turned it over and over in my mind, until I arrived at the conclusion that it was not a matter of being "in love with love"; it was more about being "an advocate of love."

Which sounds even worse, I think. There is nothing cool or sexy about being an advocate of love—or anything of the sort, really. Yet, it is important. Love is important. It moves the world, and the lack of it does, too. In my view, love has to be understood and addressed if we are to survive and evolve as a species, and it will also need advocates. Despite its centrality to human existence, many of us seem to be less than keen to acknowledge it or study it—not even in disciplines such as psychology, where it should occupy a central position. Love is not very present in science as a whole, despite the fact that no scientist is exempt from longing for the acceptance of a parent, the fascination of a lover, the unconditional admiration of a protégé. In fact, such "longing" may be precisely what draws some people to science in the first place. The same goes for politicians, CEOs, and other people in power. In fact, *their* "love issues" and profound "love" insecurities are threatening to place our planet in checkmate. And still,

this force, which moves us to be who we are and do what we do, has not been adequately addressed or studied.

As far as I am concerned, understanding the workings of love is essential to understanding human nature. Even more important is the study of love in the context of romantic relationships. Couples have been widely ignored by science. Yet, in my opinion, they constitute the most important social unit in our society.

Within the couple, in its many different shapes and forms, lies the most fascinating and extraordinary social structure there is. This minimal expression of a human system integrates and embodies every important characteristic and facet of human life, from the micro to the macro, across disciplines and across time. It is all there. To understand the couple is to understand our nature and the whole of human history. Everything starts with the couple. It is the system that conceives, gives birth to, construes, and sustains our world. After more than twenty years working in mental health, I have come to believe that everything—what works and what does not work—about our society boils down to the dynamics that emerge within this unique, intimate relationship.

We are each the product of a couple. Most of us were born, raised, and forged within its microcosm. Everything that is lived and witnessed within it, or was indirectly delivered to us through stories about it, molds us into who we are. We carry this relationship within us—the reality of it, its narrative, or the fantasy of it. No matter what, it is there in our minds and hearts, and defines who we are, how we move in this world, and how we relate to ourselves and others.

In family therapy, mental health issues are more often than not related to couples issues. In my practice, I have not yet come across an individual (child or adult) presenting a severe mental health disorder whose parents' relationship was lived as a happy, loving one. Healthy brains require good parenting, and good parenting is heavily dependent on balanced, constructive relationships between the caregivers. Yet the study of couples has so far not been central in psychology—nor in any discipline, for that matter. It seems to have gotten lost somewhere between the divisions and cracks of academia. Maybe this oversight is simply a reflection of the fact that the more scientifically inclined among our species are scared of intimacy. I do not know. I do think, however, that any version of a better world will require policymaking based on the impact of love or the lack of it and on people (individuals, couples, families, and communities) having the tools and know-how to build and sustain wholesome, healthy relationships.

I have been working specifically with couples for more than a decade now. As the director of an international psychotherapy center in a cosmopolitan city, I have had the privilege of working directly with (and of supervising indirectly) hundreds of couples of all ages, walks of life, cultures, races, and sexual orientations, from all over the world. Together with my team, I have been able to observe how powerful these relationships are for the individuals who compose them and for those indirectly or directly involved with them. I have witnessed and worked within their extremely constructive and destructive potential. I have observed what makes individuals and couples different from one another, and, even more important, I have had the opportunity to explore those aspects that are universal. This book focuses, above all, on "the universals." Given the infinite variety of dynamics within and between individuals, this book is also unavoidably limited. Nevertheless, it is my hope that all readers, no matter their particular characteristics, will be able to find parts of themselves and their loved ones within its pages.

Toward a More Unified Theory of Love and Coupledom

There is a huge, very well-established division in our minds, traditions, and, consequently, educational institutions between the arts and the sciences. These two spheres, both in the service of promoting knowledge and human development, were once fused. In the times of the ancient Greeks, to give an example, philosophy encompassed all bodies of knowledge, including aesthetics and natural philosophy, the mother of all sciences. Nevertheless, the arts and sciences have since evolved in apparently different directions. More than two millennia later, the two realms are barely on speaking terms. There are exceptions, of course, and the need for integration is increasingly acknowledged, but at this moment the arts hardly ever employ the language of science, and the scientific realm rarely acknowledges the accumulated wisdom of those fields defined as the arts and humanities. Psychology uncomfortably straddles this divide.

Such dichotomy may have been useful in our quest to obtain certain types of knowledge. At the same time, divisions can easily turn into traps. The separation of art and science has also ended up gravely hindering the development and evolution of our understanding of the world as an undivided whole.

One of the many consequences of this division is that the disciplines within the two realms have developed in very different ways. The implementation of the scientific method within the fields labeled as "science" has led to broad areas of consensus between the professionals that comprise them. In the realm of the arts and humanities, the opposite is the case. There is very little consensus on practically anything. The more we approach the human factor, the less the common ground (i.e., universal agreements on theoretical premises) we find. Thus, most scientists will agree on a great deal of things in fields such as physics, math, geography, geology, biology, and, to a large degree, medicine. The opposite is the case in almost any field that explores the human condition, mind, or behavior. For example, although medicine is generally categorized as "science," psychiatry—one of its specialties—is a field of study with little consensus. There is no universally accepted theory on what drives human behavior, nor is there a universally accepted theory on psychopathology.

Psychiatry is a battlefield. There are huge differences in criteria for practically everything related to both diagnosis and, even more so, treatment. The *Diagnostic and Statistical Manual of Mental Disorders*—the bible of mental health diagnosis, used internationally—is simply descriptive for this very reason. It categorizes symptoms and gives them a name, without attempting to explain their underlying causes. Despite this dangerous oversimplification, there is still no consensus. We continue to disagree over the descriptions, over what constitutes or does not constitute a mental disorder. If no agreement can be reached on how we name what we observe, then reaching consensus on the causes has been simply—and sadly—impossible. To this day, there is no globally embraced framework that explains the human mind and behavior.

What does this mean for the professionals who dedicate our lives and work to "treating people"? The main issue is that we have no solid ground to stand on. We can never be (and should never feel) totally certain about the premises that inform our practice. Each of us has had to create a theoretical map to serve as a guide through this extraordinary yet still quite confusing territory. The pioneering explorers reached it from different directions, approached it in different ways, focused on different parts of it, attributed different names and labels to what they were seeing, and came to very diverse conclusions about their experiences.

The clinician's map will therefore be biased and limited. It may even exist in opposition to another's map, as it will be based on their particular training, the academic literature they have been exposed to, the pioneers they have "endorsed," the institutions they have worked for, and also their personal belief systems. Most of our clients do not know this. This peculiarity compels some professionals to share the theory that informs their intervention; most do not. It is a complicated and tiring enterprise to revise the ABCs of one's work over and over again.

So, one of the first reasons for this book coming to be was purely practical. I needed a text that summarized the theoretical premises of my work. It started with my clients asking for more information and references. They would often express great interest in the concepts we were working on and wanted to learn more, but when I referred them to the sources, most people found them too dense and too difficult to absorb. Then I would refer them to more standard self-help books. However, in those texts, the theory that informed my practice was almost nowhere to be found.

With the passing of time, I also came to realize that my theoretical framework had considerably expanded. I had come to a particular synthesis of theory that was not expressed in any other text. And so this book came to be, initially intended for my clients, and then also for my students: a brief synthesis of everything I learned in almost three decades of ongoing studies and two decades of clinical practice.

The main axis holding together and integrating these theoretical approaches has always been my clinical and life experience. Psychological theory only makes sense, in my view, if it is lived. When I was a university student, becoming acquainted with different approaches (cognitive-behavioral, psychoanalytic, humanistic, transpersonal, systemic, etc.) and divisions within psychology (social, neuroscience, abnormal), it felt as if I was moving between different worlds. It did not even occur to me then that all of that knowledge actually connected. Now, many years later, the accumulation of personal and professional experience, in combination with the invaluable contributions of theorists who have proposed extremely wide and integrative epistemological maps—including Eric Kandel, Boris Cyrulnik, Ken Wilber, Dan Siegel, Luigi Cancrini, and Lorna Smith Benjamin, to name a few—I have finally found a way to piece things together and come up with a theory in which, at least in principle, most ends meet.

It is important, in my view, for clinicians and researchers to join forces in order to integrate the maps available and aim for a global view of the human being that incorporates data and accumulated knowledge of existing disciplines and schools of thought. Sociologists, psychologists, psychotherapists, psychiatrists, psychoanalysts, neuroscientists, neurologists, and medical doctors cannot simply continue existing in parallel universes. The lack of unity and integration between and within disciplines is probably the most serious problem in the field of mental health, to the point of being, in my view, dangerous to the people we are supposed to benefit. As long as we worship different "gods," while only attending our particular academic churches and fighting or ignoring the discoveries and developments of neighboring communities, there can be no peace and no real progress. So this work also reflects my particular effort to build bridges and integrate knowledge. It is an adventurous and creative synthesis of theory. The conceptual pillars that have inspired it include systems theory, the theory of evolution, attachment theory, interpersonal reconstructive therapy, systemic family therapy, and transpersonal psychology, with echoes from Jungian analysis, psychoanalytic theory, and transactional analysis. Concepts and knowledge coming from biology, evolutionary biology, neuroscience, and interpersonal neurobiology have also been particularly influential. For those who wish to gain a better understanding of how the above approaches and theories have informed the ideas presented here, a brief summary of the main points has been included in the appendix at the end of the book.

This is not a scholarly text. There is no need for the reader to have any background information in order to understand the ideas presented here. As the author of a book for the general public, I've endeavored to make it as user-friendly, easy to read and understand, and enjoyable as possible.

My wish for this work, which I have greatly enjoyed putting together, is to serve as a source of knowledge, insight, stimulation, and also entertainment for anyone who wishes to become better oriented in the realm of human relationships in general and couples in particular. I hope that the information within these pages is useful to those who are looking for change, feel lost, or struggle in their relationships, setting a foundation for more constructive, mature, and loving ways to approach our partners—and ourselves, too. The aim is not to give advice or to tell readers what to do, but rather to explain and provide a useful map, so that one can feel more familiar, hopeful, and confident within what is still a mostly unknown, often misunderstood, yet fascinating territory.

May you enjoy the journey.

PART I

LOVE IN THEORY

I do not know how Archimedes felt when he screamed, "Eureka!" but I definitely felt a rush of excitement when I became acquainted with proponents of systems theory twenty years ago. I had already finished my degree in psychology at the time and was seriously thinking of abandoning the field altogether. Psychology had felt interesting and attractive but had not impressed me enough. Systems theory did. It was like discovering the works of Einstein after devoting years to the study of Newtonian physics.

The systemic-relational approach blew my mind. It was a cross-disciplinary theory that provided a lens to infinite connections. Not only did it help me unify all that I had studied, experienced, and learned up to that point, but it also invited me to go far beyond, as the theory enabled a holistic view of all existing systems on the face of the earth—in fact, the entire universe.

Systems thinking offers synthesis rather than analysis, a vision of the global rather than the dissection of the parts. It introduces causality in circular rather than linear terms. It studies the interaction of the elements rather than the elements themselves. Actually, the divide between "being" and "acting"—identity and behavior—ceases to be relevant, as action determines form, and form conditions action in a continuous dialectic. In other words, it provided me with a way to explore and understand the world as an undivided whole within the realm of science. And this has occupied my work and thinking ever since.

The ideas proposed here are based on the understanding that humans belong to the universe that they emerged from and that our makeup is inevitably and intimately related to the makeup of the rest of nature. We are conditioned and defined by forces that are all too common in the workings of the world.

The Primal Couple

Journeying all the way to the beginning of the universe with the big bang theory, we encounter forces that initially formed a dense, unified whole. Their separation meant the birth of the universe; their interaction, its expansion. The world—indeed, the entire universe—we could say, initiated its existence and evolution thanks to the emergence, differentiation, and interaction of interdependent forces.

The interplay of such forces is what we will be looking at, all the way from the big bang to subjective human experience. From a systemic standpoint, emergence—the appearance of something novel (something that has properties that its parts do not have)—requires a system. The evolution of the world is very much about the emergent properties of systems. So if everything that has emerged following the big bang is contemplated in systemic terms, we look for a common denominator that could link any system to any other.

Such a denominator may be found in the very makeup and definition of a system. A system, in order to be defined as such, requires that the different elements that compose it are interrelated. The elements need to be both connected and, at the same time, differentiated from the rest of the components, in order for the system to form and function. This requires two forces: the force that connects and the force that divides.

Connection is the force that brings things together, pushing toward fusion, unity, the undivided and undifferentiated whole. *Autonomy* is the force that separates, that creates new elements, new entities. It is the force that promotes differentiation.

In terms of the system's definition as a "cohesive conglomeration of interrelated and interdependent parts," connection is the force that ensures the "interrelated and interdependent" side of things. It makes sure that things stay together. Autonomy cares for the parts. It ensures the integrity, identity, and structure of each element that composes a system. The interaction of *connection* and *autonomy* as a pair of opposing, complementary forces could therefore constitute a binary code for any existing system.

The idea of opposing forces is not new. To quote Newton, "For every action, there is an equal and opposite reaction."[1] According to Newton, forces always come in pairs known as "action-reaction force pairs." American philosopher Ken Wilber described the world as composed of "holons" that are both wholes and parts at the same time, each consisting of two "drives": *agency* and *communion*. Agency preserves the unit's integrity. Communion ensures its connection as part of other wholes.

The idea is that *connection* and *autonomy*, as defined here, constitute a "primal couple" that conditions and defines the expression of all living and nonliving systems alike. Systems such as our brains, divided into left and right hemispheres, or the autonomic nervous system, made up of the sympathetic and parasympathetic nervous systems, are thought to correspond to the interplay between these two forces within and between systems. The very way humans have understood and defined the world may also be related to this primal couple: life and death, day and night, male and female, active and passive, reason and emotion, order and chaos, masculine and feminine. Politics has been largely understood as divided into the right and left wings, academia into science and art, and science itself into hard and soft sciences. It could be that connection and autonomy have a lot to do with the binary expressions of the world as we have defined it.

These forces appear to be opposed, but they are, in fact, codependent. They define and regulate one another, igniting and sustaining life as well as driving the evolution of the universe. Let's explore this pair of forces within the human realm, in ways that are familiar to us.

Connection

Imagine that an individual is an open system and that, as all other open living systems, one must stay connected to the bigger (eco)system for survival. How do humans do it? How do human systems connect?

We connect every time we breathe. We take in air, and part of it then forms part of our body. We connect every time we eat. We take in food, and it is then transformed to form part of ourselves. By breathing and eating, we take in a little bit of the world, and then we expel it. Without this constant communion with our context, life is impossible. We die. We need to stay connected and actively form part of our environment.

With just a simple glance at our bodies, we can observe that we are shaped to be in constant communication and interaction, a never-ending give-and-take with the world. We are designed as open systems, like everything in nature. We cannot survive unless we are linked, "charged," and sustained by our context at all times. Nature has devised a great number of ways for us to stay connected to our environment.

Within the human community, connection manifests itself through experiences that we access through our emotions. We connect when we look at each other lovingly, through a kind gesture or gaze, when we hug, when we smile at one another, when we hold hands, and when we communicate, share ideas, and feel understood. Every time we feel loved, accompanied, protected, or cared for, we connect.

We connect when we play or laugh together, when we have a common project or goal, when we fight for the same causes, or when we support the same team or flag or religion. We also connect every time we emulate our loved ones and our mentors, when we follow their rules and wishes, or when we meet their expectations—good and terrible alike. There are infinite ways to emotionally connect with the people and the world around us. The way we do so may vary widely. What is universal is the need itself.

Connection is essential to life. We cannot survive or flourish unless we keep an active, constant, and emotionally nurturing bond to our context. There is ample scientific evidence to support this notion. Harry Harlow, with his famous experiments on rhesus monkeys, was one of the first to introduce to the scientific world the importance of social contact.[2] Through his experiments, he showed that caregiving and companionship are paramount for cognitive development, social ability, and emotional balance. John Bowlby, another majorly influential psychologist whose work is closely related to Harlow's, dedicated his life's work to the study of human attachment. Among his immense contributions, he proposed that a warm, intimate, and continuous relationship with a parental figure is necessary for a healthy psychological and emotional development. The research in the field has exponentially grown since then, and it is now widely accepted that when individuals are deprived of emotional nurture and social contact, especially in the earlier stages of life—even when the basic needs for food and shelter are met—their cognitive, neurological, emotional, and social development are affected or even severely impaired.

Connection, then, is the force that binds us and is fundamental to our survival and well-being. Let's now have a look at its counterpart.

Autonomy

Autonomy opposes yet complements connection. It represents independence, differentiation, separateness. It is about being visible as a separate entity to whoever or whatever surrounds us. It is the part maintaining its identity and unique properties within the whole. Thanks to autonomy, the "I" is distinguished from its context. It is the force that provides us with a "skin," limit, and border. Autonomy facilitates definition.

We would be invisible if we were not defined, named, differentiated. We would be part of an amorphous whole. It would mean death: "Ashes to ashes, dust to dust." Life forms need to "hatch," in one way or another, into the world. As we name and define people and things, we make them visible and we attribute to them a separate identity. Definition itself is an act of autonomy. We could say that definition is an act of separation.

Autonomy is about experiencing ourselves as different from others, about having an identity that distinguishes us from the rest, or having thoughts and agency of our own. Our immune system would be, in these terms, the guard of our autonomy on a physical level, keeping our organism safe and separate from entities or organisms that seek a destructive fusion with us. Autonomy between humans is about self-affirmation: the acknowledgment, acceptance, or empowerment of one's separate identity. It is present when we strive to become better, to grow stronger, to accomplish personal goals, and when we compete or yearn to be seen, to be acknowledged, or to stand out.

There is a lot of literature on autonomy in psychology, especially in the relational and systemic fields, mostly defined as *differentiation*. Mental health is heavily related to our level of differentiation from our family of origin, according to system theorists such as Murray Bowen, a pioneer in the field, who described the process in his book *Toward the Differentiation of Self in One's Family of Origin*.[3] The more untangled the "I" is from its original context, the better the mental health of the individual. Lorna Smith Benjamin, an interpersonal, psychodynamic theorist, has defined it as a differentiation from the "family in the head," claiming that all severe mental health conditions, such as personality disorders, are a failure of differentiation from the internalized representations of our caregivers.[4]

Much as physical health is about preserving the integrity, wholeness, and separateness of our physical body in relation to our environment in general (while always maintaining the connection), mental health depends on maintaining the integrity, separateness, and wholeness of our self and personal identity, primarily in relation to other humans (while, again, always maintaining the connection). Within the human realm, autonomy, in its most constructive version, is expressed when we "give wings" to ourselves and to others, when we allow people to be different without feeling attacked or attacking them, when we can view and accept others (especially our loved ones) as separate entities from ourselves, when we praise or celebrate someone else's identity or existence, with the understanding that they do not belong to us, nor do we claim their accomplishments as our own. Giving autonomy tends to be far more challenging than claiming it for oneself. As with connection, the give-and-take of autonomy may be expressed in a great variety of ways in our lives. What is universal, again, is the need itself.

We have now defined the two fundamental needs: connection and autonomy. Both are essential to keep us alive. Yet extreme expressions of the one or the other can severely threaten our lives, our mental health, or both.

Belonging and Autonomy "in Action"

These two opposite forces keep us moving, growing, and evolving. Our brain is largely structured and shaped to cater to each of them. The right hemisphere is predominantly about connection. The left hemisphere is an autonomy specialist. Together, they make sure that our different needs are met, despite (or thanks to) their apparent opposition. In a way, this collaboration between the left and right hemispheres represents an original "coupling" that operates from within our very own skull!

Our bodily processes are also shaped to cater at all times to connection and autonomy. Glucose regulation is an example: When sugar is low in our body, our sense of hunger is activated. We respond to this need by consuming a fraction of our surroundings, transforming other organic matter into ourselves as it fuses with us. Every time we eat, we are, in essence, merging with the world around us. If the sense of hunger continued indefinitely, we might continue to eat until we died. But nature has also provided us with the opposite mechanism—satiety—that helps us maintain some distance and separation from the world (and a few hours of autonomy) by allowing us to feel "full."

The "dance" between connection and autonomy works in a very similar way in interpersonal terms. Let's take a look at the behavior of little kids during playtime. They may go off and play by themselves for a while, taking a few steps away to explore, but they will, sooner or later, seek contact with their caregivers. Children will move between connection and autonomy all day, every day, depending on their needs at different times and in different situations. When they have enough of one, they will seek the other. If one part of the cycle is missing—if they are not able to connect, or not able to explore, for whatever reason—they will become tense and express discomfort. And if the absence of either part of the cycle becomes a constant, their development may be at risk, to the point of being severely compromised or impaired.

Another example of the belonging-autonomy dance is found in the structure of our daily life. We go from a place of belonging (home) toward autonomy (the world outside), and we then return home, repeating the same "circle" day after day. A world without a home is scary and dangerous; a home without the world can be suffocating, like a prison.

As with food intake and glucose regulation, our organism does not appreciate going too far in either direction. We do far better when we can move between the two opposing poles. There is no "perfect medium" either. Standing at the door, finding and staying somewhere in the middle between autonomy and connection, will not do the trick. We need to move continuously—to "dance"—from one territory to the other: from home to the world and from the world to home; connection-autonomy, autonomy-connection. This may be an explanation of why political parties have never really worked very well. A fixed position on the left, right, or center does not and cannot cater to the needs of the whole. We need the dance individually and collectively, too.

The power and tension between the two needs is found in probably every significant experience in our lives. A lot of our problems and inner battles are intimately connected to situations when these two forces are in conflict. These are moments when we feel "split" in two: To stay or to go? To eat or not eat? To call or not call? To speak up or keep silent? To say yes or no? To be or not to be? Such tensions urge us to "decide" what is a greater priority for our survival and well-being at each given moment.

A simple example could be the ultimatum of a partner (e.g., "If you go on that trip, we are over") or a parent (e.g., "If you choose this profession or that partner, you might as well forget about this family"). Automatically, one is faced with the impossible task of resolving the need for connection and autonomy within a situation that does not allow room for both. Do I lose myself to the relationship or do I lose the relationship to defend myself? Our "primitive" (reptilian and limbic) brain, in charge of our survival, approaches such dilemmas in very simple terms: a choice between death or death—that is, death if I go (I cut off my main source of connection) versus death if I stay (my autonomy is compromised).Our reactions can therefore be extremely intense, even in cases where, at first glance, the issues themselves do not seem to be particularly significant or important. Unfortunately, we have not yet been trained to recognize this dilemma for what it truly is, so most of our attempts to resolve such tensions tend to focus on trying to control one of the two needs or to make one go away, inevitably leading to greater tension, distress, and, quite often, far greater problems.

Sometimes, the tension created between the forces goes beyond the normal and the ordinary, creating important blockages or deadlocks, extreme ambivalence, or impossible dilemmas that we are called to resolve but cannot. It means war: inner wars within individuals; interpersonal wars within couples or families; or greater wars between communities, nations, or races. No matter what the battlefield is, at the heart of every conflict within an individual, a couple, a family, a state, or the world lies an unresolved tension between these two needs. We will now look at how these forces give shape to and act upon different systems in general.

On Parts and Wholes

Transpersonal and systems theory provide language and a wide enough framework that allows us to observe how human systems and human experience relate to an infinite variety of other systems in the universe. According to these theories, the world is made up of units that form parts of wholes (systems) that in turn form parts (subsystems) of other wholes (bigger systems), ad infinitum.

There is a brilliant term for this phenomenon, coined by Hungarian-British theorist Arthur Koestler and further described by American philosopher Ken Wilber: the *holon*. This term refers to an entity that is a whole and simultaneously a part of some other whole. Geometric fractals, with their self-similar patterns that are repeated at multiple scales, illustrate this concept quite effectively. Thus, everything we define as a part is also a whole, and every whole is also a part of a different whole that is also a part of something else. This implies that nothing is totally whole, nor is just a part. Every whole-part has a different identity, properties, and purpose in relation to the parts that it is made up of and the whole that it belongs to.

In the human realm, we could use the human cell as an example: The cell is a whole in itself, with its own specific properties. At the same time, it is part of a group of cells that, let's say, form an organ—a whole in itself—that has properties and functions that are different from that of the individual cells. The organ is, in turn, a part of a body with a distinct identity. That individual in turn may be part of a couple, with its own identity, history, and purpose, that is also part of a bigger society, and so on and so forth.

In short, everything in the world is a part and a whole at the same time. Nothing is fully whole and nothing is just a part. There are no absolutes. Everything will, in one way or another, depend on some other entity, organism, or structure. At the same time, everything will maintain some level of independence.

Why is all this so important? We could say that within these fundamental concepts lies the essence of the couple's nature and dynamics. The dance between the parts and the wholes is the very dance that takes place within and between individuals, couples, families, and human communities of all kinds.

Each one of us starts off as both a whole (individual) and a part of a whole (family). And then many of us go off to become a part again of another whole (couple) that itself creates and becomes part of a greater whole (family with children). The parts that the whole produces (children) will heavily depend on the whole (family) for their survival, but when ready, they will leave the family nest as wholes eager to begin new projects as parts of other wholes (e.g., couples).

We will be asked, by life, by nature, and most likely by ourselves, to make everything—every holon—work. And they will all be pulling in different directions. The two forces, connection and autonomy, will help us both maintain the connection of the parts in order to create a whole and, at the same time, allow us to maintain the frontiers of each whole-part, so that every part and every whole survive. This means that each holon, in order to maintain its integrity (i.e., preserve both its "wholeness" and its "partness"), will need to be connected and separate at the same time (separate, in order to maintain the integrity and unique qualities of the part; connected, in order to serve and survive as a part of the whole and promote its qualities too). The two forces will therefore be present in every single interaction between elements in order to ensure their survival and evolution.

As we learn to understand our lives and the wider picture of nature in terms of these dynamics, we start to drift away from notions of "good" or "bad." Judgment ceases to be relevant. We may be more or less constructive (or destructive) in the ways we employ to meet our needs of autonomy and connection, but there is nothing inherently good or bad about the needs themselves. Everyone will do their best to resolve their "partness" or "wholeness" within a given context. The context will shape the individual, and the individual will shape the context. It is a dance of holons and a universe in constant movement and evolution. As we come to see it and accept it, we will be able to marvel at the world in all its expression—including the denizen creatures (those holons named humans) as they strive to survive and evolve.

A New Synthesis

Placing these insights within the frameworks provided by the study of biology and evolution, we find that within every individual and couple—every "holon"—are the drives to survive, to evolve, to conserve, and to transcend.

Survival

Survival is about self-preservation. It requires the ability to distinguish between threat and safety and the means to deal with threat as well as find safety. Our drive for survival involves the forces of autonomy and connection, best reflected in our autonomic nervous system (ANS). Our ANS is made up of two "expert parts": the sympathetic nervous system (the threat specialist) and the parasympathetic nervous system (the safety specialist). The first—also known as the fight-or-flight system—helps us maintain autonomy and our integrity as a part. The second—also known as the rest-and-digest or the feed-and-breed system—is activated in conditions of safety and facilitates connection.

Evolution and Adaptation

The drive to evolve pushes toward an optimized version of every living being and every species—a version that adapts as optimally as possible to its environment and functions better than its predecessors. This, in systems theory language, is defined as *morphogenesis*, and it refers to the process that occurs when a system reacts to a perceived change by moving away from its status.[5] When discussed in the context of couples or families, morphogenesis describes these systems' abilities to grow and adapt to change.[6]

Conservation

The pull toward conservation is reflected in the systemic thinking through the idea of *homeostasis*, which refers to a system's push toward internal equilibrium and stability, compensating for changes induced by external stimuli. The concept is broadened here to encompass the idea of homeostasis in living systems across time. Every living creature maintains strong bonds and links to their ancestors. Past knowledge and information lie within all of us, encoded in our DNA—a bridge with the past that defines and conditions our present and future.

Transcendence

The concept closest to transcendence, within the theoretical framework of systems thinking, is *emergence*. Life itself is considered to be an emergent property. The mind, it has also been argued, can be understood as an emergent property of the brain. Emergence involves the appearance of something new, which goes beyond the properties of the elements that compose a given system. In biological terms, it would correspond to the emergence of new species, and it has been defined as "creative evolution,"[7] "quantum evolution,"[8] or "emergent evolution"[9] by theorists who maintain that evolution is more than adaptation and natural selection. They argue that the process of organisms adapting to their surroundings within the same species is different from the processes involved in the emergence of new species. Such ideas have, of course, been—and still are—extensively debated.

Siding with this view, this aspect of evolution is referred to here as *transcendence*, a term borrowed from the realm of transpersonal psychology. According to Ken Wilber,

> Evolution is a wildly self-transcending process: it has the utterly amazing capacity to go beyond what went before. So evolution is in part a process of transcendence, which incorporates what went before and then adds incredibly novel components. The drive to self-transcendence is thus built into the fabric of the Kosmos itself.[10]

According to this book's particular framework, all four drives—survive, evolve, conserve, and transcend—are present within every living system, animal, couple, family, nation, or species. Such ideas are not new; the novelty is in the way they are structured, proposed, and integrated. This particular synthesis is put forward here for the first time. It may be informed by what is known and established but it does not belong (nor faithfully reflect) any of the frameworks that it draws from. Attachment theory, for example, where the concepts of connection and autonomy originally stem from, does not employ these terms in the way they are used here. Secure attachment is about healthy upbringing and also—lately—healthy adult relationships, but it is not studied or understood within a systemic framework. Attachment styles are related to individual needs only. Systemic relational theory, on the other hand, does not encompass the neurobiological or the intrapsychic. It talks about the family as a system but does not conceive the individual as a system in itself. The theory of evolution does not account for the pull *back*—the drive to conserve and maintain the organism's status quo—as a fundamental part of the process of evolution, nor has it officially embraced the pull of emergence or transcendence. Systems theory does not refer to DNA transmission in morphogenetic or homeostatic terms.

Within the realm of transpersonal psychology, holons are described as possessing both agency and communion, which correspond to autonomy and connection. There is also reference to four pulls: "the pull to be a whole, the pull to be a part, the pull up, the pull down: agency, communion, transcendence, dissolution."[11] There is a lot of correspondence between the pulls as they have been defined by Ken Wilber and as they have been described here. There are differences, of course, but the integration of the two maps seems possible. Yet the couple or the family has not been conceived, as far as I know, as a holon worthy of careful study within that realm. The transpersonal, as many other approaches that encompass spiritual ideas, goes directly from the Self (the individual) to the social or to self-transcendence, missing out on the couple or the family unit. This phenomenon may have something to do with the stories of Buddha leaving his wife and son behind in search of enlightenment. Maybe enlightenment is more of an attainable goal than establishing a healthy, working relationship with a partner. In any case, the synthesis of theory presented here is new territory.

An Interpersonal View of the Brain

In his book *Psychiatry, Psychoanalysis, and the New Biology of Mind*, Nobel Prize winner Eric Kandel strongly urged the psychoanalytical world to draw connections between psychoanalytical knowledge and neuroscience. Any sound psychological theory should be reflected in the brain, which is, after all, the "home" of our identity and our operations' center, where all the action takes place. French neurologist Boris Cyrulnik, with his ground-breaking work on trauma and resilience, has been one of the first to study and integrate the interpersonal with the neuroscientific. Within the field of psychotherapy, there is a strong current, especially in the United States, moving in this direction.

The field of *interpersonal neurobiology* or *relational neuroscience*, initially developed by American psychiatrist Dan Siegel in the 1990s, also aims to connect the neurobiological with the relational. It is an approach that seeks to describe how our brains and minds are shaped and how they function, based on the interplay between genetics and social interaction. There are more approaches that seek to connect the brain with the interpersonal—or the psychological with the neuroscientific—such as Porge's polyvagal theory or Bruce Ecker's Coherence Therapy. In parallel, there is a rising number of neuroscientists who are integrating psychological knowledge into their research and practice, such as Joseph E. LeDoux. These currents are nevertheless quite recent, so there is far more criticism going back and forth between disciplines than bridges being built. Those who try to build bridges are questioned both from within their field—as they move away from the parameters of their epistemological territory—and from other fields (as they approach realms they do not "officially" belong to or have not fully mastered). In any case, as more scientists, theorists, and clinicians move toward an interdisciplinary understanding of the human being, a day may come when this vast wealth of knowledge is integrated, enabling us to finally share an epistemology that is common and accepted by all.

In this line, here are a few ideas linking the brain with the interpersonal and systemic realms that might serve as conceptual connecting points across disciplines. If we approach the brain as a system, for instance, its very structure can raise some interesting questions.

The Horizontal Axis (Right-Left Brain)

To begin with, the brain is made up of two hemispheres. Why would this be? There is usually a logic to the way different systems and life forms are structured. If connection and autonomy are fundamental forces in any system, it could be that the division between the left and right hemispheres allows the brain to cater to both forces. The left hemisphere, in these terms, is primarily concerned with maintaining the integrity of the part, the "I," whereas the right hemisphere is the specialist in maintaining the connection to the whole. In order to better explain this, I will "borrow" the voice of Jill Bolte Taylor, a brain scientist and best-selling author of *My Stroke of Insight*:

> One of the jobs of our left hemisphere language center is to define our *self* by saying "I am" . . . It is the home of your ego center, which provides you with an internal awareness of what your name is, what your credentials are, and where you live. Without these cells performing their job, you would forget who you are and lose track of your life and your identity.[12]

Here, she describes left hemisphere functions that hint at its role in our drive toward autonomy, such as critical judgement and analysis, or the act of comparing ourselves to others in every possible way. The left hemisphere, according to her view, "revels in our individuality, honors our uniqueness, and strives for independence."[13]

Similarly, a lot of parallels with the drive toward connection emerge in her description of the right hemisphere, which softens borders between elements in both space and time:

> [O]ur right mind perceives each of us as equal members of the human family. It identifies our similarities and recognizes our relationship with this marvelous planet, which sustains our life. It perceives the big picture, how everything is related, and how we all join together to make up the whole. Our ability to be empathic, to walk in the shoes of another and feel their feelings, is a product of our right frontal cortex.[14]

The way the two hemispheres relate to one another is also consistent with the behavior of holons, which act both as wholes and as parts of a whole:

Neuroscientists have learned that the two hemispheres perform differently when they are connected to one another than when they are significantly separated. When normally connected, the two hemispheres complement and enhance one another's abilities. When surgically separated, the two hemispheres function as two independent brains, with unique personalities, often described as the Dr. Jekyll and Mr. Hyde phenomenon.[15]

This kind of functioning is also discussed in systemic theory. According to systemic therapists, for example, within the context of a relationship, the partners become subsystems within a bigger system. They occupy different roles and positions, becoming specialist parts of a greater whole. In other words, each individual, very much like each brain hemisphere, can function both as a whole and as a part of a whole.

Given this ability of each hemisphere to operate independently, it was previously suggested that each hemisphere was an independent brain. But now, thanks to the development of more advanced tools to study the brain,

The world of science supports the idea that the relationship between the two cerebral hemispheres is more appropriately viewed as two complementary halves of a whole rather than as two individual entities or identities.[16]

I would argue that the same reasoning applies to couples. Within the context of a relationship, it is more appropriate to view and understand the individuals as two complementary halves rather than as individual entities. One conditions, regulates, and complements the other. In order to understand the functioning of the couple, not only do we need to understand the individuals that compose it, but, most important, we also need to look at the relationship as a whole, as one entity—much like the brain.

In sum, the left and right hemispheres may have formed in order to respond to our fundamental, complementary, yet opposite needs for autonomy and connection, our conflicting needs to be a unit in ourselves and part of a greater whole. The polarization that, as we will see later on, takes place within the couple can be understood as a way for the members of the new entity to address its needs to be connected and autonomous both internally and externally. This means that the partners will almost naturally gravitate toward the different poles, with the "left hemisphere" partner in charge of the autonomy side of things and the "right hemisphere" partner in charge of fostering connection.

For example, let's say that Jason has been single for a few years, and during this time he has had to figure out a way to meet all his different needs. In order to achieve this, he had to work, socialize, cook, clean, take the dog out, go to the gym, fix things, water the plants, etc.—all activities that could be roughly divided into the two categories of autonomy and connection. At some point he meets Helen, falls in love, and moves in with her. Jason and Helen have now created an entity that is more than the sum of their parts, a new whole with its own needs. That new whole requires inner connection (Jason and Helen staying together), outer connection (contact with the outer world as a couple), inner autonomy (Jason and Helen keeping their separate identities), and outer autonomy (an identity as a couple that differentiates them from the rest of the world).

Once the couple is formed, Jason and Helen will gravitate toward the roles that they feel more comfortable with, gradually becoming more proficient and efficient in the tasks they are better at and less involved in those tasks that the partner is doing. If all goes well, Jason and Helen will not only continue to cover their individual needs, but between them they will also manage to cater to the needs of connection and autonomy of the couple (in all its different levels and dimensions). This kind of organization and specialization within the couple may reflect aspects and functions not only of the couple as a system but of systems in general—one of them being the brain.

The Vertical Axis (Higher-Lower Brain)

Each brain hemisphere also includes both cortical and subcortical structures. Again, why is it that our brains have developed this way? Why did Mother Nature not decide to completely reform the contents of our skull when the "new technology" (i.e., cortical brain) made its appearance? Consider the pulls of morphogenesis and homeostasis, defined here as the pull toward the new (to grow and evolve), and the pull toward the old (to conserve and regress). As I see it, our brain functions as a small community, a prototype that reflects the primary forces of connection and autonomy (symbolically female and male), as well as the "regressive" pull of homeostasis and the "progressive" pull of morphogenesis (symbolically, the child and the parent). The parts of the system are not supposed to merge or lose their particular identity and function, nor are they supposed to separate. The goal would be for this "community" to work as an integrated whole, each part maintaining its integrity and identity, at the same time complementing and enhancing the functions and purpose of the rest.

Some parallels have already been drawn between the brain and certain stages of human development. For a very long time, ever since psychoanalysis appeared as a discipline, the importance of childhood experience was stressed and underlined as paramount for the individual's later development. Neuroscience is now showing in a quantitative way what psychoanalysts have always known qualitatively.

Childhood and adolescence, the most crucial stages regarding personal, emotional, and interpersonal development, also happen to be the moments when the brain undergoes the most important changes and transformation. The existence of the unconscious mind can also now be explained in neuro-scientific terms. Soon—it is already happening—science will be in a position to show that the chemistry and structure of our brains is also massively interpersonal. From then on, I believe that we will come to understand that mental health is also interpersonal: People are not born crazy; we drive each other crazy. We prefer to blame Mother Nature for the shortcomings of our children, as it is a terrible responsibility for parents to assume.

We now know that music, meditation, or even driving a taxi in London has an impact on our brains. Well, our interactions do, too. Their impact is ongoing, extremely significant during the first years of our lives, and probably the most important influence on our brains than any other external stimuli. Healthy brains, therefore, require healthy relationships.

PART II
THE SEEDS
OF LOVE

The story of the individual commences, primarily, with fusion—with connection. Our journey begins in our mother's belly. There is no sense of a separate self at this point—at least that we know of. Nevertheless, autonomy also begins there. Once the sperm connects with the ovum, they cease to be part of the organisms they came from and a new, different organism emerges. Nine months later, our birth provides us with an occasion to celebrate our first day of "independence." The cut of the umbilical cord marks another step toward autonomy. We are given an identity of our own, a name, and a place within our family and the world.

Apart from the above, autonomy is not much needed at the beginning. Belonging and connection are more important. If all goes well, we will remain very connected to mom (or our main caregiver). We may be breastfed, cuddled, hugged a lot, loved a lot. We are designed to require a very strong connection to our main caregiver(s) in order to survive. At the very beginning, there are no clear boundaries between the "I" and the "you" of the caregiver from the baby's point of view. Babies are more likely to start off feeling at "one" with mom, with nourishment, with the universe. This interpersonal enmeshed bliss, of course, is just a stage that will be experienced for a very short period of time, if such bliss is experienced at all.

At this early stage, what is important regarding autonomy is more related to the caregiver's viewpoint. It is vital that the baby is perceived both as "part of" the new family, as well as someone different, with needs of his or her own that are distinct from those of the caregivers. Otherwise, the integrity of the part (the holon) can get compromised.

Autonomy becomes slowly and steadily more important from the child's point of view as she starts to move, walk, talk, and explore the world. Parents will need to accompany the process and adapt to it accordingly. With the passing of time, as children grow and pass from one developmental stage to the other, the balance in their needs for belonging/autonomy will change.

What at one stage is functional and appropriate may be dysfunctional and totally inappropriate at another. For example, bed sharing with a child at the age of one or two may be a brilliant idea; bed sharing with an adolescent is not. What at one moment is caring and nurturing may be invasive and controlling at another. Big doses of inappropriate connection are a direct and very real threat to one's emerging identity. Big doses of inappropriate or untimely autonomy may equal neglect.

What is important to note about the ideas above, at this point, is that this part of ourselves—the baby that requires nurture and connection—will accompany us all through our lives. It will be there in our old, subcortical, limbic brain. No matter how brilliant we become in higher, "cortical" terms—no matter how old, wise, or independent—the "infant" we used to be will stick with us through our lives. Jill Bolte Taylor has wonderfully summarized this concept in the following quote:

> Although our limbic system functions throughout our lifetime, it does not mature. As a result, when our emotional "buttons" are pushed, we retain the ability to react to incoming stimulations as though we were a two-year-old, even when we are adults.[1]

In other words, as long as we operate from a physical body, the "primitive" will live within us. Not only that, but this part of ourselves is always going to come first. It is our system's first priority. It will also be the first to process all incoming stimuli. As Bolte Taylor explains, "Although many of us think of ourselves as thinking creatures that feel, biologically we are feeling creatures that think."[2] First comes the limbic brain, and then the cerebral cortex. We need to cater to our primitive needs first before moving on to anything else. And these needs will be present and will demand attention irrespective of age.

The baby needs food during childhood and will carry on needing food as an adult. It needs emotional nurturance and will also need it throughout his or her life. Survival is a lifelong goal. For this reason, everything we learn in our infancy about these needs and how to deal with them will guide us through our entire lives. We draw on these initial teachings in a similar way that we do with our native language.

We continue being baby-like and dependent during all our lives. And furthermore, the way these aspects of ourselves manifest in our adult lives will be heavily conditioned by a number of things that are determined during childhood. It is true that, under this light, we may seem too vulnerable or too much at the mercy of people and forces out of our reach or control. It may be that this is the very reason that we have opted to ignore some of our most basic human needs. We do not yet know how to deal with our own vulnerability. It could be that when we become conscious of, accept, and embrace our dependent, vulnerable, interconnected nature, we will fare better and succeed as individuals, couples, families, and nations. Paradoxically, the consciousness of our own vulnerability could make us a wiser and more resilient species.

The bottom line is that our primitive "baby needs" stay with us. This applies to CEOs, world leaders, religious figures . . . everyone. The baby, apparently invisible later on in life, will seek, as intensely and forcefully as it yearned for mother's breast and affection, ways to satisfy his or her needs for connection and autonomy, within the body of an adult.

Creating a Safe Haven and a Secure Base

The interplay between the needs for connection and autonomy set the "music" that will accompany us, every step of the way, all through our lives. This is very well described in the early human development concept of the Circle of Security™. After more than ten years of research, a group of clinicians and investigators from the United States (Bert Powell, Glen Cooper, Kent Hoffman, and Bob Marvin) arrived at a seemingly simple formula about child development and caregiving. According to their findings, successful child development requires a caregiver who can consistently provide both comfort (a safe haven) and encouragement (a secure base from which to explore). Or, in other words, it requires a reliable, consistent provider of connection and autonomy.

Safe haven is described as "relatedness-within-autonomy (*keep the 'me' and 'you' in 'us'*)," or "welcome my coming to you."[3] It is a source of comfort, protection, emotional regulation, and empathy. *Secure base* is defined as "autonomy-within-relatedness (*'be with me so I can do it by myself'*)."[4] It involves supporting the child's exploration and providing a source of esteem, enjoyment, delight, seeing the world through the child's eyes, and being there to support their individuality.

The way a safe haven and a secure base are accomplished are also wonderfully explained by the same authors on pages 51–56 of *The Circle of Security Intervention*. Given that the baby we used to be stays within us and is most present in our intimate relationships during adulthood, the description of a nurturing parent–child relationship also reflects essential aspects of the dynamics of a well-functioning couple.

Secure Base

The Circle of Security Intervention lists the following interpersonal requirements for ensuring secure base conditions (autonomy-within-relatedness):

- "Delight in me as I explore."

- "Watch over me as I turn to new sights, sounds, and touches."

- "Look at the world through my eyes and talk to me about it."

- "Wait when I look away so I don't get too wound up,"[5]

In situations when the infant is upset, they add a different set of interpersonal requirements:

- "Give me just enough help when I get frustrated so that I can do it."

- "Wait when I look away so I can practice using myself to calm down."[6]

Partners, unlike babies, will find themselves in both the parental and infant positions. Now, if it were the child (within the adult) defining the interpersonal dynamics of the couple, it would probably sound like this: "Be happy for me as I move in the world. Celebrate with my personal or professional achievements. When we are apart, be mindful of me, stay connected. Accept me as someone different from you and show me you can see the world through my eyes too. Stay kind and patient when I become more silent or seek some private space. And, in times of distress, just show me you are with me; do not always step in with something useful to say or do (when you do, it often sounds as if you are telling me that you are able and competent, and I am not). At the same time, please do not avoid me or ignore me. Stay present, even when I am upset. Keep calm in times of friction, and please do not interpret my need for space as a rejection. I just need the space and time to self-regulate and calm down."

Partners, just like babies, will present a continuous alternating pattern of seeking proximity and distance from their loved one in a variety of ways. When they feel happy and safe in a relationship, they will use it as a secure base to develop further (personally or professionally). What is "key" in promoting autonomy is ensuring that it is always done "within-connected-ness," whether in times of peace or under stress. "Self-esteem—the sum of an individual's self-representations—involves a sense that someone is delighted in you for who you are, for your being, in addition to feeling good about what you do and accomplish."[7]

Safe Haven

Skillful connection is essential to establishing a nurturing bond and a working relationship. Yet, "if the price of connection is the loss of autonomy,"[8] there will be suffering. So connection must be established within a framework that allows for autonomy too. If we take a look at how a masterful connection is achieved between a caregiver and a baby, we can get a pretty good idea again on what is needed between partners. Here are the interpersonal requirements defined by *The Circle of Security Intervention* for skillful connection ("relatedness-within-autonomy")[9]:

- "Delight in me as I fall in love with your face."

- "Show me you get it by matching my emotions with your voice, face, and touch."

And, in times of distress:

- "Comfort me."

- "Organize my feelings by accepting, sharing, and naming them."

Within a romantic relationship, from the point of view of the infant-within-the-adult, the above might translate as follows: "Delight in me as I approach you, look at you, and fall in love with you. Be open to sharing intense positive emotions with me. In times of distress, please be there to comfort me, being both empathetic and emotionally stable. Help me organize my thoughts and feelings by acknowledging them—even when you do not particularly like or understand them." Maintaining connection in times of friction (an expression of the "I" fighting for itself) is a way to stay bonded, albeit differentiated. This, in turn, sets the foundation for co-regulation to take place and for the painful emotions to be soothed within the interpersonal context.

If we were to identify champions of connection or relatedness-within-autonomy during adulthood, those would be the lovers in times of contentment, and I'd say therapists (not to mention some bartenders, hairdressers, and others with exquisite therapeutic interpersonal skills) in times of discontent. Connection is about being with the other, mirroring the other, gazing into his or her eyes and sensing a special bond, but also sharing ideas, hobbies, or time together. There are many contexts in which we satisfy our need for connection or relatedness-within-autonomy in our adult life: family bonds, romantic relationships, friendships, caregiving, sexuality, groups (community, politics, sports, bands, clubs, nations), religious experiences, or other similar experiences facilitated by art, dance, music, science, and literature.

Nevertheless, for most people, there will only be two versions of safe haven or main sources of connection-within-autonomy:

1. Our primary caregivers* (during childhood and adulthood)

2. Our partner (in adult life)

Family and partners are the two "organisms" that are called upon to "feed us" in this sense. Most of us mortals, once we hit adulthood, will fulfill (or try to fulfill) our need for connection via our partner, in conjunction with a lifelong "tribute" to our family of origin. The latter refers to staying connected and loyal to the most important people in our lives (usually mom and dad). We do this, according to American psychologist Lorna Smith Benjamin, by (a) being like them, (b) pairing up with people like them, and (c) treating ourselves the way we were treated.

No matter how far we live from them, how angry we may be at them, or whatever the situation may be with our parents or caregivers, they will always be with us. This lifelong connection is a way to preserve our roots and heritage. Evolution, after all, requires the mixture of the old and the new.

Connection-Autonomy Failure

Addictive behavior is an excellent as well as dramatic example of our less constructive, sometimes desperate attempts to soothe these two fundamental needs. The following also make for very poor substitutes: compulsive eating, tobacco, alcohol, sex, drugs, gambling, video games, shopping, and social networks, as well as the less recognized but the most destructive and dangerous of all: compulsive power and wealth accumulation.

Behind every addictive behavior lies our primary needs for a safe haven or a secure base, for relatedness-within-autonomy or autonomy-within-relatedness. The baby within seeks and longs for an experience that does not come—and, in most cases, was never properly established in early childhood.

Actually, the failure of our primary sources of nurture (main caregivers, family) to deliver a secure base and to equip us with the essential interpersonal skills to love ourselves and others, and skillfully navigate the fundamental

*In an internalized version and possibly also in a real-life version if there is a functional relationship.

connection-autonomy interpersonal dance, is reflected in probably every expression of human-to-human or self-inflicted suffering.

Not all adults resolve their primary need to connect through a partner, of course. An exception can be seen in the spiritual devotion of religious figures such as Buddhist monks. In this case, the need for connection seems to be satisfied through meditation and mindfulness practice, which leads to a sense of "oneness" with all there is. As with other religions, adherents probably also experience a sense of connection within their social context, as they follow the traditions and teachings of their attachment figures.

What is interesting in the case of Buddhism is that the teachings point in the same direction as the findings of attachment research, in terms of connection and autonomy being intimately linked and interdependent. The research defines secure attachment as directly related to human well-being, achieved—as we have seen above—by providing both "the comfort and protection of a safe haven" (connection) and "the encouragement and confidence of a secure base" (autonomy).[10] In the case of Buddhist spiritual practice, nirvana could be perceived as the highest—and simultaneous—expression of autonomy and connection.

Nevertheless, the process is normally sequential. As described by B. Powell et al.,

> Young children alternate between these two fundamental needs dozens, even hundreds, of times a day. They go round and round, dabbling in discovery and then running back for comfort and protection. They fill their cups with renewed confidence and then dart off again.[11]

Old knowledge and current findings also suggest that the two forces do not exist independently.

The relationship between attachment behaviors and exploratory behaviors is one of reciprocal inhibition. Imagine a seesaw, with attachment behaviors on one end and exploratory behaviors on the other. When a child feels unsafe or overwhelmed by incomprehensible emotions, attachment behaviors activate and exploration terminates. When the seesaw tips so that attachment behaviors go up, the exploratory behaviors go down. Once the child feels safe enough, attachment behaviors stop and exploratory behaviors engage, so the seesaw tips the other way.[12]

In other words, the two forces condition and define one another, a bit like the ancestral concept of yin and yang.

The Whole Within the Part: Copying Our Caregivers

We are born into the family organism, both as a whole (individual) and as part of a whole (family member) at the same time. Within the family organism, during our childhood, we learn about life and survival. How?

Mainly via copying. We copy all that is available around us, without thinking about whether we like it or not. We learn our native language without questioning any aspect of it. We learn about emotions and interactions without questioning them either.

During childhood, what we learn is whatever is made available to us. Nature has designed it this way. We are meant to absorb the teachings of the previous generation—our caregivers—no matter what these teachings are. They are the surviving generation, after all. According to nature and evolution, they know best. So mom says, "Do not touch the stove," and we learn not to touch the stove. We hear mom and dad talk, and we absorb their language. We hear them fighting, and we absorb the fighting. Their voices and their teachings become part of who we are—literally. We may not remember them consciously, but they will nevertheless be "hardwired" in our brains. Early experiences with our primary caregivers have a powerful impact on brain development.

 *(handwritten marginal note: PRIMARY SCHOOLS?)*

And so we absorb and, also, we practice. We practice being and behaving like our parents in our minds and in our play, both when alone and when with our peers. If mom often says, "What a beautiful girl you are," her child is very likely to repeat the phrase in relation to toys, peers, and, primarily, with herself. If mom and dad fight, their child is likely to practice fighting. If dad says, "You are a killer . . . You are a king," the child will then internalize the affirmation and may start shaping all his life and the world around him according to those teachings.*

---

*This last example appears in *Lost Tycoon* by Harry Hurt III.[13]
  The father is Fred Trump; the child is Donald J. Trump.

Parents teach by what they say and by what they do. If their words do not coincide with their actions, kids (and adults) will attune mainly to the latter. This is one of the five axioms of human communication postulated by Austrian-American psychologist Paul Watzlawick, colloquially expressed in the maxim "Actions speak louder than words."

In sum, our caregivers get installed in our brains from very early on. It happens primarily through their actions and behaviors but also through what we are told about them or how we have imagined them to be. Any parental figure who is significantly related to us will be represented in our minds, even if they were not present. The parent who passed away, who left or was never there, the divorced parent who is not allowed to see their children, the biological parents of the adopted child—even the sperm donor—will also have a representation in our brains as parental figures. In his book *Psychothérapie de Dieu* (*God's Psychotherapy*), French neurologist Boris Cyrulnik claims that God, too, is a very significant and powerful inner representation for many people.[14]

In cases where the parental figure has not been lived or experienced directly, the representation will be defined by what we have been told about them or, if there has been no such information, they will be defined by our imagination, fantasy, fears, or desires about them. The stories themselves will have a great impact on us—sometimes as great as direct experience. Stories also activate and shape our brains—in this case, in ways that give shape to some of the most significant, impactful representations within us. The extent of their power, for example, may be found in God's representation in the mind of a young child named Jesus.

A less biblical yet powerful example is to be found in the recovery—or the beginning of the process of recovery—of the severely distressed adopted child who discovers that her biological mother has not abandoned her but "entrusted" her, out of love and an awareness of her difficulties to raise a child, to people who could. Such stories are very common in the work of Luigi Cancrini, who has dedicated his work of the past decades to the care, protection, and therapy of children.[15]

I could therefore not emphasize more, as a side note, the importance of what we tell our children about their attachment figures. I have witnessed amazing recoveries of people with severe mental disorders who were told their mothers or fathers were monster-like figures and discovered a very different story later on in life. Therapy itself is about transforming the most terrible parental representations into alternatives that one can at least live with. It is important because these representations, whether monster-like or divine, will live within us and define us, as they mentally occupy the position of parents. And parental figures, external or internalized, teach us about the world and inform us about who we are, about whether what we do is good or bad, about whether we are intrinsically "good" or "bad." They do it both in real life and then, intensively and intensely, all through our lives internally, producing massive amounts of self-talk, brain activity, and corresponding chemical changes in our bodies.

Our caregivers will also be the ones who will teach us about autonomy and connection and about how couples work. The way they have forged and worked through their relationship will leave a great imprint on us and will strongly inform how we will go about our own relationships.

In sum, we all end up with inner parents "speaking to us," informing our decisions and actions up until we die. If you have ever wondered where all these voices in your head are coming from, now you know. To a very large degree, they are versions of the caregivers' voices that you have internalized. And within their voices are the voices of their own caregivers, giving them instruction on life, self, threat, and safety—in constructive and destructive ways. These voices are the echo of generations . . . of the whole history of our families and humankind.

Now, what happens in adolescence?

Adolescence: The Transformation of the Holon

Family shapes us to be who we are both as a whole and as a part, and each member of the family takes up a role and function within the family organism. We could continue like this forever, forming part of the organism that created us, feeding it and being fed by it. But nature has planned it differently. Evolution requires the creation of new organisms. Therefore, the individual will eventually need to move away from the original system. This will involve two essential processes:

1. The information to be passed from the old generation to the new, so that the latter has more chances to survive

2. Inherited information to be transformed for new forms of being and doing to emerge

Adolescence marks the beginning of this process of leaving the family and setting off for new adventures. The process is a little bit like learning how to drive or, indeed, learning any other skill. At the beginning, the car is more under the control of the instructor. The latter provides us with information about driving and also shows us how it is done. Once we have assimilated the teachings, the instructor starts giving us more and more autonomy. And then, once we have really absorbed the information and have copied his or her ways, the instructor can let go and let us drive the car. We could say that instructors only leave the car once their lessons are well established in our minds.

A very similar process takes place with parents. The main difference is that it is far more powerful because it is about our entire lives—our roots, connection, survival, and evolution.

The mechanism for it is as simple as it is powerful: We learn about life and survival from our caregivers by copying them, absorbing and internalizing their teachings—a process that prepares us to later on build our own project. The new project will be based on and include what is already learned, and at the same time we will feel the push of evolution in the sense that we will experience the urge to do better than what went on before. Nature has decided that around adolescence, the teachings are more or less complete, and we can start exploring the idea of "connection" outside the family. Our aim is to do something different, something better.

Autonomy will have been explored and practiced in very many contexts and situations during childhood and will continue during adolescence: through play, at school, in extracurricular activities, and so on. As we learn about the world, we learn about ourselves, about our place in it, about what we like and what we do not like, about who we are and what makes us unique.

There are many paths to autonomy. However, there is just one or two primary paths to connection. "Home is where the heart is," as the saying goes. Home is family. It is where the "I" transforms into a "WE."

One home is the family we come from. Actually, without the push of evolution, we might avoid the "mess" and complexity of leaving this home and getting together with a totally different human being, sidestepping the risk of starting a new project. But evolution is about diversity, about mixing and matching, about growing and shifting, about transcending the old and testing new life forms and life structures. During puberty, nature "officially" activates two projects that could also be conceived as one:

1. The "autonomy from the family of origin" project

2. The "new connection" project

The latter is the project that will eventually help us create and establish a new "home," which will in turn provide a new source of nurture away from the family. The magical substance that initiates and drives this project is sexuality.

Getting "Charged"

The onset of puberty signals that the time has come to shift our baby needs into the romantic realm. And so we "transfer" our need for connection from our family to the idea or the reality of a partner. As emerging sexuality gets us "charged," we gradually feel less connected to the family system and more "connectable" to external systems. In relation to the external world, we turn into a charged part in search of another charged part who can create with us a new whole—and a new "home."

The process of absorbing mom and dad during childhood involves internalizing their masculine and feminine sides, their roles within the relationship, and the interplay of the masculine and feminine as it has manifested between them. All of it—the whole "package"—will become part of ourselves. In other words, we will internalize:

1. The caregivers, individually and their relationship as a whole

2. The feminine and the masculine (connection and autonomy, respectively), in the way it was expressed in individual and relational terms

3. The way caregivers related to one another and the way they related (e.g., attribution of value, meaning, hierarchy), in terms of the masculine and the feminine, to the rest of the world

Around adolescence, the emergence of sexual desire and the pressing need for self-definition in order to go out into the world will force us to take a stance. Adolescents may have been exploring and shaping their identity in terms of roles and positions all through childhood, but at this point, more than ever, they will be called to define which parent they identify with more, and which role within the relationship they feel closer to. This, in turn, will gradually determine which part of the internalized whole is going to be the visible one (acted out) and which will remain more silenced, in terms of their interpersonal identity. Thus, the adolescent will:

1. Define oneself as man, woman, primarily masculine, or primarily feminine, or other, in relation to gender

2. Choose a role within the relationship: feminine or masculine (guardian of connection or guardian of autonomy)

This "choice"—an emotional, instinctual rather than rational choice—will then condition our sexual preferences and orientation.

As adults in the making, adolescents will be called to define which will be their dominant "poles" in terms of primary identity and relationship role, which parts will be externalized, and which will remain silent. So the child who has been "playing with" and exploring the parental roles will now also have them manifest in their personal lives. The family dynamics transform into an inner constellation that will condition the way we approach intimate relationships. Our chosen pole will be more visible than the other in the realm of a given relationship. We could say that one pole is the "pilot" (i.e., the more active agent), while the other pole takes the copilot seat—powerful but passive, less visible. We function a little bit like magnets in the interpersonal sphere. Although we embody both poles, within a relationship one of them will be primarily activated. In principle, we will seek partners with aspects that are familiar to us yet often "silenced" in ourselves. It can be a fascinating experience to meet and get to know someone's partner. In a way, we are given the chance to glance into someone's psyche and get in touch with a significant part of somebody no longer visible.

It may be better understood with an example: Maia is an only child. During childhood she internalized both mom and dad. Mom was primarily installed in the feminine and dad in the masculine poles of their relationship. Maia identified with mom as a woman but perceived the feminine pole as the "losing" one, which in turn made her feel more comfortable occupying the masculine (autonomy-within-relatedness) pole in her relationships. After having sexual experiences with both men and women, occupying the masculine pole within every relationship she had, both hetero- and homosexual, she got together with a man who was comfortable occupying the feminine (connection-within-autonomy) pole. She identified with mom as a woman, occupied her father's position, and got together with a man who would enact her mother's position, in a heterosexual relationship.

Given that the masculine and the feminine lie within every caregiver and every relationship, the variations of the ways one relates to gender, role, pole, and sexual orientation, later on in life, are varied and numerous. It is a process that is not static either, especially during adolescent years.

In order to further clarify this, allow me to introduce John and his family. To keep things simple, I have chosen a "classic" model of a family with a father and a mother, each occupying traditional roles. Now, the whole family comes from TANGOland, and as such, John knows really well how to tango. He has been learning it all his life, dancing with mom and with dad, seeing them dance with one another. In adolescence, John identified himself with his dad and the masculine (autonomy-within-relatedness) in terms of pole and, also, gender. Having internalized mom and femininity, he sets off into the world as a heterosexual, masculine tango dancer.

Now let's meet Louise, who comes from SALSAland. She knows really well how to "salsa" her way through life. Like John, she has internalized the salsa moves of mom and dad, having danced with each of them and having seen them dance together. Then, in a similar way to John, she has identified with one of the parents and has put the other in the back seat. In her case, she went out into the world as a heterosexual female, mostly identified with mom, having chosen the feminine (connection-within-autonomy) to be her dominant pole. The masculine pole will nevertheless be present within her at all times and will manifest itself in infinite ways within a future relationship, as well as outside it.

There could be many variations to this: John or Louise could identify more with a) men or b) women. They could position themselves more on the a) feminine or b) masculine pole. And, depending on how these and other inner and outer elements combine, their sexual preferences could be predominantly a) heterosexual, b) homosexual, or c) other.

Defining the Self: Initial Challenges

Getting charged, entering the world of the adults, becoming sexually active, having to take a stance, and seeing oneself in the position of a caregiver can turn into an extremely painful and complex affair when there has been suffering in early life. Parenting may have worked, and the child may have received sufficient attention and nurturance from the caregivers during the childhood years, but if the parent(s) have suffered in their relationship, whether this relationship was actually lived or narrated, this will almost always lead to serious complications in the child's adult life, especially within the interpersonal realm. An example could be the child who will later be defined as a narcissist and who has absorbed the totality of the relationship of his or her parents. Such a relationship includes demonstrations of both narcissism and submissiveness. The child will identify with the primarily narcissistic or primarily submissive parent such that one will be visible within him or her and the other not . . . until we meet the partner. The inherited level of submissiveness will reveal itself in the other. The narcissist may not be allowed to own or accept certain parts of the parental dynamic, but he or she will be able to continue to relate to them through the partner. Likewise, the apparently submissive spouse will have received a similar inheritance. In this case, it is the ambition, the abuse, or the thirst for power that is silenced but sought. In short, if we cannot own it, we are compelled to marry it.

Equally dangerous will be a definition—by either caregiver—of the masculine or the feminine that is dismissive or derogatory. Intimate relationships will be perceived as a very risky enterprise, and this may result in significant amounts of suffering and ambivalence regarding the masculine and the feminine, in the way they relate to oneself and others.

In some cases, it will come down to having to choose between the position of a perceived aggressor or that of a perceived victim: "To be them? Or to marry them?" Should one identify with the powerful but destructive masculine or the weak yet loving feminine? (It could be the other way around, of course.) A relationship that involves aggressors and victims presents extremely difficult conundrums that kids who have internalized these dysfunctional relationships will be called to resolve later on in life. Let's say I am a woman, and my childhood experience has shown me that men are "bad" and women are "weak." If I identify with the "weak," then—within the outline of the relationship that I have internalized—my partner is likely to be "bad." Or I may decide to position myself on the masculine pole to avoid suffering. Then, it is likely that I will feel little respect for my masculine partner positioned in the feminine pole and that I will perceive him as "weak." When the relationship that has been internalized is dysfunctional, it will pose a challenge no matter which sexual orientation or pole the individual gravitates toward within their future partnerships.

Our partners, in general, reflect very significant aspects of our own makeup. Take Jack, who witnessed and experienced an abusive relationship between his parents. He was the youngest in the family and the one giving support to his mother as he was experiencing and being told how terrible men could be. As an adolescent, he identified with mom, positioned himself on the feminine pole, and defined himself as heterosexual. Although he rejected his father's role within the couple, he unconsciously sought a "very tough" woman who occupied his father's position, a relationship in which he eventually ended up feeling abused.

On Gender and Sexuality

Gender and sexuality are areas that we have not "resolved" yet as a species—"resolved" as in coming to a paradigm that the human community and most of its members (no matter how they define themselves in this realm) are more or less comfortable with. It is almost impossible to talk about gender, sexual orientation, or sexuality without generating tension or controversy. Humans appear to be extremely fragile in this realm.

This fragility—and the suffering that goes with it—is, in my opinion, universal and involves individuals of every race, gender and sexual orientation. Are there any men on the face of this planet who have not had to face issues around their masculinity, femininity, or sexual orientation? Are there any women who have not felt angry, frustrated, or hurt about gender issues? Is there anyone from the LGBTIQ+ community who has not experienced some pain around such issues during their lives? The mere fact of being exposed almost daily to swear words and derogatory nomenclature associated with gender, sexuality, or sexual orientation is a constant reminder of how much pain we continue to generate in this sphere.

Nevertheless, due to the great controversy the subject generates, theorists generally—and unfortunately, in my view—avoid it altogether. We should all take a bit of a risk instead, in my opinion, in the spirit of advancing the conversation on the subject. It is an important subject. And sharing ideas, I believe, is a good and healthy exercise, so long as we humbly understand that we may be proved wrong.

We do not know, to this day, what determines the way we define ourselves in terms of sexual orientation. It is possible that, as with everything else, both nature and nurture have some role to play in it. As a relational therapist, I do not have much to say about nature. My focus has always been the impact of nurture and how our environment can shape us into who we are. And, as with everything else (our genetic makeup included), I think it makes sense to argue that context may significantly influence the way we define ourselves in terms of sexuality.

So, what is it about our context that may be creating so much suffering around our self-definition in these terms? Again, I do not have the answers. What I do know from my work as a therapist is that suffering is almost always present when the masculine and the feminine are experienced to be at war with one another, when one pole is defined as "good" and the other as "bad," when one or both of them are experienced as toxic, and when the masculine and the feminine are not equally embraced and celebrated.

For those immersed in such contexts (probably the whole of the human species, to different degrees), the conflict between the two poles can raise important and deep inner dilemmas in terms of defining who we are and who we want to be with. We all live, after all, in a society in which the masculine and the feminine appear to be in constant tension, endlessly compared, judged, and questioned. I have come to believe that the greater the conflict, the more difficult it is for each one of us to embrace ourselves fully—both the masculine and the feminine aspects of our nature—and, consequently, to feel comfortable occupying a pole in a relationship and to be at peace with ourselves, our gender, and our sexuality. In my view, the whole of the human species is, in different ways, suffering in this realm, and this suffering is heavily related to the unresolved manmade conflict between the two poles that, unfortunately lives within us all and continues to define our society.

When there has been violence at home (or elsewhere, but especially at home), for example, the child who has witnessed and experienced it will feel reluctant to go out in the world later on in life, in the victim's or the villain's role, to suffer as one parent did or to be as monstrous as the other was experienced. There is usually a strong urge to avoid their model and differentiate from both.

Take Bruce, for example, who had a violent father and served as the protector of his continuously abused mother. The idea of being a man, being masculine, or putting himself in his father's position in a heterosexual relationship was frightening and aversive to him. The idea of being in his mother's position in either a heterosexual or a homosexual relationship was also scary for all the suffering it involved. Or Becky, who was the firstborn of yet another unhappy marriage between an authoritarian, alcoholic father and a mother who was perceived as sweet yet powerless. There was nothing of what she lived that she wanted to repeat in her adult life, feeling uneasy both toward the masculine and feminine poles, as she had experienced them.

Malvina hated the place women had in her culture, and she struggled to come to terms with being a woman herself. Max, an intellectual white man, was reluctant to embrace his masculinity, which he was made to believe was inevitably toxic. Neil, the youngest of five, had a high-powered father and a mother who stayed at home and took care of them. Neil was "her baby"—her confidant, the one she would turn to when she felt alone and, even more so, when she felt pain arising from the numerous extramarital relationships of her husband. As such, he cancelled any version of masculinity in himself that reminded him of his father.

Everyone mentioned in the examples above decided to explore alternative scripts in terms of gender and sexuality to those their parents had modelled for them. They sought to evolve—in my view, successfully—toward more constructive relationships and scripts than those lived in their families. It may not be a coincidence that homosexual men and—especially—women, for example, have more egalitarian relationships than their heterosexual counterparts.* In any case, and irrespective of how we choose to define ourselves in this realm, I believe that a lot of unnecessary suffering would be avoided if we focused on embracing and celebrating all genders and poles. This way there would be nothing to defend or to be afraid of. Each of us could feel freer and happier in our definitions, no matter what those might be.

A few years ago, I read a beautiful novel by José Luis Sampedro titled *La Vieja Sirena* (*The Old Mermaid*) that portrayed a society that existed almost two thousand years ago in which gender and sexual orientation did not trigger controversy.[16] To be precise, it was set in Egypt, during the third century CE. Indeed, there have been times and cultures, like in ancient Greece, where sexuality and gender could be lived in many different ways, all of them respected and understood as part of normal human experience. I do hope that someday we will manage to evolve to at least where we were some thousand years ago.

---

*According to *Systemic Sex Therapy* by Katherine M. Hertlein, Nancy Gambescia, and Gerald R. Weeks,[17] citing several studies, "The most striking difference between mixed and same sex couples found consistently in research, is that gay male and lesbian couples are more egalitarian in almost every way than male-female couples (Gotta et al, 2011; Solomon, Rothblum, & Balsam, 2005; Peplau, 2003)."

Leaving Home

No matter how we define ourselves in terms of gender, masculinity and femininity, or sexual orientation, if the family system has functioned more or less well, leaving home will form part of our path as an individual and will be perceived as a natural stage in our (and everyone's) process. Nevertheless, even for the most resilient and balanced families, the moment when the members of the new generation leave the "host" organism and set off into the world to create a new one may entail pain and distress for all. The impact is usually greater on the parent who has been more in charge of "connection," whose role involved holding the parts together. The caregiver most connected to autonomy may also experience hardship, especially if their offspring make strong statements of differentiation in terms of identity. An example for this would be the child who chooses to be an artist when he was supposed to become a businessman like dad, takes on an unexpected change of surname, or chooses a partner of a different ethnic or cultural background. It may be okay to leave, but not okay to lose the parent's imprint on us. No matter the case, the whole organism will undergo major transformation and face challenges at this stage.

The most important challenge is related to the survival and continuation of the family project. Individual autonomy is important, but it will only be promoted and facilitated if the survival of the whole (the family that will be left behind) is ensured. Otherwise, the individual may not have the chance to separate and live independently. The adolescent will instead stay with the family and postpone or abort his or her emancipation. Inevitably, such movements that defy the natural course of things usually come at a very high price.

The main and most common price to pay is the new generation's mental health. We can almost literally split into two, trying to be both a part of the whole (our family) and a separate entity in its own right. The most "expensive" version of this tension involves not only compromising or aborting the emancipation of the individual, but also the whole project of construing a separate self. The life and identity of the offspring, in such a case, is put to the service of the survival of the whole.

If, instead, the individual is "allowed" to move away from the family (to a lesser or greater degree) and enter the adult world as a separate, "charged" entity, the experience of a love story becomes possible!

EROS AND AGAPE

There are two kinds of love that we will experience during our lives. The Greeks have a different word for each, which is quite handy: eros and agape.

Eros is the love we experience when we are "in love." It is the love that is activated by the little angels' arrows. It is the risky kind—the love that can hurt, the love that transforms, the love the pushes us forward. It is a love we do not control. Being "in love" is like being caught in a powerful current to unknown destinations. Eros is a self-centered kind of love; it is about personal growth and identity, more about the part rather than the whole, more about the "I" than the "WE." It tends to ask for more than it offers, and it involves change and transformation. Sex and romance are essential components. Eros can be intense, sublime, and unforgettable.

Agape is understood as universal love, the love that connects. It is the love for the mother, the father, the child, the friend, the world, and the partner too! It is more about the whole rather than the part, more about the "WE" than the "I." It gives more than it expects to receive; it is less exciting but more enduring. Agape is a love that we can control, that we can offer consciously and decidedly. Related to attachment, it is also a "safe" love that soothes, brings stability, preserves, and heals.

If love were an entity with poles, eros would occupy the autonomy side, whereas agape would represent the connection. Interestingly, the gender of the words in Greek correspond accordingly. *Eros* is a masculine word, whereas *agape* is feminine. If love were divided into primitive and higher terms, eros would be the more "primitive" one—and actually is reflected to be a child, the little angel with arrows—and agape the more "adult" kind of love. If love is the force that creates, moves, and conditions human systems, then eros would be the love that triggers morphogenesis, and agape would be more in charge of homeostasis.

As we go down the path of life, if we are fortunate enough, both kinds of love will accompany us at different stages, in different combinations and intensities, adding to the quality of our experiences and making memorable our passage through this world.

THE POWER OF LOVE

LOVE TRANSFORMS, LOVE CONNECTS, "LOVE CONQUERS ALL!"[1] Love is reflected in almost every aspect of human experience—art, music, literature, religion—but it still occupies such an irrelevant space in science. Love may be the blindest spot of our civilization. We talk, write, and sing about it, live for it, die for it, and yet love does not inform the way we structure our society, whether in terms of education, health, technology, politics, or policy making—not explicitly.

Love, connection, dependence, emotion, relationships—actually, pretty much everything that would fall into what is generally defined as the "feminine realm"—eludes our society's radar. We have managed to digitally connect the whole planet but still struggle when it comes to understanding how basic human interactions work. Our society has focused far more heavily on reason, autonomy, agency, identity, and differentiation, which are important, but it's only half of the human story.

So let's talk about looove, baby!

The Bliss and Terror of New Love

A stretched arm. An invitation: "Shall we dance?" And then . . . we join hands, and we are not individuals anymore. We form part of a whole—a moving system that has its own properties, structure, and flow.

Intimate relationships involve two individuals who do not share family or DNA, and sometimes not even culture or race, creating a new organism, a new "WE." It is quite an extraordinary and complex enterprise—perhaps the most complex there is.

Eros will be of great help at the beginning of the process. Eros will help us separate from the family (or any other system we happen to be part of) and connect us to somebody else, thus ensuring that we always have a "home."

Romantic love will also set the foundation for partners to become the best versions of themselves, at least at the very beginning. It will present us with an opportunity to grow and evolve, to fulfill our potential and go beyond our initial programming and teachings. It is probably one of the most, if not THE MOST "transformational substance" there is in the human realm, as it has the power to make, break, and totally transform human systems.

When we fall in love, we "let someone in." We allow a "foreign entity" to penetrate our emotional "immune system." It is not just me and (the rest of) the world, but WE and the world (or against it). Although there are a lot of other "WE"s of which we may be a part (e.g., culture, religion, nation, sports, clubs, political parties, friends, etc.), the most significant ones by far are the ones related to the family we come from (in its multiple expressions, shapes, and forms) and the family we will potentially create (which may also have many shapes and forms but will usually involve a partner with whom we may—or may not—have children).

In romantic terms, especially at the beginning, a new WE marks a stage of bliss, of sweet, childhood-like enmeshment. Even if it is just for a brief period of time, we enter the romantic realm longing for, as we have seen before, what the father of attachment theory, John Bowlby, termed a "secure base." We look for the she or he who will provide a source of warmth, care, and safety (connection) as well as a base for play and exploration (autonomy).

Once we come across that person, it will feel wonderful but also scary. Like any baby at the first stage of attachment, we experience both the bliss of connection and the terror of losing our attachment figure. When the partner is there, we feel good and secure. And then we also experience the almost absolute dread and helplessness of a baby when we realize how much power the other has on us, especially at moments when they do not "deliver" as we hope or expect. Our happiness and well-being depend to a large degree on someone else who we do not control.

It may take days, months, years, or a whole lifetime—if ever—to feel safe. In this relationship more than any other, we feel vulnerable, as it is in this relationship, more than any other, that our primitive needs—the same needs that we have had as kids in relation to our parents—will be at play. This is the relationship that will activate the most "regressed" version of ourselves, and here is where we will also express, once again, all the needs, insecurities, blessings, and curses that we have experienced in our own families. This reenactment of our most vulnerable, baby selves will be one of the main challenges that the couple will be called to address and overcome.

When people say, "She is never like this normally" or "He behaves this way ONLY with me," now you know why. We may manage to keep our baby side from our peers, but not our partners. Romantic relationships are the one interpersonal space where our infantile side is most present and active—just think of all the love songs with the word *baby* in their lyrics!

So the two main sources of nurture, belonging, and connection are:

1. Family love

2. Romantic love

Romantic relationships will be, on a very fundamental level, our parental substitute. There is no other relationship in which we are more regressed and in which we feel more needy, vulnerable, or exposed within our adult lives. The implications of this are immense, and we will be looking at them later on. When the individual seeks emancipation from the family and then looks for a new source of nurture and connection in a partner, two parallel processes start to unfold. On one hand, we perceive the other as this amazing human being who will respond to our fundamental needs, wishes, and desires. This is the primitive, childlike brain, observing and experiencing.

Now, if we imagine my inner child observing my partner, and my partner's inner child observing me, we essentially have two kids looking at each other, perceiving two amazing creatures who may or may not actually exist! During the time we are in love, we are looking at a 100-percent wonderful adult who will love and care for us like no one has, and, on the other hand, a 100-percent grateful child who will receive us in their lives as their savior, providing the care and safety that no one has delivered to them before. During the initial stages of coupledom, in other words, we live in a fantasy—the fantasy of two perfect "parents" who will have superpowers to deliver everything needed and the fantasy of two perfect "kids" who will be wholeheartedly grateful for all that they will receive.

Despite the delusion that characterizes young love, such fantasies (or maybe visions) can have an amazing effect on both members of a couple. Under another's loving gaze, we may manage to activate our potential—that is, our "birthright self," the adult we were meant to be or have always wished to become—and open up to receive love and care or to experience life with hope, optimism, and intensity again, as a child does.

I believe that we do perceive something authentically marvelous, divine, or transcendent in our partners at the beginning of a relationship. We also connect with those aspects within ourselves, which is probably another reason why falling in love feels so wonderful and enchanting.

The WE's Mission

The couple's relationship is a dance of parts and wholes, of the primitive and the transcendent, of autonomy and connection, of the past and the future, of morphogenesis (evolution) and homeostasis (conservation), of the old and the new—all within an ever-changing framework of space and time.

Consider John of TANGOland, whose agenda will consist of many fascinating projects:

1. SURVIVAL

   a. OLD WE → I (autonomy): Differentiate from his TANGO family so that he can claim his identity and "wholeness" in relation to the previous project

   b. I → NEW WE (connection): Establish a new "home" that will serve as a new source of nurture and connection, where he will operate as part of the new project

2. EVOLUTION (morphogenesis): Be a better TANGO dancer than the previous generation

THE OLD-NEW-BORROWED-BLUE TUG-OF-WAR

An easy way to remember all of the pressures that a couple encounters can be found in a well-known wedding tradition in which the bride has to wear "something old, something new, something borrowed, and something blue" at the wedding.

We can compare these four traditional elements to the various forces exerted on the individuals ("parts") within a couple, as well as the couple as a whole:

- Something old: the pull of the past and the families of origin ("homeostasis")

- Something new: the pull of the future, growth, and the development of the new systems ("morphogenesis")

- Something borrowed: the pull (and DNA!) of the partner, including the give-and-take of autonomy and connection

- Something blue: the pull "up" of the will toward transcendence, the will to create something different

3. CONSERVATION (homeostasis): Ensure the survival of TANGO

4. TRANSCENDENCE: Create a new "dance" that goes beyond the TANGO he has known

So John goes out into the world with the complicated task of finding that special someone who will foster his goals of survival, evolution, conservation, and transcendence in the following ways:

1. a. Offer something new and different from TANGO that will help John differentiate from his own family

   b. Feel familiar enough to TANGO in order to facilitate a new source of connection

2. Support him in his project to take TANGO further and improve it

3. Respect or be fascinated by TANGO, which will reassure John of his identity and help him maintain the link to his origins

4. Collaborate on something new that transcends what he has known, offering the opportunity not only to improve things but also to take steps beyond what has been lived and previously experienced

What makes relationships so remarkable is not that they often fail, crash, and burn, but that they actually manage to get off the ground on so many occasions. When an agenda as demanding, complicated, and apparently contradictory as the above works—even for a short period of time—we could consider it a miracle. And it is not just one agenda; it is actually three: John's, his partner's, and the couple's as an entity of its own accord.

Like any other entity, the parts of the couple will need to work together in order to form a coherent whole that ensures the survival of the greater organism. We become "specialists" within the whole—a bit like cells forming different parts of the body or different departments making up an enterprise. In a functional system, roles and labor are distributed in a logical manner. It makes no sense to duplicate functions. We do not have two brains and no heart in a body, or two foreign affairs ministries without an interior one in a government. If one cooks, the other might set the table. If one plays the piano, we do not expect anyone to sit on top of the pianist and do as they do. According to Pauli's exclusion principle, formulated by Austrian physicist Wolfgang Pauli in the first half of the twentieth century, two identical elements (e.g., fermions [quarks and leptons], the particles that make up matter) cannot occupy the same energy state at the same time. Within a society too, our roles and chores are widely distributed. We do not do it consciously. We generally just occupy the spaces available within given contexts.

The viability and well-being of the whole, as well as the parts, in the case of a couple, will depend upon factors such as:

- How comfortable we feel with our position within the whole.

- How comfortable our partner is within his/her position.

- How well-defined and flexible the whole is—or can be.

- How well-defined and flexible we are.

- How well-defined and flexible our partner is.

- How valued and respected our position is within the whole.

- How valued and respected our partner's position is within the whole.

In other words, the couple will survive and do best having a well-defined, strong yet flexible structure that enables it to adapt to its environment and ever-changing circumstances and situations. The better equipped the partners are to occupy each other's roles, the greater the chances of the couple's survival, and the sense of confidence and security in relation to the project. One may be a great driver, for example, and the other one a magnificent cook. Both will naturally gravitate toward the roles, functions, and positions that they feel most comfortable with. The one who likes to drive will probably do the driving most of the times. Same with the cook. Now, if there is an unexpected situation, where the driver or the cook cannot fulfill their part of the equation for some reason, the couple will do best and experience the least amount of stress if each partner has the ability to also occupy the other role for as long as it is needed.

And this will be the case in relation to aspects such as autonomy and belonging, the feminine and the masculine, or the "child" and "parent" roles. Within the couple we are likely to occupy primarily one side of the pole, as what happens with magnets when coming together. It may be more or less rigid for different couples, but the distribution will be there, irrespective of sexual orientation. In general, within the couple we are likely to get "pole(a) rized." The greater the respect and appreciation given to every role, pole, and function within a relationship, the richer, happier, and more resilient the relationship will be.

THE POWER OF SEX

OH THE JOYS AND WOES OF SEX! Together with romantic love, sex defines the very essence of the human couple. We could say that romantic love and sex are the two "substances" that distinguish couples from any other human system. And they do so even when they are not present, even when they are not practiced within the couple. A couple is a couple when, at least in principle, eros and sex *can* manifest within its boundaries. On the contrary, eros expressed or sex practiced outside of the couple threatens its identity, viability, and existence.

Sex at its best expression, which is when it actually comes in a pair and forms a couple with eros or agape, could be considered a sort of magical merging. It is a "gate" to everything. Within its interpersonal space, we can experience connection and autonomy, being a part and being a whole, nurture and transformation, regression and transcendence.

As a force that makes, breaks, and transforms human systems, sex is less present when the main need of the organism is conservation, safety, or parental attachment. It is more present when the interpersonal space is a laboratory of exploration, transformation, and experimentation. It is central during the couple's initial stages, even when it is not practiced, even when it only lies in the realm of fantasy. It feeds and empowers the parts and is more needed at those times when the I's seek to grow. Still, it continues to be important and relevant throughout the couple's life cycle. Sex is the glue that "seals" the organism of the couple, and the couple is the only inter-personal context within which humanity is generally comfortable with its practice. Any other setting or space is commonly associated with some kind of controversy, resentment, or rejection.

Given sex's power (there may be no other force as effective in the making and breaking of humans and human systems), we would greatly benefit as a species by understanding it more thoroughly. While we know a lot about the reproductive and biological aspects of it, the psychological side and functions of human sexuality remain largely unexplored, despite its centrality in our culture and the fact that its reproductive function is hardly ever relevant in its practice nowadays. So what do we need sex for, other than reproduction? This is precisely where we lack theory, which is in itself quite an interesting phenomenon. It indicates that despite sex's importance, we have been reluctant to approach it in these terms. We—especially men, I would argue—are extremely vulnerable, fragile, and dependent creatures in relation to sex, which may help explain the lack of theory. Regardless of what the reasons holding us back may be, it is still essential that we explore it. Sex is one of those forces that literally "makes the world go 'round," often in the most destructive ways. A deeper, more wholesome understanding of human sexuality could help us extract its amazing transformative power, as well as protect ourselves from what can be "deadly," traumatic, and destructive.

The theory presented here is, of course, limited. In lack of answers myself, I primarily aim to raise questions as well as to suggest an alternative vision of and approach to sex and sexuality. These ideas have been shaped through years of practice, thanks to the many brave and meaningful conversations I have had with the people I have been attending.

Sex and the Individual

One of the conversations I feel particularly grateful for took place just as I was writing this chapter. Joan (who was happy for me to use his real name) and I were discussing sex when at some point he paused and remarked,

> We need to make a distinction here. Sex, in my view, is about two different aspects: (1) one's sexual value, and (2) the actual experience and practice of sex. Both are important, but they are not necessarily related. One can have high sexual value, that is, be very attractive and desired by others, and at the same time be a lousy sexual partner. They may not even like sex. On the other hand, there are people like myself, who have very little

sexual appeal to others but always care for every sexual experience to be special and for the partner to enjoy it. One can be a good lover without having sexual value and vice versa.

He then went on to talk about beauty being a great asset to one's sexual value, as well as status, money, and power—the latter especially in regard to men. I found Joan's definition, which distinguished individual sexual value from sex as an experience, to be an incredibly important insight. Not only did it "fit in" with the theory, but it also provided a "key" conceptual component for sex to be understood within both individual and interpersonal terms. On one hand, we have individual sexual value—that is, the value of the part. On the other, we have interpersonal sexual value, as it is expressed within the system. Our culture seems to be obsessed with the individual sexual value, considerably favoring it over what would be its interpersonal counterpart. In terms of the theory presented here, we could define it as our "connectivity value." The more attractive, young, strong, healthy, rich, and so on we are, the more likely it is that others will want to "fuse" with us. The more "fusible" we are, the greater our value in connection terms. As long as the value is high, we will not need to worry about connection.

High connectivity value means that if we get to feel the need to fuse with someone, someone will be available to connect with us. Most women do not worry about their connectivity value because they can usually obtain connection any moment they feel like it. They can even get paid (or exploited) for the connection they provide. Within the sexual realm, those in more desperate need of connection are actually men. Their need renders them significantly more insecure and vulnerable, generating a dependency that has had grave consequences throughout human history.

Now, our connectivity value or individual sexual power, as Joan pointed out, is not directly related to the actual practice of sex. Most individuals will make a lot of effort to enhance and preserve it, even if they are not drawn to sex at all. "Connectivity value" is more of a marker of one's status within the social context, rather than a marker of sexual desire or sexual availability. When it is high, one can say to the world, "I am great. I can connect with whomever and whenever I want. I may not want to, but I can."

PART III: EROS AND AGAPE | 63

The more "connectable" we are, the greater our chances of survival in the jungle of life.

So, in modern society we seem to understand sexual success as, basically, an individual affair. There is definitely a lot of truth in this, yet the interpersonal dimension of sex is of paramount importance.

The "Dance" of Sexuality

In interpersonal terms, every sexual experience will involve a dance between connection and autonomy. How (and how frequently) partners "dance" will vary according to various factors, such as gender, age, context, or moment in the life cycle. Sex is likely to be far more present, for example, at the early stages of a relationship, when a strong connection between the parts that compose it needs to be established.

In my view, there is also a significant difference in the way men and women go into the dance, no matter what their sexual orientation. Men seem to seek fusion as a means to primarily nurture the part, their "connectivity value." It is about the "I" more than about the "WE." Women seem to seek sexual fusion as a means to nurture the "whole." It is more about the "WE" than the "I." Women generally experience less anguish about their "connectivity value," as they usually have plenty of it—sometimes more than they wish to have. Men tend to be less worried about the bond, often also wishing to have less of it. They are more likely, on the other hand, to experience a lifelong anguish about their "connectivity value," seeking sexual experiences to reaffirm themselves as desirable parts, sometimes to the end of their days. I have found this particularly relevant in the lives of homosexual men. The research in this field, little as it may be, supports such observations. Blumstein and Schwartz,[2] for example, revealed that lesbian women's sexual activity was far less frequent, on average, than that of other couples (gay men and heterosexual). The way I interpret it is that women, no matter what their sexual orientation, have less "connectivity value" anxiety. Far more confident than men as individuals in that respect, they do not need sex as a means to affirm themselves.

Within the context of any particular dyadic sexual experience, no matter the biological sex, gender identity, or sexual orientation of each partner, both poles will be present: masculine and feminine. Each member of the couple—whether heterosexual, homosexual, gay, lesbian, trans, queer, or any other way gender and sexual orientation are defined—will occupy a pole, even if it is just momentarily. The masculine and the feminine poles serve one another as they merge during the sexual act. The feminine side will offer connection within autonomy; the masculine, autonomy within connection. One offers roots; the other, wings. Individuals may shift poles within a partnership or change poles depending on the partner they happen to be with. Whatever the circumstances, the basics of the dance, at least in my view, are quite universal.

The tasks and challenges involved for individuals on each pole was wonderfully described by a client who defines himself as a heterosexual male, also occasionally drawn to sexual encounters with transsexual partners.

> When I have sex with women, the initial anxiety is about performance. I am the one giving and I feel I need to do it well. I need my body to respond to the task, to perform well, to provide satisfaction to my partner. When, on the other hand, it is about sex with a trans person, I am on the receiving end. My anxiety is about trust and being treated with respect. It is an experience of surrendering myself to the other.

When at the male pole, he offers sexual power (autonomy); when at the female pole, he offers sexual surrender (connection). In a good sexual experience in interpersonal terms, each pole will be at the service of the other, merging in order to nurture and empower one another.

Regression

Sex involves, to a large degree, an experience of going "home." The intense fusion and momentary lack of boundaries between the parts activates both the most regressed side of us (the infant) and the most transcendent and least conditioned by our physical body (the [fantasy of the] divine). Sex is where the most primitive and most divine expressions (or little-god-fantasies) of ourselves meet.

Without a doubt, sexuality sets the interpersonal space where we most regress. It is necessary that we do. In order to receive nurture, we need to be openly dependent. Nature has provided us with this space for it. There is no other interpersonal space in our adult lives where we are more infantile. Sexuality allows us to establish a communion with the other and receive nurture from a position and degree of such fragility and dependence only comparable to our childhood.

This means that we are not very adult in our sexual encounters. There is very little (if any) of our mature, adult side in this context. It takes as little as a simple look at how everything is staged—how we speak, the games we play, or the way porn is promoted—to realize that it is not our mature, higher selves that we seek to "celebrate." It is our regressed states that take over. It is about being childlike and primitive again, now within an adult body. Sex may be the only interpersonal space where adults are allowed to act out as kids again, expressing their needs as primitively as they do.

Given that our strongest memory of nurture is our childhood, our sexuality is very likely to be defined by what we lived during the earlier years of our lives. We seek, now as adults, to have experiences of primary love and connection. So we are very likely to stage, reenact, or fantasize what we experienced in childhood as primary love and connection. We seek the familiar: if we were caressed, to be caressed; if we were abused, we are likely to be drawn by abuse; if we witnessed violence, to seek violence.

It has always impressed me to observe how closely linked our sexual life is to early life dynamics with primary caregivers. This unfortunately also means that if the primary relationships were adverse, such adversity is very likely to be reenacted within one's sexual life too, in the form of fantasies or actual sexual experiences. As these sexual experiences often also trigger orgasms, which make for very powerful positive reinforcement, we condition ourselves to stick to those scripts, and we act them out not only in our sexual relationships but also in our lives and the way we relate in general. I remember American psychologist Dr. Lorna Smith Benjamin saying at one of her seminars: "How can one work with a narcissist who wishes to move on, while he continues to have orgasms fantasizing about abusing women? It is therapy versus powerful operant conditioning. It is almost impossible to move forward this way and change the pattern."

Is there a way "out"? There is no way not to regress, but we can always care for the primitive side, the child within. We can try out different fantasies, explore different options. The partner can play a significant role in this, providing safety, respect, and therefore healing that will in turn help trigger new primitive experiences, new fantasies, or new "turn-ons." The idea is to take care of the primitive—the children that live within us and, even more so, the children that live around us, the latter by simply keeping them far away from our regressed states.

Transcendence

And then again, there is another dimension to it. Within the sexual experience, boundaries become hazy. Fusion means a momentarily loss of the part to the whole. It may feel like a connection to infinity. We get a "taste" of ourselves and of each other that goes beyond our identities, our bodies, our social personas, our ages, and our circumstances. There is a sense of timelessness as we seem to participate in the flow of life and the workings of the universe. In this light, sex could be one of the most joyful, celebrated, and respected expressions of adult human experience. After all, nature celebrates its sexuality every spring. Why not humanity?

PART IV

THE JOURNEY OF WE

L ike any dance, or any piece of music, the couple will also have a beginning, a main theme, and an end. The tunes and the issues that will occupy the interpersonal space of the couple will be different as the partners move along from one stage to another.

THE STAGES OF LOVE

THERE ARE THREE STAGES IN THE LIFE OF A COUPLE: CHILDHOOD, ADOLESCENCE, AND ADULTHOOD. The primary task of "childhood" is to establish *connection*. The main task of "adolescence" is to establish the partners' *autonomy*. Adulthood is about the skillful interplay between connection and autonomy, both within the couple and externally—that is, in the way the couple relates with the world. When accomplished, adulthood sets the ground for *emergence*—for the partners and the couple to evolve, develop, and grow; to move beyond their past; and to eventually be of service to the greater whole.

Some couples will manage to transition from one stage to the other, while others will not make it beyond childhood. Some couples will reach adolescence and die quickly afterward, while others will remain stuck in that stage for a very long time, perhaps forever. Adulthood is neither inevitable nor guaranteed; it is not even a desired stage for some. There are those, for example, who prefer to go into and out of childhood eternally, changing partners all through their lives.

STAGE 1: Childhood

John and Louise have fallen in love. They are amazed and mesmerized by one another. They tick all of each other's boxes, they have a lot in common, and they experience a sense of closeness and familiarity, as if they have known each other forever. At the same time, they are attracted to each other's differences too, as they marvel at all the new and wonderful things that each brings to the relationship. There is so much to share!

Things are flowing well. John and Louise are happy dancing together. They are also happy dancing each other's dance. At times, they may not even know or care what dance they are dancing or what it is they are doing as they are fascinated by the experience of being with one another. They may talk about individual projects and reassure each other that they will "be there" for mutual support. They may reveal their past pains and promise one another that they will be different, that they will really care. They may look into the future and invent different realities or dream of common projects. They feel happy. Most boxes are ticked at this point in time, or so it feels. Differentiation from the old and reconnection to the new is happening, together with a promise of evolution and transcendence.

Our couple is now happily enmeshed in a new world, a new organism that they are building together. They may get excited or even honored to also officially enter and become members of SALSA/TANGOland, meet each other's parents, and get a taste of the origins of their respective dances—or not. There is a sense of completion, of not needing much else but the other's presence.

We could say that the first period in the relationship of a couple—its childhood—is very much like the individual's childhood. It is fun, exciting, and wonderful, when things go well. Everything is experienced more vividly than at any other time:

"You and I are one!"
"You are the world to me."
"Nothing can come between us!"

The inner child has found its new "placenta," so to speak. At the same time, partners feel more powerful than ever. They are seeing the best version of themselves reflected in the eyes of the other, and they are seeing something otherworldly, something divine in their partner. This translates into an experience of great strength and extreme vulnerability, all at the same time.

We idealize the other as we idealized our parents when we were little kids. We idealize ourselves too. Our expectations from ourselves and from the other are also as demanding and often as unrealistic as the expectations of a baby who perceives the caregiver as a godlike figure. So we expect them—and we also expect ourselves—to be attentive, caring, strong, protective, smiling, ever thankful, available, and so on.

Simultaneously, we are extremely fragile—as fragile as a baby. Maybe if it were not for this fragility and almost utter dependence on the other for our well-being we would never abandon this stage. It is the happiest time when things go well, but it is also the most dreadful and painful when they don't. Again, the dynamics at play are similar to childhood. We are at the other's mercy. If they do not deliver, pain and frustration are almost guaranteed.

There are no clear boundaries during this stage, either; the boundaries of the I's are less important than the territory of the "WE." We all start off with fusion, like a mother with her baby. Yet we cannot afford being immersed in enmeshment for too long. At some point, we will need to set boundaries and claim our identity. Life moves on. Things evolve. Babies grow. And so does the relationship.

Almost like a pendulum, the forces will push toward a new "balance" and state of affairs. This is where most romantic films or great dramas end. It is either summarized as "love conquers all," with the couple overcoming obstacles until they come together and live happily ever after, or, despite the intensity and depth of their love, they are unable to live and experience their apparently perfect bond. The world comes between them, as in the case of *Romeo and Juliet* and many other tragedies. Sadly, we lack in music, literature, or movies that dwell upon the greatness of couples who manage to continue dancing all through their lives.

STAGE 2: Adolescence

John and Louise have been dancing together for a while now. It has been exciting, adventurous, creative, fun. Like in childhood, the early stages of coupledom are great in many ways but require *a lot* of energy. At some point, they will seek—or start falling into—patterns, routines, ways of being and doing that require less expenditure of energy to keep things moving between them. In short, the couple will need to delegate parts of its functioning to "automatic," "default" modes—the kinds of modes that require less thinking and less effort. We could say that it is the organism seeking an eco-friendly modality.

Let's say that John invites Louise to move in with him, and Louise happily accepts the invitation. After a while, she starts moving things around in their place so that it feels more comfortable and more like a "home" to her, as she understands it. In principle, this is wonderful. "Home is where the heart is" and where belonging lives. However, the home Louise will gravitate toward will inevitably be influenced by SALSA. Those who have danced SALSA all their lives will quite naturally step into SALSA mode even without meaning to—even if they have consciously decided not to dance SALSA ever again. It just happens. SALSA is Louise's default mode, we could say.

So there may come a moment when John will find himself immersed in SALSA and may think, "When did *THAT* happen?" It may seem to him that their interpersonal space has all turned SALSA overnight. Or it could be the other way around. It could be him saying one day, "Louise, you are with me now, so you should behave in such and such a way, which is the right way." It may happen wilfully or not . . . but it *will* happen.

The patterns we seek to install will be our own, familiar patterns. And we will invite our partner, perhaps without meaning to, to dip into them. At this point, enmeshment involves a very different experience: the threatening kind. When immersed in foreign territories, we feel insecure. If they are also felt as hostile, they can be perceived as a direct threat to our survival. It is the kind of enmeshment we cannot afford: the enmeshment with an enemy. Intimacy, in these terms, if the integrity of the parts is not guaranteed, can become a very frightening affair. So an experience that feels like a motherly, loving cuddle, can suddenly turn into something as frightening as fighting for survival inside the mouth of a predator.

When the primitive brain sounds such an alarm, defense mechanisms will be activated. John will defend his integrity, and Louise too. They will seek some sort of differentiation from one another, and they will move toward their respective familiar territories: TANGOland and SALSAland. Their defense mechanisms will reflect and operate in accordance with all that they have learned about threat and safety in childhood from their caregivers. They will go "home" in their attempt to defend their integrity and identity. This regressive pull toward the roots will open the door for the houses of TANGO and SALSA to now enter and officially become part of the relationship.

This passage is inevitable. Enmeshment will call for differentiation at one point or another. The enmeshed baby will eventually become the adolescent who seeks independence. We have seen that adolescence in an individual is initiated when the "family," the whole, is properly installed in the adolescent's mind. The adolescence of the couple will be about both respective "houses" getting included in the relationship before it can move on to adulthood.

This is the stage Romeo and Juliet missed. We do not know what would have happened had their story continued. What is certain is that, had they lived, they would not have escaped it. We cannot move forward unless we incorporate our past into the new organism. Cells can only create a more complex life form if, on one hand, they have defined identities as differentiated cells, and, on the other, if they carry *all* of the information of the whole within them. Similarly, there is no way for a part to create a new whole unless it is differentiated from the previous whole, and the previous whole forms part of the new equation one way or another.

The adolescence stage of the couple is, primarily, a period of negotiating with oneself and the partner on how the respective "houses" will be incorporated into the relationship, in terms of personal or family identity, roles, hierarchy, and much more. What will vary is the level of fear, ease, or tension with which the couple manages to handle these movements. With a much heavier load now, John and Louise are called to continue their journey.

It is an extremely challenging journey and mission—one that the whole of humanity has struggled with throughout history. There are no good scripts, no role models—hardly anything that will help the couple manage and successfully negotiate this process. This extreme lack of useful references takes us very far back in time and is reflected in all realms, including spirituality and the way the divine is understood and represented in different religions. Couples have not constituted entities to be worshipped in themselves—at least not the way individual gods or groups of gods have been worshipped. They have not represented paradigms to be reproduced "as in heaven so on earth," so to speak, either. We have Adam and Eve, whose only well-known interaction gained them eternal damnation. And Mary and God, whose relationship is impossible to reproduce. It may be easier to reenact the short-comings and eternal problems of Zeus and Hera, but this less-than-ideal couple from Greek mythology is not precisely the best model to follow. We then have Buddha, who, as mentioned in part I, left his wife and son behind to pursue enlightenment, and Muhammad, who had thirteen wives. These two spiritual leaders may have achieved great things individually, but their approach to relationships would cause great concern to any contemporary therapist if they came in for a consultation.

The human species clearly lacks powerful role models of balanced, functional couples. As such, we draw from our respective parental models, the couples we grew up with or were surrounded by, which are all too often examples we'd prefer to avoid rather than follow. We are also influenced by the highly unrealistic examples of couples, still in the childhood stage, that lived "happily ever after" in romantic movies.

Since John and Louise have likely had poor examples of healthy, long-lasting romantic relationships, as very few parents or artistic, religious, and cultural works have managed to provide it, they are more likely to get stuck when the relationship officially enters adolescence, the identity-seeking stage. The duration of "stuckness" may vary from a few months to a whole lifetime. All too often couples remain stuck for years. The frustrated adolescent countenance remains, even after a divorce, or until death do they part (and maybe even after death, who knows?)! There is a global epidemic of human couples and ex-couples stuck in the stage of adolescence, with grave consequences for all involved—especially their children.

Bringing the Past into the Future

Adolescence marks the beginning of a new period and, therefore, also involves closure. It is the "death" of childhood, of innocence, of sweet, careless enmeshment. It will inevitably involve some pain and suffering, as we will need to let go of one stage as we enter another. The cycle of life is about birth and loss, and loss involves pain. Nevertheless, a lot of the pain can be avoided if we are skilled at helping one another move forward.

Let's imagine that John and Louise have had it much better than most mortals. Both of them have had a good family experience. They have been taken care of and loved (connection) as well as encouraged to explore and discover what makes them different and special (autonomy). All caregivers involved have had a well-developed feminine and masculine side. The care-givers have also been capable of moving from one pole of the relationship to the other without problems, providing connection and autonomy when needed, while highly appreciating what each one represented and brought to the equation.

At the moment their kids were ready to leave the family, they allowed for the transition to take place, confident that they would be able to readjust to their new reality. When presented with their son- or daughter-in-law, they would welcome them even if they did not see eye-to-eye with the choice of their offspring. They might express their concerns respectfully but, in the long run, as parents they would take a step back, knowing that the new organism is a priority now. They would participate in the couple's life when invited, providing connection and support when required, and allowing for its autonomy at all other times.

If John and Louise's family stories and experiences were reflected along these lines, then our couple would probably not face any serious challenges during the adolescence stage of their relationship. They would allow TANGO and SALSA to "hatch" and manifest in it and then jointly decide how to include them in a constructive manner, neither of them forcing their will on the other. They would have no fear about their future together because they would have learned that there is nothing to fear.

Yet, the vast majority of people have lived with an understanding that there is a lot to worry about regarding relationships, and that partners (like parents) are not to be fully trusted. The adolescence stage of the relationship, in this case, will pose greater challenges. The process is very similar to adolescence in its exhausting and often frustrating back-and-forth with the partner, defining and negotiating one's own identity and role within the relationship, as well as defining and negotiating the relationship's identity and role within the context of the larger family, the community, and the rest of the world.

This stage of identity and definition (inner and outer) is a "rite of passage" for the couple. And, crucial as it is, this is where most problems emerge and where we usually get stuck. The need for definition demands answers that we sometimes seem incapable of producing:

- Who are you? Who am I to you, or you to me?

- How will connection and autonomy manifest in our relationship?

- Who will provide what, when, and how?

- What is your role? What is mine?

- What is the value that we attribute to each other's roles?

- Who is in charge of this or that?

- Who are we to the world? How do we relate to it?

- Who are we to each other's families? How do we relate to them?

- What is our project? What are our priorities?

Some answers will come easily, while others will be very difficult to resolve. Some others may take years or decades of elaboration. What is certain is that this stage will inevitably take place, and such questions will arise and will need to be addressed in one way or another. It can be at the beginning of the relationship, before or after getting married, when becoming a parent, or when the kids have left home. Any time may present itself as a time to (re)negotiate identity, roles, boundaries, and loyalties—transitional periods and times of crisis being key moments for this.

The main aspects that we define and negotiate are:

1. Our identity, roles, boundaries, and value in relation to one another

2. The relationship's identity, role, boundaries, and value in relation to the families of origin

3. The relationship's identity, role, boundaries, and value in relation to the world

In terms of autonomy and connection, and the dynamics between the parts and the whole specifically, the couple will need to define:

- How the roles will be distributed. That is, whether one or both will be in charge of connection, and whether the other—or again, both—will be in charge of autonomy. In other words, how each will occupy what we have defined as the feminine and masculine poles within the organism, in order to ensure its survival.

- How much autonomy and connection will be permitted within the couple. How much value will be attributed to each pole and the different roles and functions related to it.

- How rigid or flexible these roles and functions are going to be.

- Hierarchy. What, when, and how needs are expressed and by whom; when and how they will be met. When it is okay to be "one up" and when not. This includes determining which partner will be in charge of the nurturing, at which times, and what kind of nurturing is available or acceptable, and under what circumstances.

- How rigid the system will be in terms of hierarchy.

In relation to the "outside" world, the couple must determine:

- How rigid or flexible the boundaries will be between the couple and the outside.

- Who will be more in charge of connecting to the outside and who will be the one maintaining the boundaries.

- How enmeshed or autonomous the couple will be in relation to their respective families of origin and how they will be reacting to them, among many more aspects.

We may not realize it, but the number of variables that we have to negotiate as part of a couple is vast. Surprisingly, we actually succeed at times. Even more miraculously, we can get there without explicitly talking about any of it. We do it as we discuss or fight about who is going to take out the garbage, when or whether to marry, who will look after the kids, where we will go for holidays, who will drive the car, and how money issues and bank accounts will be dealt with. We do it implicitly rather than explicitly, positioning ourselves mostly without reflecting upon or explaining our position—very much like what happens during an impromptu dance.

This implicit, poetic, indirect way of dancing with the partner—marvelous during the stage of "sweet, childhood enmeshment"—can pose important obstacles during the adolescence stage. Verbal, higher brain communication will be key now, especially in times of friction. Talking things through with adolescents, approaching them respectfully and honoring their autonomy as if they were adults, makes them feel respected; it works with the partner, too.

As mentioned earlier, some couples will make it through this stage, some not. Adolescence can carry on indefinitely until a) both partners manage to "hatch" and feel comfortable within the organism, and the relationship as a whole manages to define itself in relation to the families of origin and the rest of the world, or b) the couple as an organism dies.

It is either transformation or death. The factors that will determine the outcome is, basically, the ability of partners to communicate and negotiate, their capacity to see the world from the other's point of view, and their ability to go beyond the self-centeredness of a baby or the reactiveness of an adolescent. The task will require a partnership that is strong and mature enough to allow for both parts to claim their legitimate need for "wholeness" within the new system. The intensity of the struggle will also be determined by the degree to which each individual has managed to accomplish this task initially, in relation to one's own family.

STAGE 3: Adulthood

John and Louise look at one another and smile. It is the smile of two accomplices. They have now been through enough together to know that neither of them is a superhero; they are limited human beings, like their own parents, who will never meet each other's—or their own—expectations. They now like each other better this way. They can laugh—when they do not cry—about their shortcomings. They feel connected and they feel free.

John and Louise know now that the other will be there when a need arises. They operate as a team, taking care of their project from their respective, changing positions. Louise supported John in building his career. When John lost his job, Louise was there to comfort him and reassure him. She took over the burden of keeping them afloat financially. John took care of their household for a while. Despite the challenges and frustrations that life has posed, they have managed to stick together and resolve the friction and the differences between them.

There is still hardship. Life is not easy. What is different is that, within their organism, they recognize each other as a vital part. Alarm bells have almost ceased to sound in relation to one another. They do not pose a threat to each other. And when they do, they approach it as a misunderstanding that they then address and resolve—or they simply let it pass.

John and Louise are there for those around them, too. They came together when John's father needed their financial help and supported him. They took Louise's mom into their house when she fell ill. And when their parents started to interfere with their business, they set respectful yet clear limits. Both partners helped each other see their respective parents as lovable creatures with their own limitations. John helped Louise have a better relationship with her father by making her see how much her dad loved her, despite his inability to express it. Louise was there to help John unwind after—as it seemed to him—his mother's incessant whining about everything. They are respected and accepted within their social context and have some good friends. Their focus now is less about reaffirming themselves in relation to one another and the world that surrounds them; it is more about giving—to one another, to their children, and to their respective families, friends, and the community. Feeling safe in themselves, as wholes and as parts of the couple, the organism they have created together, they are now able to contribute to the whole.

Guiding the Horse

Adulthood is not about getting older, interpersonally speaking. Nor is it about ceasing to be childlike or, even less so, about letting go of the "child within." We could say that an adult in relational terms is someone able to make children (the inner children, the primitive side of oneself, and the partner) feel safe, comforted, and happy to be, experience, and explore. An adult in these terms is mature and psychologically strong enough to care for somebody else apart from themselves. This includes caring for the children within (and the real ones if they exist), as well as regulating their own emotions to an acceptable degree. In sum, adulthood within a relationship is about skillfully caring for different kids:

1. The child within (our primitive side)

2. The partner's inner child (their primitive side)

3. The children we give birth to

This requires that we acknowledge and accept the primitive sides of our own parents and all human beings.

The brain is a good metaphor to explain this. We could say that our subcortical brain is the child and our cortical brain is the grown-up.* When we are born, we are not developed enough to take care of ourselves; even less so, to regulate ourselves emotionally. We will need our caregivers for this. It is the caregivers' brains, subcortical (primitive cues, such as tone of voice, gaze, touch, and rhythm of breathing) and cortical (such as attributing meaning to the experiences, guiding, explaining, and knowing what to do) that the child is helped to organize and regulate emotions.

We could say that the subcortical brain is like a powerful stallion that can take us to the most amazing places but will need our guidance to do so. The cortical brain is like the jockey, a lot more skilled and intelligent than the horse but far less powerful. Babies do not have a skilled jockey for their horse at the beginning. Their jockey will develop skill through the years by absorbing the learning and instructions of the caregivers. So, at the beginning, it is the caregivers caring for our "horse," and later on our jockey begins to take over, having been instructed by the caregivers themselves first. This means that the way we will be treating our "horse"—ourselves—throughout

---

*Not the adult; the grown-up. An adult is someone who can see and appropriately care for children. A lot of grown-ups never manage to get there.

our lives (especially at the beginning, before incorporating other influences such as those of teachers, partners, authors, therapists, coaches, etc.) is going to be almost identical to the way our caregivers treated us.

When an individual seeks therapy, the relationship between rider and horse is usually in great difficulty. Both parts experience hardship. The "horse" is usually in great pain and the rider is about to fall off, overwhelmed by the situation. Quite often, the experiences we have had with our caregivers have not promoted happy, strong, confident "horses," and the lessons we have learned from them have not produced skilled, confident, animal-friendly riders either. Or maybe they have, but life sometimes can be so overwhelmingly painful that our coping skills are just not enough. At such times, we seek comfort and help from another source—a source that can provide a safe haven for the "horse" while also supporting the "rider" to feel more confident, so that he or she can then take over.

This is what a therapist does, but it is actually a very common human behavior. When a friend in grief comes to us after having suffered a loss, we give them a hug and a shoulder to cry on, we connect and acknowledge their suffering (care of the horse), and then, at some point, we start supporting the "rider," too, by reminding them of their attributes or telling them that we see them as capable of moving on.

Interpersonal adulthood is about being able to provide care, nurture, and guidance to "the horses" of the world—one's own, the partner's, the friend's, and society's. It is about understanding, soothing, containing, giving voice to, and guiding the primitive. Life can only be lived and enjoyed when our primitive side is both safe and fully engaged.

A couple at the stage of adulthood is itself a safe haven—a refuge from external stress, a place to rest and recharge batteries, a space for healing and comfort, and also the starting point of new explorations. Each individual will find the nurture and support they require in order to grow and thrive personally, professionally, and socially. This is now a space for both (and, if there are kids, even more so for them) to get nurtured, grow stronger, and feel safe.

Interpersonal adulthood requires a working relationship between the cortical and subcortical parts in the way we relate to ourselves and others. It is not an easy enterprise for anyone. It entails assuming responsibility and acting respectfully. It requires strength and confidence. It involves approaching wild animals—the primitive in ourselves and others—when hurt, and still being able to provide safety as they show us their teeth. Above all, it requires a broader view of the relationship—a view that goes beyond the duality of good and bad, right or wrong; it requires a vision that can encompass the whole social system and the structures within it.

WE IN THE LIFE CYCLE

THERE IS NOTHING STATIC IN NATURE, AND RELATIONSHIPS ARE NO EXCEPTION. As with all other forms of life and matter, they change and transform through time. The main themes and issues that will occupy the interpersonal space of the couple will be different as the partners move along from one stage of life to another.

We have already looked at the inherent stages of a relationship—its inner, emotional "clock": the childhood, adolescence, and adult stages. The passage of time will introduce yet another set of variables—and challenges—to the couple.

Morning: Awakening, Experimentation

"To WE or not to WE?" Falling in love is a high-risk enterprise that only the bravest will have the courage to traverse. Our first experiences are usually quite powerful. We do not forget our first loves and heartbreaks. These relationships are schools of life that force us to grow, that get us out of the home and help us see ourselves from almost every possible angle. Within them, we will get in touch with our light and our shadow, our strengths and our weaknesses, the most divine and the most primitive within us. Slowly but surely (and often quite painfully), eros, or romantic love, teaches us about who we are. It is self-definition time.

Some people will prolong this period, passing from one relationship to another, exploring and experimenting, falling in and out of love or just having experiences for the sake of it. During this time (which seems to be getting longer with each passing generation in the Western world), individuals are likely to experiment to a lesser or greater degree until they commit to a more "serious" relationship.

Such experimentation can involve pretty much anything, from simple flirting to longer or shorter relationships with one or more partners, homosexual and/or heterosexual experiences, online encounters, long-distance affairs, one-night stands, swinging, polyamory, and so on. As we have the opportunity to experience ourselves in different interpersonal contexts, we start having a clearer idea of who we are. The experiences will help define (among others):

1. Sexual orientation and sexuality in general

2. The interpersonal position we favor within the model most familiar to us (mother/father) and role (masculine/feminine)

This stage is usually a "fluid" time of emotional insecurity. Belonging is yearned for and feared at the same time. We often try to appear more autonomous or self-sufficient than we really are. Some people will not move on, despite growing older, uneasy with the idea of commitment, belonging, or aging.

There are many interpersonal challenges in our first years as adults that could be summarized as: "To WE, or not to WE?" The young adult may perceive a new "WE" as potentially hostile territory. They have just managed to step out from home and have not yet learned to skillfully care for and defend themselves and others interpersonally. They are likely to still feel their parents' powerful position in relation to them, which will also be reflected in the way they approach their partners.

The greatest challenge will be for those who come from a troubled family experience—for example, those who have been very needed within the family of origin (e.g., being the only emotional company to a lonely or abused parent) or have learned to operate more like a part rather than a whole. The previous family organism has needed them for its survival, and so has "taken" more than it has "given" to them. The sense of Self may be quite fragile too—and romantic love is too powerful a business for fragile selves. The individual may refrain from falling in love, cultivate only platonic relationships, go into relationships and sabotage them shortly after, or be a "serial" partner, moving on swiftly every time a "WE" starts to define itself.

Learning how to deal with our defense mechanisms will be another big issue. During early adulthood, we are like kids with heavy weaponry when it comes to intimacy. We are scared little creatures with powerful munitions in our hands. What do we do with our defenses? Keep them down and get maximum nurture, risking maximum hurt? Or stick to our guns, taking minimum emotional risk but putting at stake the very essence (and point) of having a partner? Going into a love relationship defended is similar to arming a little kid and sending him or her off to play.

"I have been hurt before, so I must protect myself (from you)" is the kind of thing we say. This could translate into, "I have been in a situation where I felt attacked. I now see you as a predator too, so I have already put up my defenses, just in case."

Afternoon: Construction

"What kind of "WE" are we?" Once we decide "to WE" rather than "not to WE," the next challenge will be to define the identity of the new WE. As we move on in life and become older and more secure, we are likely to allow ourselves to have a relationship that is more settled in its structure and definition. The inner and outer functioning and roles of each partner are now clearer. This stage favors connection and belonging. Agape—the attachment type of love—will make itself gradually more present and have a more central role. Passion and sexual desire may diminish somewhat. The love of exploration and transformation will make space for the love of nurturance. The Self will give up part of its individuality to form a stable whole.

The relationship, as a system, will be strengthening its boundaries in relation to its context too. It may define itself as such through marriage or cohabitation. Given that it will have to remain an open system at all times, partners will be deciding at this stage the degree of permeability they will allow in relation to their context. Ideally, it will be open enough for the partners to go in and out freely and for the couple to obtain energy, connection, and autonomy in relation to its context. The fire within will grow stronger with the oxygen provided by the outside. Safety and stability may be the leading forces at this stage, but enough space will be required for the "air" to come from the outside and strengthen the fire of the whole and in each. Too much air can make the fire go so wild that it burns the whole structure down, as in the case of infidelity. Too little air, as when one partner fiercely controls the other, could extinguish the fire altogether.

Giving up individuality is the main challenge that the partners will need to face at this stage. An "I" that forms part of a strong "WE" has the advantage of having a stable foundation of nurture and the disadvantage of having reduced autonomy. As we tend to "get serious" when we are also setting off for other important projects—such as a professional career or expanding the family—the need for a safe haven eclipses the need for extra autonomy. Yet, in our quest for safety, the boundaries that we set and the control we exercise on one another can become suffocating. If we do not make sure the relationship is flexible enough, at some point it may need to transform—or die.

Late Afternoon

"Can WE survive ourselves or others?" The couple usually sets off toward common projects. The most common one is having children, but it is not the only one. This period is one of the most active, creative, and productive in the life of a couple. The main challenge during this time will be the couple's need to arrange and rearrange itself in relation to its projects and important third "parties," such as offspring or elderly parents.

The couple as a system will be more rigid at this stage. At its best, it will serve as a secure base for the partners and their projects, activating creativity (autonomy) in relation to the rest of the world. At its worst, if the parts do not feel valued or fulfilled in their life path, it will feel like an entity that can "smother" individuality, and that can be a threat to personal value and identity.

One of the most challenging transformations at this stage (which can also happen at a later or an earlier stage too), if and when it takes place, is the passage to a "parents only" WE, marked by a separation or a divorce. Separating the two functions—letting go of the romantic partnership while maintaining a functional, working collaboration as parents—will make for a time- and energy-consuming process. Similarly, the construction of new WEs involving children of previous partnerships will also demand effort and skill, so that the new organisms are able to face the new challenges and advanced complexities of the new stage.

The main challenges that are characteristic of this period are more extensively described in the next chapter.

Evening: Reorganization

"Am I in a midlife crisis, or are WE in crisis?" After years of occupying quite fixed roles and positions in relation to common projects, there usually comes a call for major change. The relationship is likely to reach this stage in life somewhat tired, as a WE that is worn out after years of effort to meet life's constant challenges. Partners may sense a need to refresh, in themselves and as a unit. When such rearrangement is needed, eros, the love of transformation, may reenter the equation—for better or for worse—pointing to a new relationship, demanding for life to start moving again, and forcing the partners to make important decisions about the course of their project. Such a moment of crisis that calls for transformation is related to the children moving toward adulthood.

An inevitable rearrangement for the couple comes at the time children leave home or are about to do so. The "whole" will have to transform again at this stage, and the couple will need to facilitate the transition so that the new generation can "open the door" to the world with confidence. It is a particularly difficult moment for the parents, as it involves a loss that was first marked by the end of childhood and the beginning of adolescence. (Bye-bye, fun times! Farewell to feeling big, strong, and important as a parent!) At this moment, the caregivers' fundamental tasks involve:

1. Supporting the autonomy of the offspring

2. Supporting one another in order to let go of the kids

3. Rearranging the couple's relationship structure

These are usually quite challenging times for the couple, as they mark the beginning of a new period that is often uncertain and confusing in terms of direction and purpose. The horizon is becoming shorter with the passing of time and can begin to feel less appealing. The partners will be called to look at one another again. The I's may have gotten quite "stiff" after years of being of service to others, working for a certain objective, or sorting out the demands of day-to-day life. Partners will need to reconnect and find a way to dance that will provide them with a sense of togetherness—a connection that was put on "automatic mode" during the project-related years. The better the foundation they built during the earlier stages, the easier this task will be. In any case, the relationship may have already gone through various other times of crisis or inevitable rearrangements related to external or internal factors: economic booms or recessions, accidents, professional transitions, taking care of elderly parents, illnesses, or the loss of family members. In such cases, once again, the capacity of the couple to adapt and transform will be the definitive factor for the relationship's well-being.

Night: Returning

As we arrive at the final stage of our life cycle, the pull toward transformation is less prominent. This period is more about reconnection—our return to Mother Earth or the "existential soup," as I like to call it. It is "agape" time again. We seek home and safety. The roles and identities are pretty much fixed at this point. The "I" is quite fixed and rigid, and it will very much depend on the "WE" that it belongs to. The identity is more solid, but the individual is far more dependent on the context than before—almost as much as when one was a child. The "I" will therefore feel less powerful and more insecure or anxious with the passing of the years. The individual is unlikely to survive well without being sheltered by the larger organism. There will be a strong need for the partner or the extended family. When one of the partners passes away, it is not uncommon for the other one to soon follow. The individual is more a part of a whole than a whole in itself. The main difference from childhood is that the parts that make up the whole and the whole itself are now pretty rigid. Changes will be felt as a threat rather than something to welcome.

An important challenge during this period is coming to terms with the gradual loss of autonomy and, also, the possible loss of existential shelter. Old age poses a threat to both the "I" and the "WE." We do not like it; we generally fight it. Quite often, a false sense of autonomy is maintained by trying to boss the partner or other people around, paradoxically at times of great fragility and need.

The objective, at this point, is to find a way to meaningfully connect, to nurture and be nurtured, to give and receive love. The greater the sense of connection, the easier it will be to let go of our partner, of the relationship, and of life itself.

PART V

NAVIGATING ROUGH WATERS

John and Louise have been barely on speaking terms lately. They have been stepping on each other's toes, in every attempt to "dance" together, whether it is salsa, tango, or, really, any dance. They feel angry, hurt, misunderstood, lonely. What do they need to do?

There are usually very important, powerful reasons that "hold us back" from finding resolutions—reasons that directly relate to our identity and interpersonal skills, which are in related to our personal history and experiences. Within the couple's interpersonal context, no one is stupid, no one is evil. We are just human beings trapped in the extremely complex task of surviving and evolving, trying to find a way to embrace and include the past in our way forward, with the partner sometimes perceived as a great accomplice and sometimes as a terrible threat.

INNER TROUBLE

FEAR IS CENTRAL TO RELATIONSHIP DYSFUNCTION. We saw earlier how extremely fragile we are within a romantic relationship. The other is practically "under our skin," as together we have formed a "WE." This "WE" binds us together and separates us from the rest. The transition from the warm and friendly to the cold and hostile in a couple can be instant—and dramatic. In neuroscientific terms, it is our amygdala that detects and "decides" upon threat and safety issues. The perceived threat level will determine the brain's focus and the mode that our whole body and chemistry will adapt in a given situation. When we go into defense mode, when the other has been categorized as a possible threat to us, our more complex cognitive functions get compromised. Our levels of anxiety get raised and we are not in a position to do anything constructive anymore. We are in fight-or-flight mode, and it is the "I"—the part—trying to survive. Consequently, the "WE," the whole, is under threat.

The Defenses

Our defenses are the WE's major internal problem. On the one hand, they are there because they are needed: they protect the integrity of the I's that compose it. Yet, if they are used by the I's to attack one another, the WE is in trouble. It is the organism attacking itself.

Our primary caregivers are the ones who teach us the fundamental lessons in life about threat and safety: what to fear and what not to fear, and how to act accordingly. If they have taught us explicitly (through their words) or implicitly (through their actions) that relationships are painful and frightening affairs, then inevitably we will fear them, too. If they have shown us that in a relationship one can be a villain or a victim, we will be on alert regarding the actions and behavior of our partner. They also teach us about what is "normal" within a relationship and what it is not, what is acceptable and what is not. The prolonged exposure to our caregivers' relationship during childhood brings with it a familiarity and a sense of normalcy—and therefore safety—that will then condition the way we approach our own relationships.

Louise's upbringing did not involve much parental control. Her parents would encourage her to make her own decisions, especially as she grew older, and rarely worried about her whereabouts. So one day, about a year into her relationship with John, she decided to go on a small trip. She did not let John know about it, however. In fact, she did not even think about letting him know, because, in her family, it was normal for everyone to do their own thing, without seeking permission or necessarily informing one another. But John was surprised and not at all happy about it. He wanted to know where she went, what she did, and with whom. In his family, it is common courtesy to keep family members informed of one's plans, and he expected Louise to act accordingly.

Now this is unknown territory for Louise. It is a script she is not familiar with. Control is not part of her family's "DNA"; in fact, she is threatened by it. To her, John is acting "crazy." Her defense mechanisms are now activated. She learned from her mom that one way to protect yourself is to "shut down." Mom would lock herself in her room and refuse to communicate with her dad for a few hours or a couple of days after a conflict. Dad, on the other hand, would usually get really angry and show it in a variety of ways—most often by becoming verbally violent. Louise learned and absorbed both kinds of defense mechanisms, among others. In this particular moment and relationship, she reacts like her mom by shutting down.

It is now John who feels surprised and threatened. To him, knowing where your loved one is, what they are doing, and with whom, is normal. This is how his family has always operated. He actually considers it as a way to show someone that you care. As a result, he does not understand Louise's behavior and thinks she is being unreasonable. The one thing he definitely cannot tolerate is her reaction, as his mom would all too often use the silent treatment. His defense mechanisms are now activated. Ironically, he now also "merges" with his mom (the interiorized version of her), employing another set of defense mechanisms she would often also employ. When John's mother felt she was being overlooked or disrespected, she would usually respond by making bitter, hurtful remarks. And that is exactly what John does.

They are now both immersed in the stories of their respective families. John's reaction reminds Louise of her dad—actually, of all that she did not like about her dad and had promised herself to avoid in her life. And Louise's reaction reminds John of his mom and all the behaviors of hers that he despised.

As they look at each other in this moment in time, they are likely to be seeing a version of the partner who feels both very foreign—as foreign as any other external threat—and also quite familiar. The familiarity connects to two different visions:

1. The other's family: "You are being exactly like your mom/dad!"

2. One's own family: "You act exactly like my mother/father used to act, and I hated it."

What they are not seeing:

- The other as a scared child trying to defend him- or herself

- How they, themselves, have activated the other's defenses

- Their reactions being exact copies of their parents' reactions—the very same ones they have loathed or wished to avoid

John is not seeing how he is contributing to the conflict. He just feels misunderstood and unjustly treated. The same goes for Louise.

This kind of blindness is universal. We are not particularly conscious of our own regressed states—if at all. We are very rarely aware of how our inner child "acts out" and impacts the other. We do not like to acknowledge the primitive within us; even less so are we attracted to the idea of the primitive in the other. We are not happy, for example, when biological mothers or fathers step in to offer their care to our partners—or, in fact, any other person. The primitive in the other is only welcome when we are both in a very loving mode, mainly during the childhood stage of the relationship, and under quite limited conditions, such as when:

- The other's "babyneeds" do not pose a threat to us

- We consider such needs appropriate in a given space/time

- Attending to the partner's needs makes us feel stronger, wiser, or more adult-like ourselves

- We are the only ones attending that baby

Take Naya, for example. She is a very competent, bright, working mother, married to Mike, a soft-spoken man, caring father, and well-respected professional in his field. They admire and love each other deeply, and, as they say, their friends see them as the perfect couple. What is striking to me is how Naya dominates their interpersonal space. She does all the talking, calls the shots, and sounds like she is also the one making all the important decisions—including who is to be considered a friend or a foe. As she speaks, Mike nods silently beside her, every now and then turning and looking at her with care and admiration. As I point to their style of interaction, Naya looks at me in disbelief. She does not understand what I am talking about. According to her, there is nothing noteworthy about the way they interact, but that sense of "normalcy" radically changes when the focus becomes Mike's relationship with his mother. Naya becomes furious at that point and talks about him being dominated by his mother, not being able to draw limits, being docile and subservient, not ever having his own voice, needing to man-up.

In sum, we cannot usually stand the dependent side of our partner unless it makes us feel more important, stronger, or better ourselves. Sometimes this need—or sense of insecurity—is so pronounced that we do actually look for dependent partners or even promote their dependency, so that we can feel bigger than them and, therefore, safer. The condition is, always, for their dependency to be exclusive and not to pose a threat to us. In other words, we only see a baby when we want to see a baby, and we only want to see a baby when it makes us feel good about ourselves, with our own primitive side calling the shots.

So we often fail to approach our partners in an adult manner, allowing ourselves to see the world from the other's point of view and being mindful of and attentive to their needs. The partner senses that. We all know when we are being approached constructively and when we are not, when it is for our own benefit or when it is purely out of interest. When we are not convinced by the way we are approached, we are very likely to also react in a childlike manner as well. The difference is that, when it comes to ourselves, we will probably come up with a very good story to explain our dysfunctional behavior. To start with, it is nothing more than a response. Our own unfortunate reactions are usually defined as the result of the other's bad actions. The cause of the other's negativity either remains a mystery or lies anywhere but in ourselves.

We are usually quite happy to hold accountable anyone or anything—the other's childhood, their mother, father, sister, brother, stepdad, boss, the therapist, the food they have just had, their lack of sleep, their personality, their mental health, their genes, the universe—but not ourselves. Each one of us is going to be the good one—the hero, the victim—in our own stories, our actions being a mere response to the other's wrongdoing. This phenomenon is reflected in *Pragmatics of Human Communication* (1967) by Austrian-American psychologist Paul Watzlawick: "The nature of a relationship is contingent upon the punctuation of the communicational sequences between the communicants."[1] This means that, when two people communicate, they structure—and therefore understand and react to—the sequence and flow of information (which, in turn, conditions the relationship) in different ways. *Punctuation* refers to the way a sequence of events is structured by each communicant, including which event is labeled as a cause and which as an effect within any interaction.

In simple terms, communication is biased in the way we experience it and interpret it.

> Disagreement about how to punctuate the sequence of events is at the root of countless relationship struggles. Suppose a couple have a marital problem to which he contributes passive withdrawal, while her 50 percent is nagging criticism. In explaining their frustration, the husband will state

that withdrawal is his only *defense against* her nagging, while she will label this explanation a gross and willful distortion of what "really" happens in their marriage: namely, that she is critical of him *because* of his passivity. Stripped of all ephemeral and fortuitous elements, their fights consist in a monotonous exchange of the messages "I withdraw because you nag" and "I nag because you withdraw."[2]

We react; *they* act. *We* are not being listened to, *we* are being treated unjustly, *we* are misunderstood. *We* defend ourselves; *they* are being mean or crazy. Louise will say that she has to go off on trips because she needs some space to breathe, because John is so pushy and controlling. John will say that he is pushy and controlling because of Louise's inconsiderate behavior.

This theory stems from the *Steps to an Ecology of Mind* (1972) by British anthropologist Gregory Bateson. Together with four more axioms, it is described as a universal phenomenon of human communication.

Fear, Control, and Neglect

Now, what sparks our defenses? Well, anything really. In the interpersonal dance of life, the sudden pull, the stepping on one's toes, the rhythm we are not familiar with, a misstep, or a lack of engagement from our partner is very likely to be registered as a threat to our safety.

Two primary fears commonly appear at the root of the dysfunction:

1. Fear of losing connection: the loss of the other, the loss of the WE.
2. Fear of losing autonomy: the loss of Self, the loss of the I.

Fear of Losing Connection

This fear is probably responsible for most of the shortcomings of our world and may be unique to the human species. Lack of connection equals death, and given that our partner is often a primary source of connection, we can easily feel that we are at their mercy. A sentimental separation—a breakup, a divorce, the rejection of a partner—is probably the most painful situation we will experience in our adult lives. It is the baby losing their attachment figure. It is a child being abandoned. The experience is similar to spinning toward a black whole of nothingness, so any movement that suggests impending separation can potentially trigger a sense of dread.

When this fear is activated, the universal remedy of preference is *control*. There are many desperate, sad, dramatic ways that we opt to maintain connection via control. And it's not just the partners who suffer; the world at large suffers and is held hostage to such power plays.

Control is the most widely applied "solution" when faced with the fear of losing connection to the other, when we feel that their autonomy poses a threat to the "WE." Men have traditionally used control in physical, practical terms. Women have used control more in psychological, emotional ways. Between us all, we have formed quite an impressive vicious circle of shared and perpetuated misery.

Control is also a direct attack on the integrity of the part. The "I" as an entity gets compromised. It loses agency (autonomy) and becomes subservient to the other "I." Such conditions are not tolerated long term by the I's under attack. Paradoxically, the more we try to achieve connection with someone by exercising power and hostile control, the less this someone is available for connection. Ask any adolescent and they will explain how it goes. Hostile control is more than a threat to the other and, as said before, sets off the other's defenses and a whole new set of problems and fears.

Fear of Losing Autonomy

Our second greatest fear is loss of autonomy, the loss of the "I" to the "WE." This is the fear of our individuality getting dissolved within the relationship. The "I" will fight to stay alive, and this struggle is what psychotherapy primarily deals with. The common denominator of individuals seeking therapy is an unresolved question: "How can I be with him/her/them without losing myself?" The only way to ensure connection for some people has been by giving up part of their "Self" or their project to have a separate self and identity. They do this because their primary caregiver was not in a position to provide connection unless they themselves were supported. Part of the individual will therefore dissolve into the whole, in order to ensure the latter's survival. The more prevalent the symptoms, the more the "Self" is compromised. We rarely ever successfully defy such assaults to the Self (practiced usually as external attacks by fathers or internal invasion by mothers) because we cannot afford to lose them altogether. Mental health disorders make for a "perfect" midway solution: neither with you, nor without you. I communicate that I am in distress; I thus claim some integrity for my Self, but I am not directly pointing at you, defying you, or openly challenging our relationship.

When the fear of losing autonomy is activated, the most common way to respond is by getting angry or building interpersonal walls. Anger is an emotion that facilitates separation; it protects us from invaders. Other adaptive behaviors involve stepping back, hiding, or keeping emotions and needs to oneself. Obviously, it is difficult for any dance to work under such conditions.

So on one hand, exercising hostile control, in any shape or form, is an attack on the other's integrity. But on the other hand, when we consciously or unconsciously ignore someone who requests our attention (such as when we are absorbed by our smartphones), we are not offering autonomy to that person. Instead, we are communicating rejection, dismissiveness, and neglect.

Neglect is the most impactful and painful communication there is for a human being, especially at a young age when the brain is still developing. "You do not exist for me"; "You are not important to me"; "You mean nothing to me"—these are among the most powerful and traumatic messages one can receive. Neglect is hostile autonomy. In a similar way, many versions of control are hostile connection. In hostile autonomy (neglect) conditions, connection is lost. Within hostile connection (control), there is no autonomy. In such conditions, the couple's dance has no chance to work and flow.

Curiously enough, men, who have traditionally represented autonomy in relationships, usually do a great job seeking it, but quite often fail to provide it to their partners. Similarly, women, who have traditionally fostered connection and belonging, frequently—especially after the appearance of children—cease to be emotionally available to their partners. In other words, we seem to make a very big deal about those very things that we, ourselves, fail to provide to the other.

Why? I guess it is because it is easier to take than to give. As we provide autonomy and connection to our partners, the risk is that they will become stronger and more fulfilled . . . and may eventually not need us anymore. Or they may not give anything back, leaving us alone, weak, and starving.

Sexual Challenges

We saw earlier that defenses pose the greatest challenge to the couple in terms of safeguarding the autonomy of the parts without compromising connection—that is, the integrity of the whole. Sex poses the greatest challenge in terms of safeguarding connection without compromising autonomy—that is, the integrity of the parts.

At times of inner trouble in the relationship, its difficulties will almost inevitably be reflected in its sexual life. Though sex may bring some of the most exciting, fulfilling, satisfying experiences in the life of the couple, it will also likely pose its greatest challenges. This is because the sexual experience can be both extremely nurturing and fatal to the I's involved. It is fusion at its most extreme expression, involving a momentary loss of Self. So, if one is to feel good and happy about losing themselves in the act, even momentarily, they need to feel confident that they will also recover themselves afterward and rejoice in the integrity of a stronger and brighter I.

How often does this happen for both? And how often do partners, especially long-term partners, go into the experience feeling that their I's are safe, valued, and respected by the other in their daily lives and routines, before they give themselves up to the sexual experience? There is no way for good sex to take place if the I's are not in a good place to start with. At the same time, if no intimate connection is taking place between partners, sex can also be terrible. At its best expression, it nurtures both the I's and the WE. It helps partners feel stronger in themselves and more connected to the other. At its worst, it is a threat to one or both partners and to the relationship as a whole, stripping one or both of their integrity and self-esteem.

There are infinite ways to get to a miserable sexual experience. If there is one thing human society has in abundance, it would be bad sex, ranging all the way from simply unsatisfactory to absolutely tragic. The possible scripts on offer here are innumerable. The one I will present is one of the least terrible ones: a classic scenario between people who love each other and mean well but fail anyway.

Louise was raised, like the rest of us, in a world where almost every swear word is related to sex. In order to verbally attack someone, one of the best and easiest ways to do it is to position the other on the receiving end of a sexual act. Getting "fucked" will therefore raise mixed feelings to almost anyone who is supposed to occupy the feminine pole. Louise cannot relate to the position society has delineated for her as a sexually active woman. Family has not helped significantly change such perception either, as there was no indication of any sex taking place between her parents in the first place and, even less so, of her mother enjoying it. She ended up feeling very ambivalent about sex. Is it an act of love, or is it a threat? Is she going to gain something from the experience, or is she bound to lose?

John was raised in the same society. He learned that if he was to be cool, he had to have sex—lots of it, ideally without even feeling anything about his sexual partners. Sex is about taking, not giving, the world around him seemed to indicate. It was defined, above all, as a marker of male value. He did not feel particularly comfortable with this but never voiced it out loud, just in case it reduced his particular value—something no male can afford.

John and Louise went into their first sexual experiences heavily biased by these social constructs and feeling in love at the same time. John felt very strongly about Louise; he wanted her to have a good experience, but he had learned to worry about his sexual value first and the satisfaction of his partner second. Louise would be more worried about her integrity rather than establishing connection. She went into the experience feeling attracted to John, but, even more so, she felt scared. Meanwhile, John totally missed out on the opportunity to center his attention on Louise first, to ensure that she felt safe, to provide a sense of autonomy, warmth, fun, or play at the beginning. He performed anxiously and forcefully in Louise's mind, while she surrendered, not due to being turned on but out of a sense of obligation: a "close your eyes and think of England" kind of experience. Or, close your eyes and think of something more important than personal satisfaction, such as the bond itself. "How was it for you, darling?" asked John. "Great," said Louise, as the guardian of the "WE" who did not want to pose any threats to it. She stood up, went to the bathroom, and cried.

Louise will learn to offer herself this way, feeling less willing and less motivated with the passing of time. At some point John may "bring her" to therapy, both claiming that she does not function. Is it biological? Is it due to past trauma? After a few years of unsatisfactory sex, Louise has decided she has had enough and told him straight and direct, as the empowered woman she has decided she will be from now on. She tells John what he has to do and what he cannot do in order to satisfy her, giving orders and, above all, making sure to point out everything he does not do well. He feels more and more anxious but does not say anything, as it would lessen his already questioned sexual value. This situation in turn has a massive impact on John's "performance." They decide he has a problem. Biological, maybe? Or is it because of his controlling mother?

A lot (practically everything, in my view) of what is currently defined as individual sexual dysfunction is actually interpersonal failure disguised. It is the interpersonal "dialogue" within the sexual act—or the relationship as a whole—that needs to be "fixed" rather than any person individually. When the interpersonal dynamic does not function properly, on any level of the relationship, the sexual experience will reflect it.

Our failures almost always involve the lack of one or more of the baseline components: respect, safety, and togetherness:

1. **Lack of respect.** "I see you, I admire you, I am here for you." Sex is, among other things, a celebration of both ourselves and our partner. If one feels disrespected, not seen, or humiliated, the experience will be a "fail." The wife who does not feel valued and appreciated is not likely to offer connection. The husband who is not allowed to connect and feels like an outsider in his own home is unlikely to offer autonomy in the form of making his wife feel great about herself, within or outside a sexual experience.

2. **Lack of safety.** The one who will introduce the other into their body will need to feel absolutely and entirely safe in themselves and within

the relationship—physically, emotionally, mentally, and spiritually. We only invite home those we trust. The door to one's own body requires a far greater sense of trust and safety. Both partners will also need to feel safe in themselves—appreciated, desired, admired— particularly the one who feels he or she has to "perform or deliver."

3. **Lack of togetherness—or lack of love.** We seek fusion via two very different—and very common—experiences: via eating and via sex. Eating involves the death of the other. It is the kind of fusion that means the end of one organism for the other to live. Sex, on the contrary, is about life and creation, as the two may become three. It is not about the survival of just one of the parts, even if it is often practiced as such. Fusing with someone without their consent and desired participation, without togetherness, is a sort of death— the death of the WE; the death of empathy, respect, collaboration, dignity, and so much more. It is one of the biggest and most terrible interpersonal fails of human existence.

Failure does not have to be epic to be a failure, and it is actually far more common than people realize. A successful sexual "dance" will involve not only the consent but also the satisfaction of both sexual partners. I would go as far as to advocate for people to avoid having sex if they do not think both themselves and their partners will enjoy it. John cannot afford to lose Louise for his individual needs to be met, nor Louise to lose herself for the needs of the relationship to be met. If one gains and the other does not, well . . . better not. The quick fix of loveless sex, inconsiderate of the other, has the effect of addictive substances: it briefly soothes but leads to serious long-term problems and worn-out souls. One of my most beloved professors, Luigi Cancrini, said once at a seminar, "Every time sex is practiced without love, I think the souls get scratched."[3] He added that maybe his views were outdated, related to his old age, but I could not agree more.

OUTER TROUBLE

"NOBODY LIKES COUPLES. NOT EVEN GOD," asserted renowned Italian family therapist Carmine Saccu in an interview for a Spanish newspaper. "Nobody likes them because (the partners) love each other, they make plans together, they keep the rest further apart."[4] He presented various examples of those who can feel excluded—among them, God. Adam and Eve, he claims, by disobeying God, formed a triangle in which they were closer to one another in relation to the Almighty. The latter was not pleased and punished them for eternity. Similarly, according to a Greek myth described in Plato's *Symposium*, couples were very different creatures at the beginning of time. They were called androgynous and were merged and mighty, with one body, two faces, four legs, and four arms. They got to be so powerful that they provoked the fear and resentment of the gods, who resolved to destroy them. And so they did: Zeus divided them into two separate entities. From that point onward, they were doomed to operate as "halves" and search for one another through life.

A couple may not be a closed system, but it is probably one of the most closed and self-sufficient ones to be found in the human realm. Those who do not form part of it (the child, the friend, the mother-in-law, or gods themselves) can feel excluded and, when they do, they will usually fight it. It is an inevitable and necessary tension, as the couple itself cannot survive as separate from its environment. Yet, its interaction with third parties will make for its main and ongoing challenges. A couple will need to stay open as well as differentiated—connected yet autonomous—from other systems, which will mean the appearance and existence of numerous "triangles" that will in turn need to be attended to and resolved if the couple is to survive. We will be looking here at the most significant ones: families of origin, children, and lovers.

Intergenerational Entanglements

The existence of a partner is, in itself, a sign of some degree of differentiation from the family of origin. The degree, however, may vary vastly among different couples, cultures, and individuals. What is noteworthy is that we seem to share with our partnersa very similar (if not the exact same) degree of differentiation from our respective families. According to pioneer American family therapists Augustus Napier and Carl Whitaker, "Some mysterious chemistry usually links partners who are virtually psychological twins."[5] No matter how different we may be, no matter how different our families may seem, we, as individuals, are probably at the same developmental level.

This may be good news for those who have achieved a decent degree of differentiation, but it can mean further complications for those who are still tangled up within the structures and workings of the previous organism. Families of origin can pose some of the most challenging triangles that a couple will need to resolve. Consider Jacob, the son of very religious and authoritarian parents. Jacob, probably in an attempt to claim a different identity to the one imposed, started to go out with Helen, who was not religious and not an acceptable partner for their son. In order to maintain ties to his family, Jacob hid the relationship from his family for many years. Helen's wish to have a baby triggered the process that led to their separation. Having to hide from Jacob's family, already very difficult for the couple, would be impossible with children being added to the picture. What would happen then? Jacob did not want to find out. He was unwilling to do anything that could make the family strings snap, so the relationship came to an end.

Unfortunately, something may have to break if the choice is presented in absolute, "either-or" terms. It is generally preferable, if there is truly no other way and no other choice, that the family's strings snap (instead of the relationship's), as it is more in line with the life cycle and evolution. This was not the case for Jacob. Interestingly enough, once the relationship was over, he could not be around his family anymore. Helen's presence in his life allowed him to have a separate self and definition in relation to his family, at least in his own eyes. Their control was tolerable while she was around. At the moment she was out of the picture, the family's pull and intransigence was once again a threat to his identity and autonomy. After the breakup, he attended to this need by seeking distance from them.

Helen's presence, as is the case with almost any partner, facilitated Jacob's differentiation from his family. However, Helen and Jacob did not succeed in fully forming their own organism. The family's pull, in this case, and Jacob's need to keep intact his original source of belonging, made it impossible for both projects to survive.

Let's now imagine a somewhat different scenario: a couple whose families were opposed to its union but who moved forward anyway. Let's say that Romeo and Juliet have managed to survive and go beyond their families' mutual hatred and contempt. They have moved further than Jacob and Helen from the previous example, leaving their families and respective issues behind. They have accepted and even celebrated their differences, which was a breath of fresh air in relation to the controlling, authoritarian attitude of their respective families. Juliet then gets pregnant and they have a child. All of a sudden, they are faced with issues that did not bother them up to this point.

Romeo says that he would really like Juliet to breastfeed the baby. His mother had breastfed him for almost two years. Juliet does not want to. She was never breastfed, and she came out wonderfully! She suggests instead that they do bed-sharing. Romeo won't have it. No one in his family ever did. He suggests that their daughter be named after his grandmother. He was really close to her. Juliet would rather name the baby after hers. She is not happy about their offspring being a Montague either, after all the suffering the family put them through. Romeo does not understand why Juliet wants to keep her family name, as they have disinherited her. Juliet wants their daughter to go to the school she went to, but Romeo is very proud of his education and would like their child to follow in his footsteps. He does not understand why Juliet wants to work. His mother never did. She does not need to either . . .

If our level of connection, loyalty, or entanglement with our families did not seem to be significant or evident before, it will inevitably become apparent with the appearance of our offspring. At that moment we are called to occupy our parents' roles, which will in turn further propel us to define ourselves in relation to our partner, and our caregivers too (those we carry in our head and the real-life ones).

The couple will need to redefine itself in relation to the families of origin, as it also searches to establish its frontiers and its own identity. Each partner will be an advocate of the other's emancipation and, at the same time, will fight for his or her own identity and roots, as we have seen before. At the same time, the couple will need to decide on the level of distance, proximity, and involvement of the previous generation in their lives and the raising of their children.

So, families of origin will significantly interfere in the life of the couple. The greater the entanglement between generations, the greater the suffering—and the more severe the mental health issues. When the parts, the wholes, and different generations mix and fuse in ways that they were not supposed to, the situations that arise can be quite dramatic for everyone involved.

The Overbearing Mother-in-Law

Those in charge of belonging and connection are the "home makers." They are the ones that build the nucleus of the new organism, which will then feed and be a source of nurture for all its components. Their mission is of great importance. Without belonging, without the glue that holds the parts together, there is no organism. Their role, therefore, is fundamental and deserves to be highly acknowledged and respected.

The guardians of the connection and belonging of each project, often represented by the mother (family of origin) and the female partner (new family project), will work—and sometimes fight really hard—in order to keep their respective projects alive. They will defend them from anyone or anything they feel could put them at risk. The most common threat is often perceived to be each other.

Walter is the older child of a widowed mother. Since his father's death, his mother's life focused primarily on him, as his younger sisters lived abroad. His mother had never had a paid job and now lived off her deceased husband's pension. She did not build a social circle and had no interest in remaking her life; she was happy living with her son. When Walter got married, she asked to move in with him, too. Although he refused, the marriage was forced to include a degree of such intense intimacy between mother and son that his wife found it impossible to bear.

When Carl's father died, his mother bought a family grave, where she and her sons were also supposed to be buried. All her children had their own families at the time and lived in different countries and continents, yet it was paramount for her, as she said, "to keep the family together"—even in death. It was only when one of her granddaughters questioned the idea that she realized that, by wanting to hold together the "original family," she was exercising a force that was having the opposite effect—a "pulling apart" force—on the new ones.

When it comes to mothers and daughters, the dynamics at play can be quite different. Having belonged to the same family, they are often aligned in keeping the intergenerational bond intact, and they often do it all too well because they are both experts at it. Jane was her mother's pride and source of support all through her life. As the younger sister of a brother with a severe and chronic illness and daughter of an unhappy marriage, Jane focused her attention on her mother. She was the one looking after her mother's well-being and happiness. Soon after Jane got married, her husband became secondary in the relationship. Almost all decisions in the new family were made between Jane and her mother. The marriage was under threat.

Such stories usually ignite feelings of anger or irritation toward the people and situations that seem to obstruct the natural course of life. We do not usually like or approve of those who pull backward instead of pushing forward, making it so much harder for the new generation to move on. It makes a lot of sense that we feel this way, in evolutionary terms. Such feelings are actually there to warn us about threat. They are there as reminders that the "show must go on," urging us to defend the integrity of the new projects.

Similarly, Louise will naturally feel uneasy every time she sees John acting like more of a boy around his mother rather than a grown man. John will feel uncomfortable when Louise turns to her family for safety and comfort. It is a natural and healthy reaction, in line with growth and evolution. We push our partners to become adults, to separate from their families of origin, to "grow up," emancipate, and commit to the new organism. This in itself is good—and necessary. It is *how* we go about it that is often unfortunate.

What is counterproductive are not the feelings themselves but, all too often, the ways we address them. If the protagonists of the stories above, and so many others, are to move forward, they need to find a way that will allow them to ensure, first and foremost, a connection to their roots. They will not be able to advance if they feel they are abandoning or betraying their origins. The previous organism is a source of life and, also, identity. If it fails, they fail.

Tangled Up with the Families Within

Another seemingly "lighter" but far more prominent and universal entanglement with the family of origin takes place in our minds. It is an inner entanglement that we then "act out" in relation to our partners. All those who, during childhood, had to struggle with their caregivers and did not manage to ever resolve or feel comfortable in the relationship will continue to struggle as adults—for justice, acceptance, acknowledgment, or approval. They wrestle internally as well as externally (with the partner), repeating the very same struggles.

Luke had a very traumatic childhood. He had to endure physical and psychological abuse by his mentally troubled mother that no one in the family would openly acknowledge and, even less so, address. These traumatic experiences became a kind of "taboo" in the family and were never discussed, treated, or elaborated on in any way. There was no justice done, not even in the form of acknowledging that Luke's childhood was anything but easy. No one ever expressed any warmth or remorse or accepted any responsibility for all the pain he had endured.

As an adult, Luke was extremely apprehensive about relationships and intimacy. He would not trust anyone. He fell in love almost in spite of himself and, after a turbulent marriage and an even more turbulent divorce, Luke's emotional life continued to heavily revolve around his ex-wife. His view of her was almost identical to that of his mother: a woman with a lot of unresolved issues who made him suffer and got away with it. He would feel at the mercy of his wife as he had felt with his mother, despite the fact that he was now an adult who was causing as much pain, fear, and desperation to others as he had experienced himself. He would verbally attack his ex-wife in almost every exchange they had, obsess over her to the point of not being able to build any new personal projects, and spend insurmountable amounts of time and money to "win" his battles against her. Little Luke within was unable to see how scary and destructive he had become. Little Luke was scared himself and needed to finally feel strong. He also demanded the justice that was never done.

David has no contact with his family. He describes his father as a tyrant and his mother as a helpless, gullible victim. He doesn't want to be anywhere near them. He feels he has been mistreated by his father all his life and received no help or protection from his mother. He stopped talking to them ever since he got married to Kelly.

His marriage was not welcomed by the family. The bride belonged to a "lower" cultural and socioeconomic level, which was perceived by his parents as an insult and a provocation to them. David, in an attempt to protect his new project, decided to isolate his new family from everyone that questioned it, proclaiming himself to be its one and only protector. He started controlling his wife and, later on, his kids in an almost identical manner as his own father had.

Laura lived in a family that she experienced as follows: Her talented mother dedicated herself to the family at the detriment to her personal ambitions and an ungrateful, successful father who was not especially interested in them. He had numerous affairs that Laura would often confront him about. The couple ended up separating. Laura has always felt closer to her mother. She even helped her uncover some of her father's love affairs. She has maintained a very close relationship with and still looks up to her mother. At the same time, she has had an almost nonexistent relationship with her father. She still has no respect for and feels great anger toward him.

Laura has now been married to Tom for more than a decade. She describes him as a loving man. Nevertheless, she is always on alert in the relationship. Anything he says is likely to be held against him. She fights him intensely and frequently, as she is afraid that she may one day find herself in her mother's position. Tom is slowly drifting away, and Laura's fear is turning into a self-fulfilling prophecy.

The list, if I were to continue, would be as long as the number of people I have come to know, both inside and outside my practice. All through our lives, we will come across different versions of our childhood experiences.

The most threatening scenes of our early years are bound to be evoked again and again within our relationships, until we manage to integrate them in a healthier way. Until we get there, we are very likely to find ourselves (and our partners) reenacting scenes from our past. At such times, we will feel trapped, scared, or blocked. At the same time, we may also understand, firsthand, the suffering of our parents. We will have the opportunity to feel more empathic about their shortcomings and perhaps more understanding, or even forgiving, toward them.

Those parents who are idealized—in ways that allow for no flaws, mistakes, errors, or any reflections of their human limitations and fragility—can be equally as compromising to the formation of a functional, loving bond with a partner. Interestingly, partners tend to feel more comfortable with the other's monster-parents (as long as they are kept at bay) than with saints or superheroes. The latter are often too present, too overbearing, forming a triangle almost impossible to resolve. Adult children can be so absorbed or so conditioned by these "deities" that it is quite common for the partners to feel like a kind of sacrificial gift at their altar.

Rob is the only son of a well-known lawyer's second marriage. He became a lawyer himself, following in his father's footsteps. Despite being professionally trained to argue, Rob has never had an argument with his dad, or challenged him in any way, once his turbulent adolescence was over. Yearning to earn his father's approval, he studied law, married a beautiful and intelligent wife, Nicole (whom his father approved of but ignored), had a son that he named after his dad, and organized his family life (outings, celebrations, holidays) to revolve around his father. Nicole did not share Rob's admiration for his father. To her, he was a selfish and self-centered man, only caring for his son when he behaved according to his parameters. He practically ignored everyone else: his current wife, Nicole, the children from his first marriage . . . He did not seem to care about anyone unless they were there to admire him or serve him.

Rob did not appear to be aware of any of the above or, in fact, any kind of limitation in his father apart from his advanced age. Nicole did not feel she had the right to question anything either. To her, there was a silent agreement in the family to treat the father with utter, unconditional respect. She felt invisible to her husband, just like Rob's mother had, her only value being reduced to giving birth to the children who would carry his family name.

The bond one has with an idealized parent is frequently even more fragile than the bond with a "monsterized" one. The idealized parents are frequently very fragile and emotionally insecure individuals. Parents who feel secure in themselves—those with strong I's—have no need or desire to be glorified. It is the fragile ones who long to be maintained on pedestals. There is usually a lot of hidden resentment in these apparently strong, respectful relationships. These parents have not been confronted for any of their faults or wrongdoings, and no one seems to have the courage to bring them into consciousness, as they are afraid of "breaking them" emotionally—or breaking the weak, conditional attachment that binds them. These extremely fragile child-gods are silently worshipped and resented at the same time, preventing their offspring from fully becoming adults themselves. The partner's position is, quite frequently, even more complex in these cases.

In general, there are no easy formulas when it comes to unravelling intergenerational entanglements (inner or outer). Such an enterprise requires a level of psychological strength and skill that can pose an insurmountable challenge even to the professionally trained. Therapists may be quite aware of such patterns, but at the moment they are called to deal with them in their personal lives, it is likely they will struggle as much as anyone. It is not easy. We are all human, after all, and it seems that part of our design is to naturally regress in the presence (mental or actual) of our own parents at all stages of life and to be on alert when it comes to the partner's family. Yet, managing to untangle things can be extremely rewarding. By getting ourselves to adult positions in relation to our own and our partner's parents, forming a powerful team that will defy the gods (like the androgynous or Adam and Eve), while simultaneously ensuring connection between the systems with  genuine respect and care, we could aspire to create a new "heaven"—this time with the blessing of the gods themselves.

The Perils of Parenthood

The biggest, most common, most ongoing, most challenging of challenges for the couple—the triangle that is bound to bring the greatest of joys and most terrible of woes to the equation—is related to the appearance of offspring. Many couples do wonderfully well for a very long time. They create remarkably beautiful love stories, they transition smoothly to having a "nest," and they take great pleasure going in and out of the emotional "home" they have created, exploring, traveling, developing professionally, and supporting or comforting one another. Their roles shift and change depending on their needs, personal attributes, and life circumstances. Both partners feel respected and equally valued for who they are and what they bring to the relationship at any given moment. And then they decide to have a kid.

A third member appears, and a new triangle is created. The way this triangle will be defined will affect the well-being of everyone involved. The baby is likely to be very close to both partners but even more likely to start off closer to one of them. This presents what is likely to be the first challenge to the WE of the couple. The previous equilibrium has to give in to a new dynamic that will continue to undergo changes as the children grow.

Happiness and general well-being—interpersonally speaking—are often a reflection of equality and flexibility in the distribution of roles within the relationship: equality, in the sense that what each one brings to the equation is equally valued; flexibility, meaning that each partner is open and prepared to occupy a different position if the situation demands it.

The appearance of children does not leave that much of a margin in terms of "shifting roles." One will get pregnant and carry the baby for nine months. The other will not. One will give birth. The other will not. And the baby is programmed to seek mom at the beginning more than it will seek dad. The roles are pretty fixed in this context, although there are always (and as time passes, more and more) exceptions. There is nothing inherently negative or destructive about fixed roles and positions. As we have seen, any organism will need structure in order to survive. Nature only allows for so much flexibility, so it has blessed women with the amazing gift and privilege of bearing children, but not men.

What becomes of paramount importance when the roles become more fixed and do not allow for much "vacillation" between functions and positions is that the "fixedness" is compensated with an equal attribution of value. For instance, although men do not have the opportunity to give birth to a child, they should still be valued for what they bring to the equation. Wouldn't it be interesting for this to be humanity's concern (how to support men in finding an equally valued place and role within society as women)? Wouldn't it make more sense? Curiously enough, we have created quite the opposite problem: Not only are men valued, but they have also been overcompensated for this inequality in nature's design. So the father who moves toward a further development of his career in order to bring more money and social status to the system will be socially and monetarily valued. The mother who moves toward motherhood will not.

There are many issues that the couple will need to face in regard to parenthood, such as greater financial stress, a further giving up of the "I" in favor of the "WE," and the (re)appearance of the intergenerational entanglements—all complex and all demanding. Yet these entanglements also having more attainable solutions to the one problem that I consider the most serious and most destructive of all: the valueless position of the extremely necessary feminine tasks and qualities, paired with the almost inevitable rigidity in the distribution of roles during parenthood. However, it seems to me that there is a universal oblivion to the relevance and importance of this issue. Feminists have fought long and hard for women to be able to move toward the autonomy (masculine) side of things, but I am still longing for the moment when connection will be so valued that both men and women will also "compete" to move toward the feminine roles and functions. That day has not come yet, however, so when it is time for a rearrangement, one partner moves toward the autonomy pole and the "outer" sphere, in order to attend to the energy (money) and autonomy (status, independence, power, agency) needs of the organism. The other one goes "in" and moves toward connection, attending to the inner workings and needs of the system. One moves toward more value and the other toward less.

Pregnancy is an extremely sensitive period for the mother-to-be in these terms. She is in a fragile, more dependent position, and her connectivity value is also lower than ever. The partner will need to provide support and a sense of great safety of the "WE" at this point—a factor that will also help determine whether the mother-to-be will suffer from postpartum depression.

Once the baby arrives, the triangle is "officially" established. Ideally, the couple will still be close, with mom maybe a bit closer to the baby than dad at the early stages. A common scenario of future disaster is a triangle with mom and baby extremely close and dad occupying an emotionally distant position. Such a constellation is often intricately related to the issues mentioned above. The partner who goes "in," often losing professional, social, and many other kinds of status or value—if not compensated by their partner in any of these terms—will compensate by dominating the "in" world. They will bring the child even closer to alleviate the loneliness, the insignificance, the lack of value. They will seek to control the family's physical and emotional space to compensate for feelings of frustration, abandonment, or powerlessness.

We do not like controlling, nagging wives and, even less so, absorbing mothers. There is a lot of literature about them, drawing quite an unfavorable picture. In general, we do not like mothers who seem to live for their children and are unable to cut the umbilical cord. We like indifferent mothers even less. And it makes sense that we do not, because the caregiving they provide is not optimal from the child's standpoint. What we do not take into account is that these mothers compensate for what society and partners fail to deliver. And what partners fail to deliver is related, to a great extent, to their own absorbing or indifferent mothers. It is a vicious circle that the whole of society has built, across cultures and generations.

As mothers lose their footing outside the family, it is highly likely that fathers will lose their place within it, leading all too often to overwhelmingly unhappy and dysfunctional situations. A silent (or not-so-silent) war is declared between the parts, which will inevitably involve suffering for the whole of the organism.

The vast majority of households fall into this pattern, in one way or another. Here is just one example: Noah and Inés had been greatly enjoying their long-term engagement. Their respective families were quite controlling and restrictive, so their relationship was like a breath of fresh air in their lives. They loved spending time together, and they were very creative with it.

Eventually, they decided to have a baby. They both wanted to have a family and saw it as another great experience for them to share. Yet, the reality of it ended up being very different than what they had expected. Inés was overwhelmed by the loneliness and isolation of motherhood, and Noah now had to work twice as much as before to make ends meet. He was feeling exhausted, frustrated, and quite lonely every time he returned home and faced Inés's anger and complaints about him not being there. He would remind her of his impossible days. Being the breadwinner and very mindful of their finances, he thought he should have complete control of the money coming in; after all, he considered it his. Inés, in turn, felt controlled and treated with arrogance, and she was very bitter about it. She did not feel like having sex with him anymore, to the point of opting to move to her son's bedroom for a while. She would control their intimacy. They had been starving each other before coming to therapy: no autonomy (money) for her, no connection (sex) for him; no status for her outside the house, no status for him inside it.

The variations of this tune are infinite. Still, it is a tune that we are all unfortunately familiar with. It is the tune of "war" between the masculine and the feminine, a background music that has been haunting our species for millennia. The feminine is devalued in the external world and the masculine in the internal. The former loses out in autonomy, the latter in connection.

A lot has been written about male dominance in the world, but not so much about female dominance at home, which feeds into and maintains the dysfunctional cycle. The partners occupying the male pole are often extremely devalued within their own homes, to the point of becoming the "odd one out," the "third party" of the triangle that is formed when children appear. Once an emotional "war" is unleashed at home, the partner on the masculine pole usually has very little chance to do well. They are quite hopeless, really, and they know it. So they "stay out," they communicate less, and they often compensate by exercising more external or physical dominance. And so the cycle of drama and endless suffering is sustained across time and generations.

The Classic Love Triangle

Another triangle that will inevitably occupy the WE at one point or another is the fantasy or the reality of "the other." To begin with, the "other" could be considered one of WE's main allies. The other is necessary for the WE's very definition, as it is actually constituted on this very basic differentiation. The "WE" is me and you. We are a WE because I have chosen you over him or her and you have chosen me over "others." If this distinction is not established, it is very difficult, if not impossible, for a WE to be established. So "the other" is a defining entity from the very beginning and it will keep conditioning, moving, and shaking the WE throughout its lifespan. The third party—the ghost, the imagination or actual presence of someone—will be challenging the WE, reflecting its strengths and weaknesses. It may help the WE to better define itself and strive for quality and constant care and growth. It may also be its greatest foe.

The "other" is usually most present during the constitution of the new organism, until the partners establish a meaningful, affectionate bond. Then it reappears as a challenge at different moments and stages in the life of the relationship, usually when one or both of the I's are fragile or weakened, or when the WE has become rigid or is failing to provide either autonomy or an affectionate, meaningful connection.

Based on the above, some of the purposes an extramarital lover can serve are to:

- Provide autonomy (i.e., nurture for the devalued "I," a boost to one's connectivity value, more freedom for the controlled "I")

- Provide connection for the abandoned "I"

- Help weaken the other partner's "I"

- Present an alternative to fear of commitment

- Prevent the loss of the "I" in the "WE"

- Keep family traditions going

- Get a stuck WE moving again

There is more to this list, which is neither linear nor exhaustive. A lot of the factors described may happen simultaneously. The lover reflects the state of both the I and the WE, and also constitutes a communication to the partner.

The Needy "I"

When the "I" is fragile, it will seek empowerment or reassurance from others. It can be within or outside the relationship. Either way, the insecure "I" is likely to move in not particularly constructive ways—actions that often involve, sooner or later, third parties.

Some fragile, needy I's will seek reassurance in the WE. The choice of the partner who will form something as special and important as a WE may have felt random or fortuitous—or not. Anyhow, for some, the question will be all too present: Why me rather than him or her? What if they find someone better? It is not that difficult, after all. Nowadays, it is basically just a click away. Such a question, if one cannot give a convincing answer, may linger on, haunting one partner—and the couple—indefinitely.

Rebecca was head over heels in love with Jake. They had met at the gym, they had "hit it off" right away, and, from what Rebecca described, the feeling was mutual. She was extremely concerned about the relationship, though. Would it last? Did he really feel for her as strongly she felt for him? Did he mean it when he said he loved her or that he had not met anyone like her before? She had doubts and would therefore put him to the test again and again. She would call him many times every day to see where he was, check his activity on social media and interrogate him about it, and secretly look at his phone. She would also surprise him during the night to see what kind of movies he watched. She would ask for proof of his feelings in every imaginable way. At the beginning, Jake was understanding and would reassure her in any way he could. Later on, he became tired of it. A couple of years down the line, Rebecca finally found the "evidence" that she was so sure she would find one day: there was someone else in Jake's life.

The less confident the I is, the more the options for another "better, nicer, greater" I out there that can occupy one's place. Individuals like Rebecca are in for eternal suffering within relationships unless they connect with what makes them unique and special. Proof of one's love to the other may be soothing and needed at times; it can actually be wonderful and something to welcome at the beginning of a relationship, while it is being built. Yet, as in the case of Rebecca and Jake, it can easily turn to hostile control of the other. Hostile control is an attack on the integrity of the I of the partner, who will eventually seek autonomy. The greater the control, the greater the need for some level of autonomy, and the greater the likelihood of the partner seeking a new "secure base." It is a self-fulfilling prophecy in the making.

Another typical version of a fragile "I" is that of the narcissist. In this case, the reassurance is sought outside the WE. He (it is most often a "he") will attempt to compensate for his sense of fragility by trying to increase his connectivity value. Unfortunately, no matter how much he tries, it is unlikely that it will ever be enough: these men (again, they are usually men) have never really felt thoroughly successful in the eyes of their demanding caregivers. They will marry the trophy wife as an offering at their parents' altar and for their own vulnerable I. They will show their partner off to their social circle for bonus "I" points. But, no matter how beautiful or desirable those women are, they are unlikely to ever be enough. These men's anxiety about their connectivity value (i.e., their grave need to feel admired), and the insecurity that comes with it, does not go away that easily. Given that therapy to them is perceived as failure, they will not come in for treatment either. They will look for alternative remedies: escort services, lovers, or marrying many different times with gradually younger women. In these cases, it is almost inevitable that there will be lovers (third parties in different shapes or forms) somewhere along the line—or even every step of the way. The good news is that the existence of a third party in these cases is often not directly related to the partner and the relationship *per se*. The bad news is that these individuals are likely to need the "boost" all through their lives, and even more so as they get older and become even more insecure. Third parties may therefore be part of their "deal." The worst news is that they have very little skill or competence in building and caring for a WE anyway.

The Smothered "I"

"I need to talk to you. It is important. My husband has a severe problem." Those were Lena's first words to me. Lena is a friend. I knew a lot about the relationship but, until then, I did not know the problem. "What is it? What has happened?" I asked. "He masturbates. I caught him masturbating. He watches pornography on his phone. He has been masturbating since he was in high school."

I could not help but smile. "No kidding! A male who started masturbating in high school," I said, laughing caringly. I knew them well. I loved them as a couple and as a family. What I sometimes wondered about was how George had managed to resolve autonomy issues that I believed should derive from Lena's control. She was definitely the one dominating the household (often not in the most positive, constructive ways), and he continued to be a very dedicated husband and father. It didn't quite add up. I tend to be more direct with those who I feel are strong enough to take it—even more so if they are dear to me—so I recalled a phrase of Facundo Cabral, an Argentinean poet and songwriter, and offered it to Lena playfully: "Masturbation is an untamed declaration of independence." I suggested it as a hypothesis to consider. Could there be some truth in it?

One's forceful control will lead to the other's search for autonomy. The ways we seek autonomy may be more or less constructive. Masturbation may be an initial declaration of autonomy in relation to our caregivers. It may happen with a partner too, as was the case of Lena and George. We are likely to seek anything that will produce or restore some sense of individuality, integrity, power, or freedom when there is a lack of it. A lover is quite a classic solution. Many women seek such affirmation in the relationship with their children, which is more acceptable but can also be more destructive. Here, George's sense of "I" was wearing off. He needed to restore it somehow. Lena had been communicating to him through the years that he was not good enough, that he had failed and disappointed her in so many ways as a husband. Had Lena continued down the path of defining George as severely disturbed for masturbating, they would be back to square one—only worse. George would now also need to deal with the humiliation of his attempt to restore a sense of Self and would probably be met with Lena's renewed and more forceful control.

The Abandoned "I"

Ingrid and Philip were very young when they got married. They now had two adolescent children. She was a powerful, successful businesswoman. Although he brought less into the family moneywise, Philip was doing quite well professionally too. He admired and was very attracted to his wife, but he felt they had lost connection ever since the kids were born. They rarely had time for each other and hardly ever cuddled or showed any kind of affection to one another anymore. She would repeatedly reject Philip in bed, which hurt him and got him to stop seeking intimacy. He felt overlooked and devalued in the relationship—and in the family too. A few years later, the situation between them had not changed. The only difference was that Philip now had a parallel relationship with a woman who was very attracted to him and with whom he enjoyed intimacy and a lot of "together" moments.

Monica was a stay-at-home mom and wife of a successful businessman named Ken. Ken spent most of his time at work, away from home, on business trips. He was quite an absent father and husband. Intimacy with his wife was limited to a few highly unsatisfactory encounters, as she would qualify them. "The moments he feels like it, he comes on to me. He has his orgasm and then falls asleep. He does not know how to approach me, how to touch me. He has no idea, I think, about how to make a woman feel good." Monica, a stunningly beautiful woman herself, started having lovers who made her feel attractive, desired, and cared for.

One's neglect is likely to be met with the other's neglect. Such dysfunctional situations will bring the WE to a precipice and will mean its death or its transformation.

The Fragile "I" Facing the Power of "WE"

The presence—real or imaginary—of a third person is a powerful message to the partner: "You are not that important. You do not have that much power over me." Behind such messages—which may be transmitted consciously or unconsciously—lies a sense of fragility and fear of loss of control in relation to the other, often accompanied by the fear of being abandoned. Consequently, these individuals try to avoid what they perceive as a one-down position within the couple. The introduction of "a third party" is a quick (yet quite destructive) remedy. When a partner has a weakened sense of Self, self-esteem, or connectivity value, they appear "safer" in the eyes of the insecure partner. With their "connectivity value" reduced, they are also less likely to abandon the WE. Thus, a fragile "I" may seek to weaken the other "I" through the introduction of the reality or the idea of someone else in order to feel more secure.

Weakening the I of the Partner

Dave was very much in love with Sonia—so much so that he had left his home country so that he could be with her. He had made an important investment in their relationship that he was happy yet uneasy about. One day, he started talking to Sonia about a previous relationship: "I was with X before we got together, but you do not have to worry about her. We talked the other day and it became clear that we could no longer see each other. She has her life established there; I live here now. You are close, she is far away." Sonia did not understand. Why was he saying all this now? She thought they were in love. She did not even know there was someone else to start with, and she did not take it very well at all. She suggested seeking help. Dave was puzzled as to why she had gotten so upset but agreed to accompany her. In the couple of sessions I have had with them, what most stood out about them was how much in love they were. They described their feelings for one another as beyond their control, more powerful than themselves. As we talked about their relationship and special connection, Dave suddenly became aware of what had made him bring "the shadow" of a third party into their WE: Sonia had become too central in his life, and he needed to feel more in control again. The power of their love was as threatening to him as it was beautiful.

Such dynamics make for quite common and established interpersonal "games." Most of us are quite familiar with another "classic" one: the guy, for example, who goes out with his girlfriend or wife and makes powerful—sometimes even obscene—remarks about other women in front of her. "Oh, look at her! She is hot. Check out that ass!" The insecure man will need to feel some control over his wife and will attack her level of autonomy, her connectivity value—indirectly, in this case—by negatively comparing her to others (implicitly or explicitly). The partner will often fall into the trap and, instead of seeing a scared little boy inside her "macho man," she is likely to feel and act insecure, ask to be reassured, and cling to her partner, who will now feel a bit more secure in his position in the relationship.

Weakening the other partner's power over oneself is probably a common factor in every equation that involves a third party. It constitutes a safety net (quite often imaginary) that brings comfort to those who do not cope well with the intensity of their own feelings for someone, of having invested so much in just one person, or of the "hold" they feel this person has on them.

Avoiding the Power of the WE

Other candidates most likely to experience an intense fear of being one-down in a relationship (and therefore avoiding to fully engage or commit to it) are those who, as sons and daughters, were drawn into their parents' difficulties. Those who have had very absorbing relationships with their mothers, for example, who have been supporting them, who were valued more for their use rather than for themselves—in sum, those who lost part of their I in the WE of the relationship with a parent—will be more reluctant to properly commit to a romantic relationship later in life. They may be even more reluctant if they have had to live through and soothe mom's suffering in relation to dad (or vice versa), or if their parents had a terrible divorce. These kids have learned that relationships are dangerous. To them, relationships are battlefields where one can get severely hurt or even lose themselves completely. Why take such a big risk?

These people may experience feelings of ambivalence. A part of them yearns for connection, and another part fears it. "No one will be able to trap me. I will be like water in anyone's hands," said Sally. I had lost count of her boyfriends and lovers. Every time she felt someone needed her or was asking for something more from her, she would look for someone else. She had been her mother's main support all through her adolescence and beyond, while her father was having numerous affairs with other women.

Repeating Patterns

Sally, as we saw above, was also repeating a pattern. Without meaning to, she was behaving very much like her dad—the same dad she said she hated for all the pain he had caused. If there has been infidelity in the previous generation, chances are that the pattern will repeat itself in the next.

Lorena only knew pain and suffering from her parents' relationship. She described her father as a violent man, abusive to his wife and children every time he would "stop home," which was not too often. He had numerous other partners whom he would not hide from his family. As an adult, Lorena had always been attracted to the "bad guys," the "players"—men with similar profiles to her father's. She got pregnant by one of them, but later left him when she found out about one of his numerous lovers. A couple of years later, she got together with and then married "a good guy," with whom she had a healthy, stable relationship and another child. With the passing of time, however, she started losing respect for him ("too nice, too attentive, too much like my mother used to be"). She said she was getting bored. She started being abusive to him in the ways she talked and acted around him, and then one day she also started seeing other people. The story was repeating itself—but this time, she was occupying her father's role.

Repeating such patterns of abuse and infidelity is not, of course, inevitable. Some people consciously resolve not to cause the same pain that they, as children, suffered due to their parents' shortcomings.

In order to avoid repeating patterns, one will need to have "made peace" with the previous generation, and interactions with both caregivers will need to have the character and fluidity of adult relationships. This was not the case with either Sally or Lorena. In the previous examples, both women were still perceiving their parents from a judgmental position that categorized them as "good" and "bad," strong and weak, winner and loser. If such is the "music" that plays within, especially when individuals have not had the chance to really get to know their parents from a more complex, adult viewpoint, it is highly unlikely that they will manage to "break" the patterns they have absorbed in the past. In other words, if our infantile view of our caregivers has not changed in adulthood, and if our relationship to them has not been substituted with a more mature bond, we are likely to be in for quite an infantile ride in our relationship with our partner.

Another very common scenario of such an entanglement is that of unfaithful men (homosexual or heterosexual) who have never managed to properly emancipate from their mothers. These men have been under their mother's extreme emotional influence all through their lives, without ever managing to set any proper limits, usually out of a sense of loyalty or guilt. The existence of a partner is often the only limit they are able to set to this "unofficial marriage" to mom. Later on, with the partner, the history repeats itself. On one hand, they have the "official" relationship that they feel attached to (but also extremely ambivalent about), and on the other, they have the lover(s) that help "resolve" the feelings of ambivalence. Ironically, the mother also often contributes to the ambivalence, as she is likely to harshly question the "official partner" or anyone she perceives to be occupying her place.

Josh, for example, had always experienced his mother as controlling and invasive but had never managed to set any limits with her. He felt extremely guilty every time he tried to distance himself from her in the slightest. He even felt guilty for his own perception of her as controlling and invasive. Soon after he got together with Corinne, a very competent and outspoken women, he started perceiving her also as someone controlling and invasive. His way of setting limits was to look for another relationship and to have someone else available at any given time—a strategy that also served as a kind of revenge or rebellion to the mother's or the partner's emotional tyranny. I have found this pattern to be quite a "classic" also for gay men, with the fusion of the mother-son relationship and the infidelity rates moving in parallel and ranking really high.

Nevertheless, it is not *what* happened in the past that matters, but *whether* the past has been successfully integrated into the present. No matter how challenging or even traumatic interpersonal dynamics have been, they will only condition future relationships when a person has not managed to live in peace with their internalized caregivers and maturely deal with actual caregivers in the present. In sum, the level of emotional maturity and emancipation one has achieved in relation to the previous generation will determine the level of entanglement and, in many cases, the likelihood of infidelity in future relationships.

Getting the WE Unstuck

Sometimes, the appearance of a third party is a way to get the WE on track again. There are moments in the couple's life when the WE, if it is not shaken, is unlikely to survive. Commonly, at such moments the relationship has become too mechanistic, too routine, too oblivious to the needs of the I's involved; thus, the evolution of both the I's and the WE is hindered. The appearance of a lover in such cases may still be a big blow to the WE, but the prognosis is far more promising.

Angel and Dana had been married for more than twelve years. They had two kids, were both successful professionals, and appeared to have a great thing going as a family. The reality of it was that they hardly ever talked about anything that was not routine or task-related. They shared nothing that was emotionally meaningful and practically stopped having sex. When Angel met Carmen, a very passionate woman, he was immediately swept off his feet. They had an intense affair that only came to a halt when Dana found out. She was distraught. Angel was distraught, too. He realized he did not want to break up his marriage. They were now forced to talk and have all those meaningful, emotional conversations they had been avoiding. The WE was being questioned. At the same time, it was being given the chance to reorganize, move forward, and do things better.

Moving On

Romantic triangles are usually seen as "symptoms" of relationship dysfunction in the eyes of a therapist. They may be approached more as issues related to the "I" or, instead, difficulties with the "WE." Most often they arise from a combination of both. No matter what the case, they almost always indicate the parts' and the whole's inability to resolve connection or autonomy issues effectively. When we do not have the tools to argue constructively with our partners—to handle things productively and maturely—we do it via "symptoms." We resort to our defense mechanisms. And so lovers appear.

Yet, sometimes the appearance of someone else is meaningful in itself. It is a case of moving on. There can be something about the new relationship that is important and powerful enough to dissolve the old "WE" and create a new one. It is the beginning of a new story.

RELATIONSHIP RESCUE

J ohn and Louise are sitting in silence, each occupying opposite ends of a long sofa. They look tired and nervous. The tension between them is almost tangible. And then someone enters the room. Their attention immediately shifts on to the person who greets them, which helps them release a bit of the tension and awkwardness they feel.

Demi is their new therapist. She takes a seat in front of them, looks at them warmly, and smiles. She knows how difficult this situation is; she has been meeting with couples for more than a decade now. She has also been where they have been herself, with her own partner. "What can I do for you? What has brought you here?" she asks after some brief introductions.

There is so much in what John and Louise express through their words, but there's even more in their expressions: anger, fatigue, expectation, disbelief, cynicism, anxiety, hope. "Problems with communication" is their diagnosis and conclusion, in a nutshell. They describe a variety of situations and contexts where they have experienced conflicts and misunderstandings—all of them painful, most of them seemingly minor (they realize that most of their arguments stem from insignificant issues). But no matter how small or how big the problems they try to deal with are, they do not really manage to get anywhere, despite their efforts.

John and Louise are trapped in a new kind of dance now: a dance of friction and inevitability. They get "pulled in" almost despite themselves. They know the moves all too well—they can even anticipate what they will say or do and how the other will react at any given moment—but they still cannot prevent any of it from happening. Once they are in the "loop," they go through the motions again and again.

Couples therapists know this repetitive "dance" all too well. Everything remains the same, even in the presence of great drama and motion. It can feel like Groundhog Day at times, witnessing the same patterns over and over. But there is a reason why going nowhere is one of the most common experiences attached to a couple: the opposing forces involved in the functioning of the couple make it one of the most paradoxical organic structures there is. It has to move forward and backward at the same time. It has to nurture the individualities and ensure connection, too. It has to create something new and at the same time respect the old. It pushes toward adulthood and transcendence, and yet it brings out our most primitive and childlike sides. Couples' problems can therefore be overwhelmingly complex, even when they appear simple. And when there is no easy way out, which is the case more often than not, partners often end up creating more and more "knots"—unhealthy interactions and patterns of behavior that are endlessly repeated—as they search for solutions.

"Today's problems are yesterday's solutions," my former boss at ESADE University, Dr. Alberto Gimeno, often says. And this is definitely the case for couples. Sometimes we see people we love (or even ourselves) suffer in what appear to be a toxic relationship, not understanding how they got there in the first place or why they choose to endure so much pain. The urge to pull them out of these situations is strong, but, more often than not, it's a hopeless endeavor. The fundamental problem is that we fail to see the whole picture. This failure then often leads to biased, miscued, judgmental stances that compound the problem rather than facilitate its resolution. Our first task would therefore be to come to terms with and accept the complexity of any given relationship, without jumping to conclusions, passing moral judgments, or even going into "rescue mode." What at first glance may seem stupid, destructive, or evil is usually nothing more—and nothing less—than a terrible and desperate struggle to resolve almost impossible interpersonal equations.

As we start looking for answers within the realm of nature and evolution, we will inevitably go beyond "human labels" and moral judgments. Our immune system's success or failure in protecting us from pathogens does not make it "good" or "evil." There is no good and bad in nature. The world just is.

Judgment poses a threat to our integrity, and we respond by activating our defenses. On the contrary, when we feel upon us the genuine curiosity of someone who really wants to understand, we are far more likely to open up and collaborate. More options then become available. Resolutions require a creative spirit, and creativity is only possible in times of peace.

So our defenses get us into interpersonal loops, and a narrow, judgmental view of our situation can get us stuck there. Acknowledging the complexity of relationships and the limitations of ourselves and our partners can set the foundation for resolution.

Parenting the Primitive

As we have seen earlier, our defenses are linked to our primitive brain. They stem from what has been defined here as the infantile or animal side within us. Learning to manage our defenses requires finding a way to constructively relate to that part in ourselves and in our partner.

Let's revisit a small extract of John and Louise's story that they may or may not bring up in their therapy sessions but is nevertheless key to their ongoing dynamics. We mentioned that Louise's upbringing did not involve much parental control, that she was encouraged to be very autonomous. When she decided to go on a small trip and did not let John know about it, John's limbic brain sounded an alarm. His emotional, childlike side—his "horse"—was uneasy. The first adult action he could take is to regulate it himself: "Pal, you have fallen for this girl precisely because she is wild and autonomous. That's just the way she is. It is not about you. She probably has no idea that you are having such a hard time. If you cannot handle it, maybe you can try and let her know how difficult this is for you. Maybe you can then figure something out together."

Learning how to be a good parent to ourselves (or a good rider for our horse) is a skill that can take us really far, individually and with our partners. We often pass the responsibility of caring for the kid that we used to be from our parents directly to our partner, and we demand from them a kind of parenting and level of dedication that we yearned for and frequently never had. When they fail to deliver, we often react defensively. By realizing that, once we reach adulthood, our primitive needs are not primarily our partner's responsibility but our own, we can be the first in line to aid ourselves. By inviting ourselves to the challenge of engaging and practicing the complex art of parenting ourselves, we also have a chance to realize how extremely difficult good parenting can be.

When the situation we are facing is so overwhelming that we cannot regulate or bring comfort to ourselves, another adult thing to do is ask for external help to soothe the child inside. In order for this to be an adult exchange, it will require higher brain activity between partners. The rider engages the other rider and signals one's own horse as the "patient." Thus, John would approach Louise and say something like, "You know, the other day when you went off on that trip . . . It was kind of weird for me. It affected me that you had not said anything about it. I guess I'm not used to it. Do you think you can let me know in the future? It would just make it easier." This is cortical John talking about subcortical John, both present and engaged, with cortical John having the reins of the interaction.

In "horse and rider" terms, John's horse and rider are approaching Louise's horse and rider in a way that her "horse" does not perceive them as a threat and allows her rider to engage constructively in the interaction. Louise will need to "negotiate" with her subcortical self later on in order to give him an answer. With this approach, it is far more likely that Louise's horse will remain calm even when it becomes aware that the whole negotiation is about giving up a bit of its "untamed autonomy."

In other words, even when the adult within us cannot attend the child within, there is still a chance for constructive interaction. We can translate our basic, primitive needs into adult language that the partner will be better equipped to understand and attend to. If we are able to keep calm, the other's limbic system is likely to match our calmness. Our partner will not detect us as a threat, and they will be in a better position to attend to our need or take in new information.

Nevertheless, this second attempt to act in "adult mode" can fail, too. John may feel too overwhelmed to organize his emotions and keep his "horse" contained enough to give an accurate diagnosis to Louise. In such a case, we will get an adolescent version of John: "You know, what you did the other day was so uncool. You should have told me that you were going on a trip. You must admit it is kind of weird that you didn't. You can be really weird sometimes, you know." His horse may be even more out of control: "Are you crazy? How can you act like this? Do you think you live just by yourself in this world without taking notice of anyone else?" The intensity may change, but the dynamic in both examples is the same: John tries to care for himself without assuming any responsibility, throwing all responsibility to his partner and asking her to care for him—not because he needs it, but because it is "the right thing to do." He is in "hostile control" mode, as the primitive within him tries to reestablish a sense of security.

In such a situation, if Louise is to react in an adult way, she has a complex task to accomplish: 1) calm her own horse, which is now under attack, 2) block John's horse from attacking her, and 3) engage with John's "rider," so that they can both . . . 4) finally care for John's horse.

Louise will need to tell herself, "Okay, he is hurt. Maybe it could be done better. Maybe there is something to learn here. Still, he is out of line in the way he is approaching me. This is something I cannot allow for." She will need to soothe the part that hurts (both hers and John's), as well as establish limits for John's horse: "I can see how my behavior may have affected you. I am sorry. I was not aware of it. I appreciate you letting me know, so we can do things differently. But you also called me crazy, and this is not okay, John. I deserve your respect as you do mine. We cannot attack each other like this."

In this case, Louise has managed to see a hurt child in John, rather than a mean adult, and she has acted accordingly. It is important to keep in mind that our partners are as vulnerable to us in the relationship as we are to them. There is a fragile side to them, even if we do not see it, even if they deny it or hide it from themselves. The very fact that one can act in hostile control mode is evidence of the existence of such a child. And the greater the acting out, the more fragile, insecure, and needy that child usually is. So as with any child, this part of oneself can be an endless source of joy, play, love, and discovery, but it can also be a great source of pain and trouble when it operates within the body of an adult.

Louise was firm and gentle. She blocked John's defensive behavior (which was offensive to her) and found the language to turn their interaction from a battle into a collaboration. Communicating with respect and empathy ("I see you") without attacking (judging, criticizing, complaining, etc.) or returning the attacks can shield the relationship from a lot of unnecessary suffering.

But Louise is also likely to fail to engage with John in an adult manner. She may also feel overwhelmed and unable to regulate her "horse," as now she also feels attacked. Her defense mechanisms are activated. It is John who is acting "crazy" in her mind. We have seen that she may also opt for the "shutdown" mechanism, possibly thinking to herself that John is being sexist, controlling, or "a chauvinist pig." That reaction results in John going further into primitive mode, his horse now reacting even more powerfully. There are no adult options between them anymore. As things escalate, they move further and further away from adult interpersonal behavior.

At such a moment, we are likely to seek help and reinforcement from someone external who will soothe our "horse." John may go to his mother to complain or have a beer with a friend. Same with Louise. Or they may go to a therapist. If they are lucky, those invited as "helpers" will themselves have reached interpersonal adulthood, and their intervention will help regulate the whole system.

An adult approach from John's mother, for example, would be to provide a safe haven for her son (care for the primitive), as well as give new meaning to the misunderstanding between them (reprogramming the rider's understanding), so that John can then approach Louise in a different, more constructive way. His mother might say: "I know how hurtful it can be, John. It makes sense that you are upset. I'd probably be as upset as you are. But I think she probably did not mean to hurt you. You also kind of like this 'craziness' in Louise. Why don't you go and talk to her? You will only know if you listen to what she has to say." Their conversation might then go like this:

John: "She doesn't want to talk to me. She does not return my messages."

Mom: "Well, maybe you could insist more. If you do care and want things to work, it may require some extra effort. I think she is just hurt. If you approach her kindly, maybe even with an apology, maybe she will respond well."

John: "Apology? Yeah, right. She should be the one to give me an apology! Why should I do it?"

Mom: "Oh, you are probably right in this. Maybe she owes you an apology, too. There isn't anything either of you should or shouldn't do. As far as I see it, it now depends on how long you feel like waiting for things to start getting better. If you step up and act, what you gain is time—and you have more control of things, too. To me, time is precious, and it is better not to waste it, but you may see it differently. You can always wait and see if she will eventually step up herself and act as you would like her to."

There are infinite possible scripts, of course, and they would also infinitely vary depending on the situation. Yet those called to provide external support often fail to produce constructive scripts and intervene in an adult mode. The most common failure is taking sides: good vs. bad, right vs. wrong. We soothe the "horse," saying how sorry we are for it to have experienced something like that, and then we judge the partner. Or, less frequently, we do the opposite: we take the side of the partner and tell the one seeking support how stupid they have been. And thus, we make the problem bigger. One is soothed; the other is not. Both are likely to activate their defenses even further. The organism is in greater trouble than before, as it cannot come up with anything constructive while its defenses are up. Plus, there is yet another threat to the system: the external "helper"—that is, the mother, the friend, the therapist . . . ourselves!

When everything fails, there is one last path to "adult mode." It usually comes after there has been so much attacking and pain that the horses are distraught to the point of not posing a threat to anyone anymore. They are just a bundle of wounds. We are then finally able to perceive the pain we have caused one another, and we may, at last, start moving and acting in more constructive, healing ways. This is quite a classic scenario, a common script of human relationships and of human history as a whole. We only stop being destructive when we are immersed in destruction, when there is nothing else left to see but the ruins our conflicts have caused. But building from there is far more challenging. Once the horses have somewhat recovered, they are very unlikely to trust the one who was perceived as a vicious "enemy." And the cycle may start all over again, sooner rather than later.

Managing Expectations

Expectations are classic defense activators, and they come in a large variety of shapes and forms:

- "Louise should have been more considerate. She should have known it would bother me."

- "John should know how I am and accept me the way I am."

- "Louise should come and apologize first."

- "John should loosen up and not be so rigid and controlling."

We often become demand-generating machines within our relationships, unable to accept that the individual within the partnership cannot and will not be able to provide everything. Sometimes we ask from our partners to be one thing and the opposite at the same time—a request that is an automatic stress generator.

Chiara is a busy professional who feels far more comfortable dealing with issues at work than at home and identifies herself as a reason- and task-oriented person. She married Steve, a warm, affectionate man who became the main source of nurture for everyone in the family. Even though Chiara valued him for the emotional support he was providing to her and their children, she would also complain about him, insisting that she needed someone stronger, a solid rock that could support the whole family. "Are you looking for a soft rock?" a friend asked her one day. "Good luck with it."

Curiously enough, we often "fight" those very attributes that made us fall in love with the other person in the first place: the softness of the loving, emotionally available man; the introverted nature and emotional inaccessibility of the intellectual; the popularity and vivaciousness of a woman whose bubbly, outgoing personality initially captured our fascination.

Every attribute has its shadow. The generous man will have less money for the family, and a very socially capable woman will mesmerize crowds but have less time to dedicate to the couple. There is no attribute that comes without a shadow. The hardness of the rock will be a blessing when it is used as a stepping-stone and a curse when it has to be used as a pillow. There are no soft rocks. We cannot occupy (and it makes no sense to ask our partners to occupy) more than one position at a time within the system. Once we come to understand and accept this, we can spare our partners and the relationship a lot of unnecessary stress.

Cultivating Connection

As we have seen, a method commonly used to achieve connection in our relationships is control, which almost always backfires. However, there *is* a way we can have a positive, desired influence on our partner. It requires, more or less, the same tools, skills, and processes as gardening does. Let's imagine the other is a plant and we are very eager for it to nurture us. First comes the realization that our satisfaction will not be instant; the process will require patience. As a first step, we will need to know and find out what our plant needs—not what we need or what we think it should need. If we do not know, we can observe carefully or . . . simply ask (this is a magic talking plant!). We then make sure that all the right ingredients are there, to the best of our abilities, and then we wait and repeat the process until the plant responds. If all goes well, we will eventually see the best version of it, and it will bear fruits that nurture us. If we do not like the kind of fruit it gives, however, it might be a good idea to start looking for a different kind of plant. In sum, if we are to see the best in the other, we need to ensure the best possible conditions for them to thrive.

So the best way to achieve connection is to actually offer it. We can do it via acting like an adult, as in the example above, or by being constructively primitive. The connection we can offer, operating primarily from the rider's position, is based on kindness, patience, warmth, and openness. It involves being mindful of the other's needs and making ourselves available as trust-worthy individuals that they can count on: a safe haven.

Inviting connection from our primitive side requires a different set of skills all together. It requires the courage to do exactly what babies—and some animals—do: trust. After having our hearts broken a few times, we often decide that it is not worth the risk anymore. We become far more cautious and suspicious in relationships, which makes a lot of sense but also sets the scene for new disasters. Think about it: Who is more likely to receive love—the trusting and loving, or the suspicious and bitter? I am not suggesting that we should be throwing ourselves blindly into relationships, but it might be worth while to make a conscious decision to trust when we suspect that we are in a relationship that is worthwhile.

One of the most emotionally intelligent, beautiful men I know defined love as a "closing of the eyes and letting go, in the knowing that the other will always be there to catch you." He was a master of the art and convinced the love of his life—a skeptical, cynical, brainy psychologist—to do the same. They lived happily ever after. And it could happen with any relationship if a bond of secure connection is present.

Cultivating Autonomy

When a partner feels controlled or smothered by the relationship and desires more room to grow and thrive, he or she will somehow seek autonomy. The partner is likely to react primitively (it is about survival, after all), employing open hostility, or shutting down and giving the "silent treatment" (as in the case of Louise), or in other more or less creative ways—affairs being an all-time favorite. Paradoxically, the more we try to control the other in the fear of losing them, the more likely we are to actually lose them. Providing autonomy is equally vital as providing connection, and it is an extremely challenging task for most.

It may be useful to keep in mind that, although we may be intrinsically connected to and form part of all there is, the world does not (nor anything, nor anyone in it) belong to us. We don't even thoroughly belong to ourselves, as our minds and bodies make zillions of decisions every day that we are unaware of, some of which we may not even agree with. And our body and minds grow old and die, going their own way despite our wishes.

We can explore the versions of autonomy-giving that work, from a "higher brain" perspective (the rider guiding the horse) and a more "primitive" one (the horse leading the rider). In "higher" terms, autonomy-giving is about being interested and curious about who the other is and what the other does, including what they struggle with or what makes them happy, what their goals and ambitions are, what they like and do not like, and how their day went. It is about paying attention to what they say or even what they do not say. Autonomy-giving can be summarized as acknowledging that the other exists as a separate entity and being able to accept, celebrate, or even promote their differences. It is about empowering the partner's "I."

We need to be quite secure in ourselves in order to allow for the other to thrive and grow. When we are, we can promote autonomy both via our adult selves, as we have seen above, and also via our primitive side. How can we help enhance our partner's sense of self and autonomy from this level? The answer reveals itself if we think about it in terms of child-parent inter-action. What do children do that makes parents feel competent, content, and secure in themselves? Quite simply, they "do well." We associate happy, healthy children with good, competent parents.

Taking care of ourselves and "doing well" is very likely to have a positive impact on our partner, too. They can get credit for our success or happiness, feeling more secure and stronger in themselves. Sometimes, however, unwilling to give them satisfaction and a sense of accomplishment, we passive-aggressively jettison our own happiness. Suzanna and Trevor had relocated to Spain due to a work opportunity in Trevor's company. Suzanna had accepted the move but was not happy about it. A few years down the line, she had not made any new friends, had not learned the language, and had not made any attempts to develop herself professionally. She did not want to. Her priority was for Trevor to see for himself that the decision to move was a bad one for the whole family.

Making the best out of the situations that we are faced with, whatever these may be, is very likely to have a beneficial effect on everyone: on ourselves, of course, and our children (if we have any)—and collaterally on our partners and even our parents. Our well-being is very likely to make people around us feel competent and happy about themselves. The "catch" is that our loved ones may feel more competent than they "deserve"; even worse, they may never learn all those lessons we thought they should learn.

And, even worse yet, they may go as far as giving themselves credit for our very own achievements!

I am still amazed by the amount of people who choose to immerse themselves in hell and hardship, stubbornly committed to teach someone a lesson (that they are not in the least interested in being taught), rather than looking to get situations unstuck and make the most out of the very little time we have on this planet.

Making Peace with Our Past

One way to ensure that we have set the best possible foundation for our relationship to work and be a place of nurture and growth is to have fully accepted and be at peace with our past—above and beyond all, with our parents and attachment figures. We need to make sure that our caregivers live happily and at peace in our minds and hearts and, if possible, in real life as well. This entails a vision of both mom and dad (and any other parental figure) as intrinsically good, valuable, and beautiful in their own way. It also requires that we attribute equal value to them. In addition, the two (or more) figures need to be able to coexist happily in our minds and hearts, even if they cannot stand one another in real life.

In real-life terms, ideally, we would need to maintain or construe a loving or at least respectful bond with them that maintains separation as well as ensuring warm connection at the same time. If there is no chance to build such a bond with the real ones, their representations in our minds are equally important. In my experience, there is no way to create a working, intimate relationship with our partners when the above (at least in inner terms) is not achieved.

We will need to find a way to understand and tell ourselves the story of our life from the perspective of a world that has no villains and no victims—just human beings, who, due to their limitations, ended up hurting each other. And us. Until then, we are likely to reenact the hardships indefinitely.

This is another very difficult point to come to terms with. We may not mind being "trapped" or determined by our parents' genes, but we are not happy being defined by our parents' actions and shortcomings as well. Still, we are better off accepting it as a fact and learning to live and deal with it rather than trying to fight it, as fighting has the paradoxical effect of binding us even more forcefully to the past we seek to escape from.

When we were little, we did not have a choice. Everything our caregivers did got hardwired in our brains. Their defenses became our defenses. In our adult lives, we are very likely to at least get as far as they did. Then, it comes down to our capacities and our decision to get stuck or evolve, which could also translate into "fight them" or "embrace them."

Let's imagine we choose to embrace. We may have fought long and hard enough and gotten nowhere, so we choose to give a different option a chance, even if we are not totally convinced. What is this "embrace" all about? How is it done?

The answer will vary for each one of us and may require very different courses of action and elaboration. Still, the principles remain the same. We will need to be both separate and lovingly connected to our parents—in the way they are represented within us, in real life, or both. We will also need to find a way to value them equally and feel okay about either of them being manifested within us or within our lives and relationships.

This, for example, would mean for Laura (see page 110), who had positioned herself in favor of her mother and against her father, blaming the latter for all the shortcomings in the family, to see her mother as a limited— yet still beautiful—human being who was also responsible for the failure of the relationship with her father. She will need to be able to appreciate her mother's limitations, recognize her shortcomings, and move further away from her and closer to her dad (emotionally and, if possible, literally). Currently, Laura is fully occupying her mother's position and will therefore continue to invite her partner to play her father's role. At the moment she allows herself to see her mother as having had a part in the difficulties of the relationship, and still love her despite her not being perfect anymore, she will be able to both be by her side and also have the freedom to move and explore other positions. She will also be freed from the burden of being perfect. In relation to her father, Laura will need to see the human behind "the monster" and, if possible, forge a new bond with him. At the moment dad turns into a human being, as worthwhile and as valuable as mom, and as much of a victim of the circumstances, Laura is more likely to also see her partner under such light. As she manages to see a more complex and humane picture of her own family, she will be able to do so for the rest of the world, too. Her view and expectations of her own marriage will significantly shift.

Our partners are usually quite good at detecting signs of "the child" being stuck, as they form an organism with us that needs to survive and move forward. So when our partner expresses discomfort about our relationship with our family, it may be a good idea to at least have a look at it. In general terms, idealized parents should be brought down to earth—not crushed down, just perceived as limited mortals. We cannot evolve if we are under the shadow of perfection. It is wise to get some (loving) distance from them.

"Evil" parents need to be brought back to the human realm, as mentioned above. The monsters need to at least be understood. Why? Because they form part of who we are. And we need to be able to relate to ourselves. Otherwise, we will deny the "monster" part that we have absorbed and probably then have it manifest within our relationships, still unable to deal with it. If we perceive our partners as potential monsters, they are likely to feel so extremely offended that they may react as such. Unresolved emotional issues lie at the core of most such self-fulfilling prophecies.

It is not that hard to understand monsters, despite the emotional challenge such an attempt may pose. If we manage to allow ourselves to come to such an understanding, a few simple glances beyond the surface are usually enough for one to see their suffering. It is suffering that transforms humans into monsters, and it usually takes immense amounts of suffering for such a transformation to take place.

The last passage to the peace-making process with our past would be to achieve a loving bond between the two parts that make us up: our two DNA strands, or the "primal couple" that has existed in our minds. If we manage to find a way for this couple to live peacefully in our brains and hearts, we will probably have the opportunity to see not only our relationship improving, but also our relationship with ourselves transforming. They are, after all, the parts that compose us. The better they relate to one another, even if it is just in our imagination, the more fluid and effortless our inner and outer functioning will be.

Loosening the Ties That Bind

Nicolas, a former dear colleague, came to the clinic one day with a handmade little craft called "atrapanovios." He would have great fun putting the thing on our fingers and challenging us to get it off. It appeared to be mission impossible. Once the thing was on, it would stick on the finger. The harder we pulled, the more it stuck—and the more amused he was. The resolution required a wisdom that none of us managed to tap into, despite our lifelong training. The only way for the artifact to loosen and come off was to push it farther onto the finger. This, I thought, was one of the best metaphors for how we can also resolve our relationships to our families of origin: go back in order to move forward.

Embracing the old does not mean getting fused with it. In order to preserve the new, our best chance for success is to team up with our partner. This way, we ensure that our new projects do not dissolve into the previous organisms. Things work best when the "WE"—the team that the couple forms—is preserved.

Here is an example of what does *not* constitute an embrace of the "WE," which then fails to function as a team. Xenia had been abandoned by both her mother and her father. When she met Max, she held tightly to him, as he was the only "home" she had. Very soon into the relationship, Xenia and Max started having problems. Max would find Xenia overly controlling and would push her away at times. He would disappear without telling her where he was. He would not answer his phone or return her messages. One of Xenia's coping strategies was to call Max's mother and ask for her help in contacting him and in scolding him for his inconsiderate behavior. And mom would do exactly that, despite him being a full-grown adult. In this case, the couple's boundaries got erased in the face of conflict. They actually ceased to be a couple, as the relationship decomposed within the family's organism.

Henry told his wife, Kate, that his mother did not like the name they had picked for their baby daughter. Could they choose another one? They were all just different sounds, he said, after all, and his mother would be happier and would leave them alone if they called their daughter after her.

Kate was very upset about this issue but gave in to avoid a major conflict, at the same time feeling very resentful of her husband and mother-in-law.

The above are clearly not examples of an embrace. An embrace is understood as the integration, not the dissolution, of the parts. It refers to a process that requires and respects the integrity of each holon (part and whole, each component and each organism). In the examples above, the new project dissolved into the old. Xenia will need to find a way to resolve conflicts by approaching and negotiating with Max, not his mother. Henry will need to fortify his relationship with his wife and make it a priority. If either project is to survive, the partners will need to find a way to operate as a team.

The In-Laws

So how are we to approach, deal with, and survive our partner's family? The objective is always the same: embrace the past and move on. What changes in regard to our in-laws rather than our own parents is our role in the process. It is no longer about us finding a way to constructively relate to our own family; it is about facilitating this process for our partner.

This task is not easy, because we are, in some way, competing organisms. The family is most likely to push for regression and reconnection; our push will tend to point toward emancipation and separation. The parents often want their child closer to them than to the new partner. The partner wants him or her closer to us than to his or her parents. It is not an easy enterprise to resolve the autonomy/connection tug-of-war between the old and new projects, especially in relation to our partner's family, but as long as the "ties that bind" do not snap, there is hope.

Let's start by examining what does *not* work. It does not work to try to free our partners from their "ties," nor does it work to push them to take positions. Polarization is not an effective strategy. In fact, it usually becomes a horrible trap that can last a lifetime. Why? We cannot move forward or evolve while leaving behind or rejecting parts of the components of which we are made. Making remarks about our in-laws to our partner, reminding them of how horrible they are or have been, is an attack on the partner's own identity and integrity—even if the claim is totally true, evidence based, and backed up with perfectly valid documentation. The in-laws are best treated with respect. The family is best understood, not attacked. Attacks will back-fire, and they always bring about some sort of suffering. When "hitting" the parents, we implicitly hit the partner—and consequently ourselves, as we form part of the same organism with them.

Paul was an only son. His mother, a widow, felt threatened by any girl-friend or relationship he initiated and would always find a way to boycott it. Her most favored defense strategy against his autonomy was to make him feel guilty for abandoning her. The idea of an imminent death would very often be evoked, in relation to his absence, so he did not get into any serious relationships until he reached his fifties. At that moment, mom really did get sick, and she had to be hospitalized for a long period of time. Meanwhile, Paul started dating someone. He fell in love. Mom sensed it and started putting more and more pressure on him to dedicate more time to her, making him feel guiltier than ever. Her neediness rendered it impossible for Paul to keep both of "his ladies" happy. The situation was tearing him apart.

We invited his girlfriend to join us for some sessions. She was legitimately very angry at Paul's mother. Still, instead of defining her as an evil witch who would not allow her son to move on and be happy, we talked about her as a guardian of connection, who would only let go if she felt that her bond with her son would endure. We considered that if she were left alone and eventually died, Paul would find it very hard to move on happily with his new project. As it turned out, despite her need for constant connection, Paul's mom had never cultivated an affectionate bond with him. She did not know how to, really. This is probably why she resorted to controlling him in the first place. Therefore, it was suggested that Paul attempt to form an affectionate bond with his mother. As predicted, mom appreciated the connection with her son and eventually gave her blessing to him moving forward. The new organism, by establishing a good-quality connection with the old, finally managed to gain autonomy.

Rearranging the Systems

In order to achieve something that had never been achieved before, Paul's partner's collaboration was "key" to the process. He was not to go back to mommy looking for her love. He was not to regress into the previous organism. Rather, it was about going back as an adult and connecting with his mother in a way he had never done before. By having his girlfriend by his side, supporting him in this project, the new relationship was not posing such a threat anymore. Paul was not regressing to a childlike state, yet the mother felt more nurtured, content, and safe in her relationship with her son than ever.

Note here that it was Paul doing the work—not his girlfriend. When there is hostility between a parent and a son- or daughter-in-law, it is the actual son's or daughter's job to resolve it. Allowing for hostility between one's parents and partner to grow is often an indication that the son or daughter has not yet managed to fully differentiate from their family of origin. The hostility thus serves as a temporary boundary or "buffer" between the partner and his or her parents.

Alison came from a small town, where nothing seemed to happen or change. Her family expected her to grow up, marry, and live all her life there, following their norms and traditions. She would never defy them openly. What she did do, however, was study abroad and marry Jonathan—someone totally "outside their box." He was foreign, younger, an artist, of a lower socioeconomic class, and an atheist. He did not even speak their language properly. They would not have it. They did not even want to *see* him, and they questioned everything about him. Soon enough, Alison started questioning him herself: Why are you not making more money? Why don't you learn my language faster? She started mirroring the attitude of her parents, despite Jonathan's efforts to please her—and her parents—at all costs. That's when they came in for therapy.

The map of relationships was rearranged. Alison realized how difficult Jonathan's position was: he was living in a foreign country, not speaking the language, trying to move forward as an artist, and, at the same time, supporting her in her career and in the relationship with her parents, without practically any support or recognition on her part. Our meetings helped Alison see Jonathan in a different light again and value him as the remarkable, considerate, and brave man she had fallen in love with and who had also put his love for her first. With their WE empowered, Alison would now stand up for him rather than attack him. As she gently yet firmly differentiated from her own family, she was able to come closer to Jonathan and create a more adult and genuine bond with her parents too. Jonathan ceased to be perceived as a threat by them after a while. Together, now as accomplices, they devised ways to make Alison's parents feel more comfortable about Jonathan and bring both WEs closer to one another.

When Ed and Christine had their first baby, his mother came in to give them a hand. Mom did not approve of Christine's parenting style and would let her know every time she could. Christine was distraught and would complain to her husband. "Oh, figure it out yourselves," Ed would say. "You are both adults. It should not be that hard."

Elena's husband, Jake, got a new job abroad. She had to work and raise their two kids on her own for a year, until they could all relocate as well. During that time, Jake's mother would come and stay with her to help. It sounded wonderful to begin with, but they did not see eyetoeye on everything. When there was an argument between them, Jake's mother would lock herself in the guest room and call her son. He would call his wife from the other side of the globe and ask her to treat his mother "better."

In both these examples, those who need to step up and facilitate a resolution are Ed and Jake. Both need to find a way to team up with their partners rather than with their mothers. They need to find a way to set a clear boundary with the latter without, at the same time, destroying their bond with them.

Here is a more constructive scenario: Colin and Sue had his mother staying over to help after their baby was born. In the middle of the night, the baby started crying. Both mother and grandmother ran to the rescue. Gran made it there first. She held the baby tight and would not give him to his mother, Sue, when she opened her arms to hold him. Gran thought she could soothe him best—after all, she had more experience in this. Sue was getting upset. Colin got up, as he now heard both the baby crying and the adults yelling. He saw his mother holding the baby and noticed the distress in his wife. "Mom, can you give little Joe to his mother, please?" he said immediately, with a serious tone. His mother felt resentful and she showed it, but she complied. Colin continued, "We really appreciate your help, but it is our turn now as parents. You have always been loving and kind, so I trust that you will understand." And that was that. Sue sighed with relief, feeling more in love with her husband than ever, while grandma continued to be thanked and appreciated for her help.

Sometimes it can be as easy as that: setting a boundary at an appropriate moment. Sometimes things are far more complicated. No matter what level of challenge one faces, overcoming it will require teaming up with the partner and respectfully differentiating from the families of origin.

The following points serve as a practical guide or quick summary of the above when it comes to dealing with meddling in-laws:

- Ensure the integrity of the organism (couple) by teaming up with the partner. It is always preferable to stay in the same boat, even when partners seem to be heading in different directions. The route can always be (re)negotiated.

- Invite understanding rather than criticism of the in-laws, even if they "deserve it," and even when the attacks or criticism come from the partners themselves.

- Intergenerational disentanglements should be led or initiated by the member of the couple or family—not the in-law. The partner, if anything, can help the process by offering support and by doing their best not to make things worse.

Tense, unresolved, or idealized relationships with the previous generation (parents, caregivers, in-laws) will block emancipation and evolution. The unresolved keeps us tied to the past and the previous organism. We remain the kids that we used to be.

Having the courage to recognize what the older generation has not done constructively (differentiation) and forgiving them for it (connection), entails being able to accept their limitations, mistakes, and fragility, even if they themselves do not acknowledge any of it. This is almost always a necessary condition for the passage into "adulthood" and a subsequent functional couple.

Parenthood: The Ultimate Test

A very strong partnership in the couple will also be required in relation to offspring—another "third party" of utmost importance that will pose ongoing and ever-evolving challenges. Again, there are no easy recipes for overcoming these challenges. As mentioned in the previous chapter, there is an inherent imbalance within every family system from a societal standpoint. The value attributed to the feminine and masculine poles within a couple—especially after children appear—is not equally distributed. The partner who will primarily dedicate themselves to parenting will lose out on both social value and personal identity. Therefore, the system's well-being will be determined, to a large extent, by its ability to compensate for this imbalance by ensuring that the partner who predominantly occupies the feminine pole receives extra value and support. If this happens, this "primary caregiver" partner will be in a far better position to both care for the children and provide the other partner with adequate connection. The couples who manage to do best and most happily transit this stage embody the following characteristics:

- They themselves attribute equal value to all sides of the partnership (feminine and masculine) and compensate internally for what is not compensated socially.

- They continue to operate as a partnership of two.

- They show flexibility in moving from one role to another, willing to support each other in any way they can.

Here is an example of a success story: Eric and Daniela had been together for about eight years when they decided to have children. They were both working at that time and were quite content and happy with their professional development. When Daniela got pregnant, Eric was delighted and was very attentive all through the pregnancy. At the moment the baby was born, he fought for and managed to get a three-month leave from work, so that he could be there and enjoy the beginning of their baby's life. They would bathe her, change her, put her to sleep, sing to her, and play with her together. The baby gave them the opportunity of having, in their eyes, yet another fun, stimulating experience as a couple. When they got back to work, they took different shifts, so one of them would always be with the baby. They would often say jokingly that having to go to work was giving them the opportunity to have a break and relax from the real work of raising their daughter. They repeated a very similar pattern when their second and third child came into the picture. Their roles became more defined with the passing of time and the appearance of more kids, but they profoundly respected and acknowledged each other's contribution to the "whole."

The rearrangement of roles and functions is a natural and fundamental part of the process. It is inevitable for this to take place, so the better prepared the couple is for this shift, the better the transition will be. The alternative would mean ignoring the reality of a baby forming part of the organism, which is simply crazy. Some couples do try to maintain the previous status quo and workings of the relationship—a situation that is usually blind, not to mention potentially dangerous, to the needs and well-being of the offspring. In any case, the organism will transform to a different "whole" and will have a great deal more needs to take care of and challenges to meet.

In the face of such a demanding and complex enterprise, I find a couple of reflections from a more philosophical standpoint to be particularly useful to keep in mind:

1. **Being good enough is good enough.** Doing one's best and trying hard is already a lot. There is no way to be perfect. It is actually better not to seek perfection, as it usually makes us far more stressed and, also, more blind to our own limitations. Flawed parents who assume responsibility for their limitations are still great parents. Flawed parents who strive to be perfect and cannot deal with their failures are a danger to their children, to themselves, and to everyone in their circle. Flaws only become problems when one tries to deny them or to project them onto others.

2. **Enjoy the ride as much as possible, despite its challenges.** We will only experience the transition to parenthood with the

birth of our first child once. If we have a second child, it will also happen once, and we will only be able to witness the beginning of the fraternal bond between siblings once. A third child marks the creation of a fraternal team. They are all significant, meaningful, powerful experiences. Babies will only be babies for a little while. Childhood is short. And living together as a family will also come to an end. If we miss our chance to enjoy the different stages and transitions, we will have lost an essential part of life itself.

Parenting through Divorce

Sometimes it is not possible to keep the WE of the couple intact, given all of the challenges one faces from within and without. The WE of the couple may die, but hopefully the WE of the family will remain as intact as possible. It is one of the most common challenges and transformations of WEs with children. Ex-partners will need to continue to function as parents. They will also need to collaborate somehow if they have their offspring's best interests at heart.

It helps to be reminded that the children's position in relation to our partner is very different than our own. We can leave the ex-partner behind. They cannot, even if they wished to. This means that the person we are separating from, who we do not want to form part of our romantic lives anymore, will nevertheless continue to form part of the children's organism and will condition their inner and outer lives forever. Therefore, the children will need the reality or the fantasy of two parents who can peacefully coexist in their minds and hearts, even if they cannot or wish not to coexist in real life.

The fights between the I's—those aggressive and seemingly eternal divorce proceedings that are so childlike, so primitive, so much about the little kids within trying to find a justice that will be impossible to achieve (as it almost always relates to unresolved childhood issues)—leave the real children unattended, in positions of extreme risk and negligence. According to Jorge Barudy, a well-known Chilean child neuropsychiatrist and family therapist, "The children who are used in divorce conflicts present psychological trauma that is comparable to having been abused."[1]

It is worth remembering that as long as the children are alive, the parental WE will inevitably continue to be both an inner and an outer reference for them. A great divorce-related investment would therefore be to skillfully transition the couple's WE from a combined parental and romantic WE to a parental WE only. Such transition will call for each individual to take responsibility for the whole family's well-being, meaningfully responding to—or even transcending—the pain of the loss or the anger they may feel so that they can best attend to the children's needs. Given that such a process sets the real kids as a priority, it pushes the adults involved (and the kids within them) to grow, become emotionally stronger, and move on. The focus here is to care for the I's of the children and the WE of the family, which will need to transform into something nurturing and constructive despite the separation. Such a process can be led by the partners themselves or by professionals such as family therapists.

Lawyers and litigations, on the contrary, generally focus on the integrity of each partner's "I," which is also legitimate and important. The I's will need to redefine themselves in relation to one another, and some legal definitions within the whole process are usually required and necessary. What is, unfortunately, all too often the case is that the whole procedure is carried out at the expense of the offspring and of "adulthood" in general. The wounded adult-kids hire lawyers as an extension of their defenses, seeking justice (from their perspective only) or aiming to directly "get to their ex-partners," becoming so self-centered and self-absorbed in the process that they forget to acts as adults and, especially, as parents. Such scenarios pave the way for disastrous outcomes for the children and bring about some amount of lifelong suffering for all. Success stories involve ex-partners sticking to their parental roles, operating as adults rather than scared, desperate, self-centered children, and, optimally, continuing to function as a team in relation to their children.

It may help to remember that what the parental WE will continue to have in common, despite all the things that keep them separate on so many other levels, is the love they have for the children themselves. They are likely to be the two people on the face of the planet who love those creatures the most. This may be the only positive thing still binding the former WE of the couple together, but then again, it may also be the only thing that really matters.

Untangling Love Triangles

> "You're beautiful, but you're empty . . . One couldn't die for you. Of course, an ordinary passerby would think my rose looked just like you. But my rose, all on her own, is more important than all of you together, since she's the one I've watered. Since she's the one I put under glass, since she's the one I sheltered behind the screen. Since she's the one for whom I killed the caterpillars (except the two or three butterflies). Since she's the one I listened to when she complained, or when she boasted, or even sometimes when she said nothing at all. Since she's my rose."[2]
>
> —**Antoine de Saint-Exupéry,** *The Little Prince*

The existence of a lover is an extremely painful situation. It is felt as a direct attack on the "I" and challenges the very foundation of the WE. I am never certain, as a therapist, whether the couple will manage to survive it, recover, and move on. It will depend on many different variables. The most important one, I think, is reflected in Antoine de Saint-Exupéry's words above: the partner with whom we have traversed part of our lives together is special—more special than anyone—precisely for having spent part of their lives with us. A new partner and a new WE may be very appealing, but, at least at the beginning, the new project is empty of shared history. Despite having been questioned or attacked, the current WE has many more stories and shared experiences, joys, and woes that bind it together and make it special.

This uniqueness can set the foundation for recovery if the partners wish to find a resolution, but it is not enough in itself. The couple will need to talk, to rearrange itself, to express and address what was not working before. Those problematic aspects that were being silenced before in fear of losing the other may be the very reason that an affair occurred in the first place. According to family therapists Augustus Napier and Carl Whitaker,

> The affair demands that the couple communicate on a more profound level than they have in the past. . . . They begin to talk more honestly *because they have to.* Their relationship is in such desperate straits, teetering at the edge of separation or divorce, that they overcome their timidity and face each other. It is now or never![3]

Turning the Page

Moving on from a betrayal can be a very strenuous process, as the partners come to the experience from very different angles. Their struggles will be different, as well as the pace and rhythm that each will require to deal with the process. The "unfaithful" partner will want to turn the page as soon as possible, potentially patching up the wound without treating it. The "wronged" partner will most likely want to take time to understand and process what has happened, treating his or her wounds but potentially preventing the relationship from moving forward.

The biggest mistake is to overlook the underlying issues that have led to the affair. According to Napier and Whitaker, "The affair, like many major marital events, is intuitively 'arranged' by the couple."[4] In this sense, the affair is orchestrated by both partners and pushes for evolution. It comes as an unconscious decision that necessitates transformation or, if that is not possible, dissolution.

No matter what the underlying reasons may be—and there are usually many—for the affair, the wounds that it produces will also need to be cared for:

- The relationship with the "other" will need to come to an end. Healing cannot take place unless the other story has concluded. The fire needs to be put out before starting to look at what originated it and also before any reconstruction can take place.

- Apologizing in a meaningful way is important. This does not mean going over the details of the affair. What will be most urgent is to start by soothing the wounded partner. This will require listening to their pain and giving them the time and space they need to express their suffering, no matter how painful it may be to listen. This may be the only meaningful way to "be with" the other again right after the revelation of an affair. For this reason, it is important for the wounded partner's "I" to be the priority and to try not to offer excuses or defend one's own questioned "I." This is a moment to offer as much of a safe space as possible to the wounded partner. Ideally, one will be able to connect to the pain inflicted, see the world through the other's eyes, and accompany the partner through it, starting with a genuine apology.

- Repair will need to take place, in the sense of taking action that shows one is committed to this WE and that all of their efforts will be invested here again.

In sum, if reconstruction is to take place, the fire will need to be put down first, the wounded attended to, and, finally, the causes of the fire explored and addressed. It is a very demanding task for both partners, the final stage probably being the most complex of all. The initial problems that gave rise to the affair "can be seen as one political event in a network of relationship struggles that can extend in all directions, but most commonly into the family of origin."[5] The couple will need to face and assume responsibility for their incapacity or lack of skill in finding constructive ways to resolve their original difficulties. They will need to examine how each has helped create, feed into, and sustain dysfunctional patterns. They must also assume responsibility for their failure to provide connection and autonomy to themselves and to the other in the first place. And both partners will need to operate as a team in order to resolve the triangle.

An affair will inevitably reflect difficulties in terms of connection and autonomy. Partners are usually "tangled up" between themselves and, most often, their own families of origin. An affair indicates a "differentiation" difficulty that is also inevitably related to a not-well-established bond of connection with the other. Partners have not been able to feel neither free enough nor meaningfully connected to their caregivers, and then the pattern repeats itself in the relationship. The task will be to create a different "dance," one that allows for greater and more honest intimacy, as well as greater independence.

Affairs challenge systems that are too rigid or too undefined, "organisms" that fail to provide connection and autonomy. The conditions most commonly encountered within a couple in which an affair takes place can be found in the following description from Napier and Whitaker:

In the interest of security, they subjugate themselves to the relationship's demands. *It is the relationship, the system, the dance that intimidates them, enslaves them. It is the family itself from which they beg freedom.* But more than freedom and independence are at stake, because the family's unity is a false one. . . . Its members usually feel a frustrating combination of personal isolation and tight restrictiveness. They do not enjoy either the freedom of genuine separateness or the exhilaration of real intimacy. They suffer a seemingly unending purgatory of solitary imprisonment in a family that they love but cannot fully enjoy.[6]

Although the authors refer to the family as a whole, it is the same case with the main unit within it: the couple. An affair will take place at times when there is no real togetherness, no real connection, and no real autonomy between the partners.

Connection and autonomy are both vital and interdependent. The greater the sense of connection and autonomy achieved within the couple, the smaller the chances for an affair to be needed. And if it does appear, the task will again inevitably involve enhancing the connection to one another, which will in turn provide the basis for a sense of greater independence and autonomy that is experienced within oneself and in relation to the other.

Sexual Healing

Sex is about connection. It gets the parts to "come together" and "fuse," creating and maintaining human systems. The greater the sense of intimacy and connection derived by sex, the greater the consequent feeling of integrity for each part.

But, as we have seen, sex can also be a dangerous and painful affair. The process of connection can seriously damage the I's when fusion does not guarantee the integrity of both parts as they merge together. The "dance of sex," if it is to fulfill its main purpose of establishing genuine connection, has to be extremely mindful of the I's involved.

Let's look at John and Louise in what would be a positive scenario, both fully enjoying and getting nurtured by their sexual encounters. When Louise is around, John feels great. Her gaze and the way she smiles at him make him feel strong and desired. He feels safe in himself, even more so in her presence, which is an important turn-on for him. Louise loves to be in the presence of John, too. His almost unconditional attraction to her makes Louise feel desired and powerful. She can feel the impact she has on him, and she thrives on it. His love and respect make her feel safe and, as he approaches softly and gently at the beginning, she feels more and more attracted. Paradoxically, the freer she feels within their connection, the more she engages, opening up to him and letting her body surrender to the experience. The more confident she perceives John to be in relation to her, the more emotionally stable and self-sufficient, desiring her but not desperate for her, the greater her own desire to surrender in his arms and feel his sexual power. The more she surrenders, the more intense the pleasure, and the more she wants to feel his strength. His sexual energy, within what now feels to be an open channel between them, becomes hers and transforms into orgasms that come as waves of sheer pleasure. John meets her at the top of such a wave, having a powerful orgasm himself. Louise feels extremely energized after every sexual encounter. She feels she can touch the stars. John usually feels exhausted but happy, having expended his energy, often falling asleep by her side, feeling safe and cuddled at the bosom of his partner.

There are probably infinite scenarios of what could be a positive sexual experience in interpersonal terms. This is just one possible script. The common denominators to any successful sexual dance, no matter how different they may be, is the existence of baseline connection ("we are in this together"), as well as autonomy (feeling respected as individuals) at all times—before, during, and after the act.

The information in the table on the next page seeks to reflect some of the dynamics commonly at play around the sexual act. It is a draft of a few central ideas, not a list of facts—and certainly not exhaustive. The masculine and the feminine are defined, not in terms of gender or sexual orientation, but rather as "positions" within the sexual dance.

	The masculine	The feminine
Baseline (most common) initial position	Secure in the "WE"; safe occupying the one-up position: *The other one cannot hurt me.* Insecure in the "I": *Am I desired? Will I be able to perform?*	Secure in the "I": *I am desired.* Insecure in the "WE": *Will I be safe? Will it be pleasurable?*
Baseline requirement	Primarily requires an established sense of autonomy in relation to the other (to feel safe in the "I"): *I feel admired; I can perform; I will not be humiliated or ridiculed.*	Primarily requires an established sense of connection in relation to the other (to feel safe in the "WE"): *I am respected; I am cared for; I will not be attacked or humiliated.*
The yearning	"Turned on" by the connection that the feminine can provide; the power of the "WE."	"Turned on" by the autonomy that the masculine can provide; the power of the "I."
The most common failure	Making it all about the "I"; losing the "WE"; sex that brings no pleasure to the partner.	Making it all about the "WE"; losing the "I"; sex that brings no pleasure to oneself.

As far as I am concerned, the entire human race would be far happier and far less violent if sex were understood interpersonally and we aimed to practice it successfully in these terms. This would involve both the I's getting nurtured, strengthened, and empowered; and both parts feeling good about themselves and within the relationship before, during, and after the act. A basis of respect, agreement, and safety can guarantee a valuable rather than miserable sexual experience—one involving pleasure, exploration, growth, fun, satisfaction, nurture, connection, or whatever the partners seek to get out of it. It does not sound too complicated. However, although things are slowly but surely improving, we could say that our species is, quite miserably, failing the task.

Communication to the Rescue

We have seen that skillfully managing our individual defenses within the boundaries of the couple helps maintain our integrity without damaging the connection. Similarly, skillfully connecting to the other (via sex or any other avenue) helps maintain the bond without damaging the integrity of the individual parts. *Skillfully* is the key word here. Happy, healthy bonds and happy, healthy I's will require and depend upon interpersonal skills. Here we will briefly revise a few basic yet central ideas.

Communication is the dance itself. It reflects our ability to connect with the other without losing ourselves and to care for our integrity without losing the other. Communication is also our only means of getting ourselves untangled. In the face of tension and conflict, we cannot resolve much while we operate from a primitive defense mode. Being primitive and childlike can be fabulous at moments of joy, exploration, connection, or intimacy, as our "animal side" helps us engage with life. Yet, when the need arises for complex interpersonal problems to be resolved, the primitive will not get us very far. It will inform us on whether the other is perceived as a friend or a foe. It will propel us to fight, flee, or freeze. And, if it is the primitive dictating our actions, it is likely to make things worse.

When Piers got up Sunday morning, he found his place unrecognizable. His furniture had moved, and some things had disappeared. "WTF?" he shouted at his girlfriend, Eileen, who had moved into his place a few weeks ago.

"But . . . I told you I had some ideas about rearranging the place and you said okay," she muttered.

"That's not what I meant! You are so inconsiderate! You always do whatever you feel like! You are so selfish!" Eileen said she was sorry and left. She needed to take a walk to wind down.

Eileen did not expect Piers's reaction. In her mind, she had not done anything wrong. She had even mentioned her intentions to him. Yet she was not aware that she had attacked Piers's "I" by taking action. Rearranging their place was the kind of action that would affect them both, but she did not make sure that they were both in it together. It is a classic mistake. We have not learned to think in "WE" terms. We are often not aware that, once in a couple, actions as seemingly innocuous as inviting someone over for dinner, moving something to a different place, making plans for the weekend, asking for a loan, or anything big or small that can directly or indirectly impact the partner can feel like a full-blown attack to their integrity if they are not taken into account.

We usually mean well, but it is not enough. It is like going to the doctor, knowing that they mean well, but not being given any information about the why's and how's of their procedures and manipulations. The information may not mean anything in itself, but it does mean a lot about the relationship with the other. It is a strong statement that expresses, "You are important to me. We are a team. I am mindful of your presence. I take you into account." Eileen skipped this apparently basic common courtesy. It happens a lot in relationships, but that does not make it less of an attack.

Thus, Piers felt attacked and started attacking back. That is also quite a common reaction. The fact that it is common does not render it any less of an attack either. There is nothing constructive about it. Attacks have no place within a relationship. It is the organism harming itself. If they do happen, they need to be blocked. There is nothing wise about counterattacking. It apparently serves to protect the integrity of the I, but as the partner forms part of the same unit, an attack on them will always backfire. When in primitive mode, the wisest thing to do is to respond as a martial arts master would: the opponent's attack is to be blocked or transformed, without losing one's balance and without counterattacking.

Eileen acted more skillfully in this sense. She apologized, which helped restore Piers's I and his safety in the WE, and then she left the scene on relatively good terms, mainly to help herself get to a place where she could then have a more loving conversation with her boyfriend. She did not directly block the attack. It is not always necessary, but it is important that verbal attacks are always addressed, so that they can be eliminated from any interpersonal dance. They can be as hurtful and damaging as physical attacks—sometimes even more so. Emotional aggressions like humiliation stay and live within us in a way that physical aggression does not. They may even change the way we perceive and relate to ourselves. In sum, there is nothing good that violence of any kind can achieve in a partnership and should have no place in it.

Eileen could say something like, "Look, I understand now why you got upset. I am sorry that you did—even more so because I thought I was doing something for *us* that would actually make you happy. Calling me selfish and inconsiderate and shouting is not the way to go. It was uncalled for. I understand your being upset, but I do not deserve this kind of reaction. I will not have it again."

The way we word things—*how* we speak and address one another—is of utmost importance. This is reflected in another one of the five axioms of human communication, as described by Paul Watzlawick et al.

Any communication implies a commitment and thereby defines the relationship. This is another way of saying that a communication not only conveys information, but at the same time it imposes behavior. Following Bateson (pp. 179-81), these two operations have come to be known as the "report" and the "command" aspects, respectively, of any communication. The report aspect of a message conveys information and is, therefore, synonymous in human communication with the *content* of the message. It may be about anything that is communicable regardless of whether it is true or false, valid, invalid, or undecidable. The command aspect, on the other hand, refers to what sort of a message it is to be taken as, and, therefore, ultimately to the *relationship* between the communicants.[7]

Every communication has a content and a relationship aspect. In other words, every time we say something, two things happen simultaneously: we verbally communicate the content of the message, and, at the same time, we define something about the relationship. What we say about the relationship will always weigh more than the message itself. If we say, for example, "You never take the garbage out," we are making a statement about the garbage, but we are also talking about the relationship. We can convey, for example, that we are not pleased that the partner has not taken care of it. Depending on the tone of voice we use, or the way we actually word things, the message may sound like a cry for help, a reproach, a critique, or a demand.

The partner will hear the content of the statement and will also hear and interpret something regarding the state of affairs in the relationship. Now, what the aggrieved partner is likely to be feeling—"I feel overlooked. I am at everyone's service here and nobody notices. I feel insignificant to you"—is probably very different than what the other partner is interpreting. And the partner will react in accordance to *their* interpretation.

So the messages we exchange are important, but *how* we deliver them is even more so. Imperatives, orders, and instructions are likely to be perceived as attacks and not welcomed by the other. That's not to say they should not be used; it's just important to be mindful of what we are doing when we are communicating, so that our actions are more in line with what we want to achieve.

Listening before reacting is another way to untangle a tense situation. Piers did not allow any room for Eileen to explain the situation. He immediately jumped the gun, made his mind up about what had happened, and reacted to his very own conclusions. The more insecure a partner is, the less their ability to "hold their horses," which will feel overly threatening and may seriously undermine any skilled, intelligent action. Nevertheless, it is important to try and calm ourselves down. Making some room for the other, giving them the benefit of the doubt, and adopting as a baseline that the partner is a predominantly friendly entity that can make mistakes but was not put there to torture us may save us a lot of unnecessary (and often quite absurd) conflict.

After seeing his place all changed, Piers could have just said, "What happened here? Why have you made all these changes without telling me first?" Then he could have listened to Eileen: why it was important to her; what made her do it this way and not the other. This interaction with Eileen could have helped him make a distinction between the act in particular and the relationship in general. Maybe, looking around him, knowing that it was an act of care rather than an attack, he would be in a better position to observe what works and what does not work about the changes. He could be practical. He could negotiate. He could even ask Eileen that she or they put everything back to where it was and then do it all over again together. It is also important, as with Eileen, to block what he perceived as an attack: "I don't like such surprises, Eileen. I am sorry, you cannot be making decisions about the two of us on your own. I understand you did not mean to upset me, but if you really want me to be happy, just talk to me first next time."

Eileen, in the actual flow of events, had the strength and maturity to stop the escalation of the conflict and then to seek a way to reconnect with Piers. Seeking and finding a way to reconnect is probably the most important and most complex skill of all. Its importance is beautifully reflected in the story below, attributed to a Jewish itinerant preacher.[8] Different versions of the story are also included in Hindu, Buddhist, and Christian folklore. Here is my version of it:

> Before dying, an old, kind man was invited to learn more about Heaven and Hell. He was taken to Hell first and was surprised by the scenery. It was not at all the kind of Hell he had expected. He saw people sitting around a big table, with the most delicious stew in front of them. They all had huge, long spoons strapped to their arms, paired with smaller plates. People could only have access to the food using their spoons. They struggled as they tried and failed to put the heavenly aliment in their mouths with their giant utensils. They were eternally hungry and frustrated.
>
> The old man was then sent to see Heaven. Yet another surprise was waiting for him: Heaven looked exactly like Hell. He was actually faced

PART VI: RELATIONSHIP RESCUE | 163

with the exact same setting—the same big table, the delicious stews, and the incredibly long spoons. Yet when people started to interact, there was a notable difference: each one would put their spoon into the soup of the one in front of them and would feed that person instead.

I find this to be one of the most telling metaphors about a couple's dynamics. We cannot feed ourselves interpersonally; we need the other, and the other needs us. It all boils down to *trust*: we need to feed the other and simply trust that we will be fed back.

"Can you guarantee me that if I do what you say, my wife will respond as I wish her to?" one of my clients once asked. The truth is that I cannot guarantee anything. What I do know is that the chances for resolution definitely and significantly increase when we feed the partner. Most couples, at the time of consultation, are waving their spoons angrily at one another, blaming each other for their hunger. Or they are staring angrily at each other, not moving, waiting for the other to make the first move. "Why me first and not you?"

Who should go first? I do not know. In fact, it really doesn't matter. Life is too short, in my view, to spend it pondering whether to do something constructive or not. As far as I am concerned, the less time we spend in our self-made hells, the better.

Within a relationship, it is not even needed for both partners to act wisely in order for conflict to be resolved. Usually, if one of the two is interpersonally skilled and mature enough, they can pave the path out of hell. They will need to do it from a position of personal strength and integrity. The *Circle of Security Intervention* authors talk about the parent needing to always be "stronger, bigger, wiser, and kinder" in order to achieve "good enough" parenting. There are no big differences in the relationship between adults. Simply, instead of "bigger, stronger, wiser, and kinder," we generally just need to be big, strong, kind, and wise. The comparative "–er"s will only be called for when the partner is in hostile, primitive mode. The same authors also state that all four qualities need to be present at the same time. If, for instance, one is only bigger and stronger, they can be perceived as "mean." If only kinder and wiser, they are likely to be perceived as "weak." Again, we need both aspects—autonomy (enhanced by being big and strong) and connection (enhanced by being kind and wise)—in order to establish working interpersonal patterns.

Unfortunately, all too often there is "no adult in the room." I do not believe this is because humans are stupid and interpersonally incompetent by nature; I just think that we have not made learning interpersonal skills a priority yet. We have been far too busy increasing our "connectivity value," far more interested in the "I" than in the "WE." So despite the vital importance and relevance the art of communication will always have in our lives, it has not been studied enough, explored enough, and therefore not taught or learned enough. In my view, it should occupy a position as relevant and universal as math or music.

Seeking Therapy

In the world, as in our skulls, the child should be our priority. For that, we need adults who have the skill and capacity to take good care of them. The primitive, if it has undergone serious trauma, will not collaborate with the cortical—the "parent"—unless it feels confident that that part is strong, caring, and mature enough to handle and help elaborate the pain. The most painful traumas will remain disconnected from our consciousness until we find a good enough caregiver and feel strong enough in ourselves to deal with and integrate them.

This is what psychotherapy is all about. It engages the "child," providing at the same time new learning to the cortical brain so that it can deliver a more nurturing and constructive type of "parenting" than the one that was copied from the caregivers. At the beginning, it is the therapist leading the process, hopefully facilitating a new, more constructive model of "parental care and intervention" for the client to internalize. If things go well, the client will acquire "therapeutic" abilities themselves that can then be introduced to the relationship with oneself and with others. In an ideal world, we would all have the ability to provide such care to one another, and even more so within the context of our intimate relationships, where the primitive is so central and yet too often misunderstood and unattended.

According to Bonnie Badenoch, psychotherapist and expert in inter-personal neurobiology, "One way of thinking about psychotherapy is as a process of mutual engagement that will change both structure and function in the brain and nervous system in the direction of neural integration."[9] She suggests "vertical integration" as a good place to begin, meaning that "the body, limbic region and cortex in one hemisphere are linked."[10] She considers the right-hemisphere process of limbic-prefrontal linkage to be central to personal and interpersonal wellbeing.

> I emphasize these processes in the right hemisphere rather than the left for two reasons: (1) During the crucial first 18 months of life, when founda-tional attachment styles and mental models are wired in, the brain favors RMP development over LMP (Cozolino, 2006)[11]; and (2) much of what unfolds in the counselling room is RMP-centered, as the social circuits in the therapist's and patient's brains dance together to rewire the attachment experience in a pattern of security (Schore, 2007).[12.13]

In other words, she suggests that if we are to care for ourselves and our health, our attention should focus on the "connection-specialist" region in our brains. Our wellbeing largely depends on our ability to connect to ourselves and to others. The end goal is *integration,* understood as the connection between well differentiated elements with a system (i.e., elements that have accomplished a high level of both connection and autonomy between them).

As Daniel J. Siegel remarks,

> As the mind is both embodied and relational, we see a healthy mind emerging from an integrated state: When elements of a system being examined—an individual, couple, family, group, or perhaps society—are integrated, that system is said to be the most flexible, adaptive, coherent, energized, and stable.[14]

Within our brains and within our relationships, we do best when all parts are interconnected, balanced, well-defined, flexible, and adaptable.

Ending Relationships

A lot of people come to a therapy consultation asking, "Should we continue on together or should we separate?" I really don't know. When do we consider a piece of art or literature finished? I trust that the artists and authors themselves know better. What one can do is to simply offer information and experience that may inspire their art and decide whether they want to write another chapter together or prepare the concluding remarks.

Ideally, the end should be considered when there is nothing more to add, nothing more to gain; when the relationship feels to have served its purpose and one is ready to gracefully move on, feeling gratitude for all of the shared experiences. But separations are usually messy. They constitute some of the most painful situations we will experience in our adult lives, in part because we will not live through them emotionally as adults. Loss and pain pull us toward self-protection, the primitive "I," so it is very unlikely for "adult functioning" to be taking place at this stage. Separation is the baby losing their attachment figure; the child being rejected, abandoned, in "free fall" mode. The experience can be similar to spinning toward a black hole of nothingness. It is very difficult for anyone to act wisely or constructively under such conditions. And this is when most people seek therapy.

Unfortunately, there are no magic pills that can take the pain away. There are no shortcuts to grieve a loss. The best thing one can do is accompany the other through the different stages: denial, anger, bargaining, depression, acceptance. Getting to acceptance is when the process really finishes, when the real ending takes place.

Some people may initially find ways to distract or protect themselves from the pain. Some go back to the nest of their parents' home; some rapidly seek a new attachment figure; some look to be soothed by going out more, meeting with friends, bad-mouthing the ex, drinking a bit (or a lot), working, working out, reading, or traveling. There is nothing inherently bad or wrong about such solutions, as long as they do not harm oneself or others. Yet, at some point, the person will need to fully process the loss in order to really move forward and reach the point where, under ideal conditions, the couple itself would have been achieved had they operated maturely.

So, as with any grieving process, there are two ends. The external dissolution of the WE is only a part of it. As Napier and Whitaker explain,

> many divorces are merely pieces of legal paper that do little to change the couple's massive entanglement with each other. So *many* couples are legally divorced but emotionally still married; they simply carry their marriages internally or through their children.[15]

A lot of divorced couples know this all too well, as they continue to have intense relationships many years after the actual separation has taken place. They do not let go. They become obsessed with the other, sometimes even more so than when they were together. They think of each other day and night, spend obscene amounts of time and money to get their point across to the other—directly or via lawyers—and all too often bring their children into the turmoil in what seems to be a dance that will last eternally. Sometimes it does: ex-partners die with no acceptance ever having taken place, fixed in their position and particular struggle.

Have such couples actually ended their relationship? Not in my view. They continue to dance together. It is a terrible and painful dance, but it is not an end. Napier and Whitaker wonderfully summarize the end goal of a proper closure thus:

> *If* (and we say it big) they are going to get a meaningful divorce, one that includes psychological as well as legal freedom to leave each other, they will need the same thing that is required in a good marriage: *real individuation.*[16]

In other words, a meaningful divorce involves a graceful separation that *preserves the integrity of both parts.* This way, the WE may get dissolved, but its memory can live peacefully within each partner. There is no wish to continue being a WE, but there can still be a gentle, respectful bond, honoring the time spent together, the shared experiences, and especially the children (if they exist). Such endings require a caring interplay of connection and autonomy. They require both "real individuation" and the acceptance of loss.

Now, if we choose not to end the relationship, there is still another "door" available: that of transcendence.

Transcendence (Moving Beyond)

To see a World in a Grain of Sand
And a Heaven in a Wild Flower
Hold Infinity in the palm of your hand
And Eternity in an hour.[17]
—*William Blake*

We may dissect the human being in every way possible, but still . . . we never know it all. The more we discover, the more there seems to be discovered. A lot still escapes the grasp of our rational minds and science, only felt and portrayed in literature, poetry, art, or music. I like this. It keeps us curious, interested in the world, in what surrounds us, in ourselves, in others.

Love ignites our curiosity and can take us to the most amazing places. It can be a window towards infinity, of "eternities in an hour." We may see a whole world in the eyes of the loved one and experience heaven when we see them smile or as we hold their hand. It is probably the most powerful, most beautiful, most precious experience one can have.

There is always, in my view, something transcendental about our romantic encounters and love experiences. There are colleagues who jokingly define them as "psychotic experiences," as we seem to lose touch with reality for a while and tune into an alternative "universe," apparently a figment of our imagination. "Psychotic" may be a good enough description, as it takes into account—with a twist of humor—the comic and tragic limitations of human romantic love. Still, I would propose yet another definition: a brief encounter with the divine, in the other and in ourselves. It may last a millisecond, an hour, a day, a year, or a lifetime. It may go away extremely quickly, but I believe, if even for a split second, we do perceive something incomparably beautiful within the other. The other feels this and "knows" it too. We fall in love with the other and with ourselves too, because we sense and connect to our own beauty and sheer potential simultaneously. For a brief period of time, we are two divine creatures meeting and recognizing one another. And then we are expelled from heaven.

Constrained by a very human and very physical body, while immersed in a very real and demanding world—having to address our needs, those of loved ones, and all sorts of other challenges described in this book—the godly figures become unsustainable. Unless the relationship is an "impossible one," protected by the timelessness of our minds, the fall from heaven is inevitable. How each will fall, crash, and burn will depend on a great variety of factors.

Now, if you are reading this book, it is likely that you have a partner. You are also likely to have gone past the stage of bliss. (When in heaven, it is highly unlikely that we will seek knowledge—only Eve comes up with such bad ideas—so you are probably out of heaven.) The partner may now be perceived as the limited human being they are, terribly annoying at times. You may be tempted to pass this book to them (if you have not done so already) so that they find their footing again, "get a grip," and learn what they need to learn so they can change. If this is the case, I suggest you take a pause. It may be true they are flawed and limited. After all, isn't that true for all?

Yet it may not be the whole truth. Relationships develop a bit like science. At the beginning, they are mostly driven by fascination, ambition, a desire to explore and to dive into the unknown. And so we begin to learn, to become more familiar with the object of our interest. And the more we learn, the safer we feel, as we apply labels to an infinitely complex and amazing universe. We like the comfort and safety of know- ing. It gives us a sense of familiarity and control. And, as any other explorer in the process of learning, we will also come face to face with our methodological, practical, mental, emotional, physical, and all other kinds of limitations. The initial experience of exploration and discovery will most likely transform, as any research usually does, into a process based on dissection, analysis, established procedures, and routine, which is actually not a problem to begin with. Structure (conceptual, procedural, or other) ensures further exploration and development. It only becomes a problem when it comes to conceptual dead ends, and further development is therefore compromised.

Science has often gotten stuck in this way. Yet we have applied a wisdom to science that we have not yet managed to apply in our interpersonal realm, which has resulted in one field developing and the other, not so much. In science, when things get stuck, the conceptual premises are revised and challenged. We go over and reassess "the stories" that have informed the structure and outcomes of our explorations rather than blame the scientists (their character or their genes) for it. And so it has managed to change course and to continue developing.

Moving forward or going beyond will inevitably involve challenging what has been established. What actually needs "fixing" are not the storytellers, but rather the stories themselves. The way we tell our story to ourselves and others, and how we project it into the future, can either be a trap or a key to unlocking its potential. Any story that involves a partner needing "fixing" is a trap. Such narrative cannot have a positive outcome. There is no moving forward, no evolution, when the ideas that sustain the relationship's script involve one of the main characters being placed in a "lower" position—in moral or any other terms. That person will understandably "fight" the proposed script and will come up with an alternative version. And we are then faced with two worldviews fighting one another; a deadlock. What is needed instead is a reassessment of the very ideas that have led to the deadlock in the first place. Sometimes this involves going back to the past and weaving in those initial perceptions of the beautiful—or, what was once seen as divine and beautiful—into the present experience. As our perception changes, our attitude—and all that comes with it (thoughts, feelings, behaviors)—does too. As the observer changes, the observed—the WE—does too.

So every WE will have a story, and the way we choose to tell that story will make a difference. Often couples ask me, "How can we, having so many problems and so many horrible experiences to tell about ourselves, turn it all into a good story?" "How can't you?" is often my answer. It is precisely those stories that make for the most interesting, engaging, valuable scripts. After all, there are no heroes if there are no obstacles. And the greater the obstacles, the more fascinating the story. The most beautiful narratives are not the ones that do not involve any hardship, failure, or pain. Flaws and limitations actually add to the narrative of life; not the contrary. Our lives can be narrated in many different ways. We often leave all that is beautiful behind when the road starts getting tougher. We can also become awfully judgmental. Yet what once was perceived as divine or beautifully human does not disappear; our light and our shadows stay with us and form part of who we are, all along the way.

Moving beyond is therefore, to a large degree, a matter of becoming authors of stories that we can love and be proud of, the kind of stories we would like to be telling ourselves, our children, our loved ones, the world. "You have the brushes, you have the colors, paint paradise and enter,"[18] wrote Nobel Prize nominee Nikos Kazantzakis, one of the most influential authors in modern Greek literature. His statement could be seen as an invitation to dive into our present and past and create (with the very same colors and brushes) a new picture for our future: a new story of ME, of YOU, and of WE.

This book, to a large extent, seeks to provide a conceptual framework that enables new, more constructive, more engaging, more human stories to emerge. Now, as with any other human story—old or new, scientific or otherwise—it will never be complete, thorough, or final. We do not ever really or fully "know" anything. There is always more to what we label and define as ourselves, our partner, the relationship, the world. Part of you may be urged to challenge and go beyond the "established knowledge" that may have now become a trap. It is a good urge. This urge can be a door to yours, your partner's, and the WE's infinite universe.

PART VII

FOREVER AFTER?

J ohn and Louise look at each other's loving, wrinkled eyes. They smile and gently hold each other's hands as they wait for their granddaughter, Alexandra, to arrive. She has asked them for an interview. She wants to write an article about couples, she told them.

It has been a long journey, they think to themselves. They have seen their children grow—and their grandchildren, too. They have said farewell to many dear people, family, and friends; they have lived through crises, illnesses, important losses. They have come a long way, but they are grateful to be alive and to still have one another.

"What would you say you have learned about relationships? What is the secret to your success?" Alexandra asks. They smile again, amused at the sound of the word *success*, or the very idea of "a secret to success." What could they say to their granddaughter that would make sense to her? How could they summarize a lifetime of learning and experience?

"A relationship is the most precious gift a human being can offer another," her grandma begins. "Those who decide to walk by your side through life are offering you their most important and precious treasure: their time."

"Exactly," her grandfather chimes in. "And both of us have always known how valuable this is. We have been grateful. And we have accompanied each other in kindness. I'd say that, if there is a secret to it all, this is it: kindness." He stops and looks warmly at Louise as he adds, "We have always been kind to one another, even when we have not."

Alexandra looks at them slightly perplexed. But her grandma continues. "Kindness and playfulness," she adds jokingly, as she gently pokes John. "We have never ceased to play. Life is too serious to be taken seriously."

Alexandra is as puzzled now as she is amused. "Guys, please, you have started talking in riddles. I would appreciate something more concrete—maybe a list of *do's* and *don'ts*, something easy and straightforward."

"Darling, there is nothing straightforward about relationships. This may actually be the most straightforward thing we can say," Louise explains lovingly.

John all of a sudden feels inspired. "Just live, experience, enjoy everything that can be enjoyed, and allow for the pain too. Give the best you have and be ready to accept defeat. Work with what life offers you and make the most of it. Do not give up when things get complicated. Things *will* get complicated. Maybe this is another secret: not to give up. What do you think, Louise?"

"Yes. It is true. But it is also important to feel that you can leave at any time, too. I have always known that I would go if your granddad did not treat me with respect. We can moan and complain and can be a real pain to one another, but there are lines we have learned never to cross. They are our dealbreakers. Your granddad has known this about me, and I have known this about him, too. We will not stick around if respect is not part of the deal—even now, in our eighties. We now need one another more than ever, but we still know we are free. We do not belong to one another. We stay together because we want to. It is love that binds us, not fear."

John looks at his wife and seems to be reminded of the passionate lady he fell in love with. This was not about the interview anymore. "You know something, Alexandra? I did want your grandma to belong to me once upon a time. I really wanted to feel she was mine. I even asked her once, 'Will you be mine?' at a particularly romantic moment, and she responded, 'Of course not. I do not even belong to myself.' Then I told her I would love her forever, and you know what she said? 'Uhhh . . . forever is too long a time!'" John starts laughing. "She may have married me, but she has never really liked any kind of long-term commitments—or whatever she herself felt was binding or controlling. She would get all wound up. It was different for me: I never minded her control. Maybe because there was already a lot of freedom between us—more than I originally expected, anyway. Maybe it was also because of our families. That's what that therapist told us, remember? What did she say? Something about control having to do with our families. She also said that we were stuck in adolescence. We were already in our thirties then! Can you believe this? I think she would be proud of us now. We have surely graduated to adulthood."

"Oh, I would not be that sure, darling," Louise says jokingly. "We have some tough years ahead. We have already started to act like spoiled little brats again in our eighties. Maybe we *will* be adolescents in our nineties." Louise starts laughing now. "Adolescents or just, purely, primitive: isn't that what that psychologist called it? Was it the primitive side? The animal side? Oh, I don't remember. It doesn't really matter." Louise suddenly pauses and looks at her granddaughter.

"Oh. But now," she continues, "I have been reminded of something else. Write this down, Alexandra, it is very important: sex matters. Get married to the best sex you can get. And make it better. Have fun with it. Enjoy it. That's another big secret of ours. I may not belong to your granddad but, oh, have I enjoyed being with him! I still do!" She turns and winks at John.

"Oh dear. You cannot be serious!" Alexandra says, laughing. "I don't know how all of this can go into the article."

"Look," John comes to the rescue. "Get the article to focus on these four concepts. They are old and go in pairs too, like ourselves: freedom and responsibility; playfulness and kindness."

"And good sex!" adds Louise.

"And good sex!" Alexandra laughs again. "Got it," she says. "I think that will do it. Thanks!"

The Bigger Picture

This book is just a rough map of the interpersonal world. Like any other map, it provides no real protection to anyone from getting lost within the territory, especially within such an underdeveloped field as human romantic relationships. Yet there are certain reference points that are particularly useful in order to get us back on track at times of disorientation and confusion. The first one is personal responsibility. It is about being aware of our personal input and impact: how we help create our own prisons and private hells.

Assuming responsibility gives us back the reins of our own lives. We gain in power and freedom. How we then choose to use this power is up to us. In other words, it is important that we are aware that our partner's behavior and general well-being are very tightly linked to what we bring to the interpersonal equation. We are actually shaping each other (and our respective brains) via our interactions. As the eminent neuroscientist Eric Kandel states,

> When I speak to someone and he or she listens to me, we not only make eye contact and voice contact but the action of the neuronal machinery in my brain is having a direct and, I hope, long-lasting effect on the neuronal machinery in his or her brain, and vice versa.[1]

In this light, where we may actually be having a long-lasting effect on the "neuronal machinery" in our partner's brain when we engage with them, I find it crucial that we are at least mindful of what we are doing or saying. At the same time, I think it is equally important to allow ourselves to mess up, too. Messing up is inevitable. What is not okay is to be blind to our responsibility, to not see or acknowledge the impact and consequences of our words, actions, and decisions. When messing up is owned and can therefore also be "cleaned up," it may be far more valuable and growth-promoting than not messing up at all—which is actually impossible, anyway. I often ask clients who are particularly worried about messing up in relationships whether they would choose a perfect parent—or partner—for themselves, or whether they'd rather live with someone who makes mistakes but assumes responsibility for them. The vast majority prefer the latter. We are generally not attracted to perfection in relationships, as gods can be cold, boring, and overbearing. Humans who can sometimes mess up are perceived as far more approachable, fun, and attractive. Yet, not at all fun and attractive is the human being who messes up and still demands to be seen as perfect. This would actually make for the worst-case scenario. As long as you can avoid it, don't be that human being. Everyone around you—yourself included—is likely to suffer.

With this in mind, if a very short formula existed to help those lost in the interpersonal territory, I would imagine it as follows:

- Be mindful of your input in the relationship (and ther own power over the other). Assume responsibility fc

- Responsibility brings with it freedom and power. Use this freedom and power to bring about change.

- Experiment with things, be playful, be creative. There are no given scripts to change.

- Do not be afraid to make mistakes. Just be ready to own them and make up for them.

- Be human.   EXCELLENT !

There are, of course, many things we are not in any way responsible for—not directly, at least. Some variables are "givens," contexts that we were born into: our parents, our societies, the human condition, our capacity for abstract thought. I have often wondered why human beings appear to be so much more troubled than other animals. Is there an inherent flaw in our design?

The Human Condition

"A human being is a part of the whole, called by us 'Universe,' a part limited in time and space. He experiences himself, his thoughts and feelings as something separated from the rest—a kind of optical delusion of his consciousness. This delusion is a kind of prison for us, restricting us to our personal desires and to affection for a few persons nearest to us. Our task must be to free ourselves from this prison by widening our circle of compassion to embrace all living creatures and the whole nature in its beauty. Nobody is able to achieve this completely, but the striving for such achievement is in itself a part of the liberation and a foundation for inner security."[2]   —*Albert Einstein*

While many animals share basic primitive brain structures with us, with our advanced cortex comes the ability for abstraction. Nature has created a being that can experience itself sufficiently separate from its context to be able to study and examine itself. It's a wonderful, amazing ability that, paradoxically, has had the effect of making us feel separate from the rest of the world. We feel less connected to our context than other creatures. Like the apple of Eden, our higher brain has come at a great price: an experience of solitude, of not belonging. And disconnection, as we have been seeing throughout this book, brings with it a sort of "death threat" to those experiencing it, which has, in turn, made the human being more anxious than any other living creature in the absence of predators. Humans may have achieved greater autonomy through abstraction, but we have not managed to compensate for it with greater connection. We long for it, but we have mostly striven for it in the most destructive and obsessive ways. And that is where all the trouble begins.

Connection has been pursued, primarily, in two ways: a) on an individual level, by increasing one's "connectivity value," and b) interpersonally, through control of the other. Not coincidentally, neither of these modalities actually leads to an experience of connection. Instead, they enhance the "I," which gets us even further into the "autonomy" realm.

Meditation, mindfulness, and other such practices have been shown to provide a sense of greater connection to ourselves and to the world. Still, the way these practices have been promoted and understood does not focus on the interpersonal sphere. It all happens within oneself, within the "I," even if the end goal is to dissolve the boundaries that define the Self. Buddha is supposed to have left his wife behind. He did not pursue nirvana by interacting or connecting with her. I believe this is because the interpersonal realm involves skills that no male god has ever been able to master. And it is not just the gods who have failed in this endeavor; it is the whole of humanity, men and women.

So human beings are particularly anxious about connection but are pretty lousy at achieving or providing it. Our need for connection is almost as high as our level of incompetence in this realm—a paradox and a tragedy that has led to humanity spending insane amounts of resources trying to achieve connection via the two least effective modes: by increasing individual "connectivity value" (but not the capacity to connect) and by controlling others, both primarily autonomy-related behaviors. As a result, we have managed to go very far in obtaining skills and information to empower the "I."

The irony has reached new, unfathomable levels in the past decades with the advancement of technology and social networks. We have never been so connected and disconnected at the same time.

This paradox, the fact that we have made immense advances technologically but very few interpersonally, is beautifully—and tragically—reflected in the film *Hidden Figures*. Three female mathematicians at NASA were contributing to getting the first men into outer space while, at the same time, they were obliged to take mile-long trips to the bathroom because, as black women, they had to use separate facilities from the rest. To me, this is one of the most representative and most graphic examples about how far have we come in one domain and how primitive and illiterate we still are in the other.

A colleague of mine, during one of the most heated discussions I have had on this matter, suggested that this unequal development was due to the fact that human brains and relationships are too complex for us to understand. Although I agree about the complexity, I just cannot accept it as an explanation. I bring to mind a vision of two prehistoric human beings contemplating the stars in front of their cave. One of them points to the moon: *Let's go there!* The other suggests something different: *Let's stay here and get to know to one another. Let's figure out relationships and what goes on in our heads.* Does the second suggestion sound much more difficult, more challenging, or more complex? I think it is a matter of interest rather than of difficulty. Why would we ever consider going to the moon as an easier enterprise than understanding ourselves?

There are many historical and evolutionary reasons that could explain why we have actually managed to get to the moon but have not managed to understand love, relationships, and human emotion, condemning us to behave so apelike (apologies to the apes for the expression) interpersonally, such as in the movie mentioned above. Philosopher Ken Wilber points to the emergence of the agrarian society and, with it, a polarization of the roles, as a possible explanation for patriarchy, father rule, and (in my words) the fact that the male and female spheres developed in such unequal ways:

*Social relations ()*began to organize themselves around the *basic forces of production.* Men then began to dominate the *public* sphere of government, education, religion, politics. And women the *private* sphere of family, hearth, home. This division is often referred to as male production and female reproduction.. . .[W]ith agrarian farming a class of individuals would be freed to ponder their own existence. And thus, with these great agrarian cultures came the first sustained *contemplative* endeavors.[3]

Within this framework, we could say that women have had far less time and "freedom" to cultivate their own endeavors. A lot has changed since agrarian societies first emerged, but certain things have not. For example, childrearing is time-consuming and laborious, and women are still central to that effort. So it could be that women, as experts on human interaction, have not yet had the chance or the time—or perhaps they have not been valued enough or taken seriously enough—to promote, develop, and push forward their area of expertise.

But I think it goes further than that. In my view, it may all come down to "connectivity value." There is far greater anxiety in connectivity terms for men than for women. Men will go to extremely great efforts to increase their "connectability," and yet it is not the interpersonally intelligent man who has traditionally been rewarded by women and men alike. On the contrary, it is the aggressive, interpersonally incompetent political leader or CEO who, despite grave limitations, manages to increase his "connectability" among both sexes. "Aggressiveness is an adaptive behavior,"[4] French neurologist Boris Cyrulnik has said, adding that, especially in times of hardship and uncertainty, this quality is usually rewarded and sought out. An aggressor (someone interpersonally incompetent) can therefore be perceived as a competent protector. And the greater the unrest, the more likely it is that aggressive, interpersonally incompetent people will be perceived as competent and will be rewarded with increased connectivity value and power.

The human species has been moving toward the "autonomy" pole for millennia, which has had a lot of positive consequences, such as the development of science and technologies, and a great part of our civilization as we know it. In more recent history, women have also heavily moved toward the autonomy pole, which has likewise been an important feat for our civilization. Women have fought hard for their right to be seen, heard, accepted, and valued within an unbalanced social context. There is still quite a long way to go in this respect, but moving toward autonomy has been a fundamental achievement for the traditional "keepers of connection."

However, the counter-task, which could be considered even more crucial in this day and age, is still pending: for humanity (and even more so, the "keepers of autonomy") to move toward the connection pole. If we are to advance and evolve further, we need to seriously focus on emphasizing connection and all the qualities that go with it. Within a spirit of great respect for the autonomy pole and all that has been achieved within it, connection-enhancing attributes and skills need to be perceived as an advantage in terms of "connectivity value" and evolutionary progress. In other words, while honoring autonomy and the masculine, we must also strike some balance and recognize the critical importance of the opposite pole. Humanity has a lot to gain by developing, cultivating, and effectively integrating the feminine.

Balancing the Masculine and the Feminine

The Greeks attempted some balance between the masculine and the feminine by introducing six key gods (Zeus, Poseidon, Ares, Hermes, Apollo, and Hephaestus) and six key goddesses (Hera, Hestia, Demeter, Artemis, Athena, and Aphrodite). At some point Hestia, the goddess of light, spirituality, family, and "home," was replaced by Dionysus, the god of wine, madness, and pleasure. Though I have nothing against madness and pleasure, I find it a very interesting metaphor about a world in which the masculine, pleasure-seeking, and materially oriented aspects of life are more prevalent than the feminine, spiritual, family-oriented qualities. We could say that the human species (men and women) has been predominantly masculine throughout its history.

We currently live in a world that does not place equal value on the feminine (connection, emotion, collaboration, nurturance, fusion, dependence, the interpersonal) and the masculine (autonomy, reason, agency, differentiation, individuality) expressions of existence. Almost everyone, men and women of all sexual orientations—many feminists included—heavily glorify the masculine. Parenting the new generation, creating healthy bonds, communicating constructively, providing love, mastering the interpersonal arts, and knowing how to heal traumatized individuals, families, groups, and nations do not have much credit or credentials attached to them. Inevitably, in every single couple, whoever is primarily occupied with the "feminine" side of things—whether it is the man or the woman—will be devalued. I see it as an inherent "flaw" in the formation of any couple. I also see it as the "flaw" behind most (if not all) mental disorders. If we think of society as an industry that produces couples, we could say that there is a very serious defect in the original design. Problems are therefore guaranteed, and they will be added to the long list of challenges that the couple will need to face. The partners who are capable of correcting and compensating for this defect are the ones who will do best—and their children too.

So long as the world is so biased toward one of the poles, I think it is bound to suffer. Given that the micro is intimately linked to the macro, we replicate the very same issues on all different levels. While the forces are competing, there is a winner and a loser. And, as they are just two parts forming one whole, the whole ends up losing altogether. We need, as a society, to work toward a world that honors, respects, celebrates, and legislates in favor of both fundamental needs and aspects of existence and keeps them balanced. In order to achieve this, we need to seriously empower all those qualities represented by the female pole, while continuing to respect and preserve those associated with the male pole. We need connection, integration, dependence, bonding, and relating to be at least as present, valued, and practiced in the human community as the currently dominant qualities of autonomy, identity, independence, and "law and order."

Becoming skillful in our relationships should be a priority. Everything is in one way or another impacted by our relationships. Learning about them should constitute a primary concern in our educational system, just as language and math are. The interpersonal language of emotion is the most universal language there is, the one that we will be called to use all through our lives. It is fundamental that we become emotionally and interpersonally literate.

There is some excellent research that associates our levels of happiness and general well-being with the quality of our relationships. The most important of all is the Harvard University of Adult Development study, one of the longest ever to be carried out worldwide. It was initiated in 1938 and it is still going. It initially involved 268 university students who were followed throughout their lives. The study later included their offspring, too. The main objective was to see which factors determined good physical and mental health, and what made people lead happier lives. Massachusetts General Hospital psychiatrist and professor Robert Waldinger, who directed the study, told *The Harvard Gazette* in 2017, "The surprising finding is that our relationships and how happy we are in our relationships has a powerful influence on our health." The article continues:

> Close relationships, more than money or fame, are what keep people happy throughout their lives, the study revealed. Those ties protect people from life's discontents, help to delay mental and physical decline, and are better predictors of long and happy lives than social class, IQ, or even genes. The researchers also found that marital satisfaction has a protective effect on people's mental health. Part of the study found that people who had happy marriages in their 80s reported that their moods didn't suffer even on the days when they had more physical pain. Those who had unhappy marriages felt both more emotional and physical pain.[5]

According to Waldinger, "Taking care of your body is important, but tending to your relationships is a form of self-care too. That, I think, is the revelation."

Building a Different Society

The survival of any organism requires finding and processing energy. In the case of the couple, in this day and age, this means money coming into the household. I consider this to be a necessary condition for a functional, working relationship, in line with Abraham Maslow's hierarchy of needs. Happy couples require a nurturing environment. Stress triggers our brains to set off the "survival mode" alarm. Defenses go up and self-preservation becomes the one and only priority. Such circumstances, if they are prolonged, create an environment in which nothing can properly develop or grow—neither relationships nor individuals.

There is a lot of research that links poverty with mental illness. A simple online search will point to millions of results. There is very little a couple ʳerty is institutionalized within a society. People who do not

ιns to escape poverty will have almost no chances to develop

and experience nurturing intimate relationships. The "I" must feel nurtured and strong enough to put itself at the service of the other. In such cases, political intervention is the most effective available solution. There can be no peace, no functional relationship or society, in an environment of poverty that equals constant stress.

At the same time, and even more importantly, there can be no peace, nor a functional and sustainable society, while insecure people stuck in an emotional adolescence are given such levels of "connectivity value" or evolutionary advantage, to the point of becoming our leaders in the worlds of business and politics. We cannot afford to allow these fragile souls to run the show. There is nothing powerful in a person's desperate accumulation of resources or influence.

The most powerful are the kind and the loving. The strongest are those who are already nurtured and secure, who do not need wealth and power to feel safe, who consciously and willingly put themselves in service to others and the common good. The most secure have no difficulty valuing and celebrating others beyond themselves or their own kind. It requires great strength to love oneself, a partner, humankind, and the planet. We could be legislating wisely, respectfully, and scientifically based on the knowledge we have acquired over the millennia of what it means to be and raise healthy humans. It would be a different world. We could create heaven on earth.

AN ACQUAINTANCE WITH THE THEORY

Once upon a time, there was a group of six wise blind men who lived in a small village. One day, an elephant was brought to the town. The wise men had heard about elephants, but they had never been close to one before. They decided to approach it so that they could gain a better understanding of the animal by examining it closely. Each accessed a different part. The first wise man touched its body and quickly proclaimed: "The elephant is like a wall." "Definitely not. It is like a thick snake," interrupted the second one, holding the elephant's trunk. The third, grabbing one of the ears, stated that the elephant was like a fan. "No, no, no," said the fourth, who had reached for the animal's leg and described it as a tree trunk. The fifth, holding the tail, claimed confidently that the elephant was like a rope. "What are you all talking about?" said the sixth, who had felt its tusk. "The elephant is like a spear." And so they started arguing and continued to argue, indefinitely, about the nature of the elephant, without ever coming to an agreement.[1]

—*Indian parable*

The theoretical premises of this book are based on an understanding that the world is one and undivided, like the proverbial elephant, and that every theory touches upon essential aspects of what would be the "whole" picture and misses others. "Unbridgeable differences" are understood to be man-made, reflecting more the workings of human nature than of nature per se. The concepts in this book stem from the idea that knowledge should come together and connect within and across disciplines to attain a comprehensive understanding of ourselves and the world that we live in. The theoretical "elephant" here is the human, seen within the scope of the couple.

The couple—and the individuals who compose it—are contemplated as inseparable parts of the context from which they arise. The couple is part of the world it comes from, giving shape to it, while also being shaped by it. Consequently, getting to a thorough understanding of the human being and the human couple requires a multilevel and thorough integration of knowledge. This involves conceptual bridges across disciplines and fields, employing theory that is consistent with the knowledge that has already been established (the blind wise men opening up to the idea that the elephant is an entity that eludes their individual experience and observations but could be perceived and understood if their different voices and perceptions are all accounted for).

In this spirit, a synthesis of theory has been attempted here in order to provide a more thorough view of the couple. In order to understand how the different theoretical approaches mentioned in this work relate to one another, it may be helpful to examine the table on the following page.

There are four main conceptual domains in which all different approaches to understanding the individual (human) can fall into:

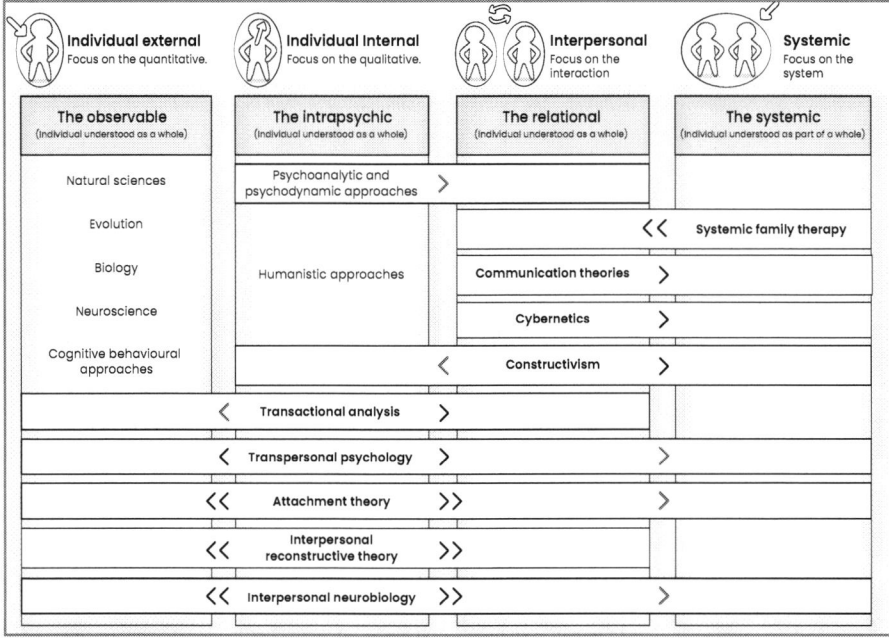

1. Individual external

2. Individual internal

3. Interpersonal

4. Systemic

The approaches that arise from the first domain approach the individual as a whole entity (rather than part of a whole), employing the scientific method and studying the observable, external, and quantitative aspects. The approaches that stem from the second domain also contemplate the individual as a whole but focus primarily on the inner, "invisible" processes and organization. The approaches of the third domain continue to contemplate the individual as a whole, but the focus is no longer on the individual. Instead, what is observed and studied is the relationship and the interaction between individuals, with an emphasis on communication and relational processes. Finally, the approaches that come from the fourth domain contemplate the individual as part of a greater whole—that is, a system. From this standpoint, individuals cease to properly exist on their own accord and can only be understood as part of other units.

In the table on page 188, you can observe which domain each of the theoretical approaches mentioned in this book falls into (some may originally come from one domain but have expanded to include more than one category). It should be noted here that epistemological frontiers are not quantifiable like geographical frontiers, which means they are subject to subjective perceptions. This very simplified classification is, therefore, inevitably influenced by my subjective view.

Within this categorization, biology, the natural sciences, neuroscience, and pretty much any approaches that involve the scientific method fall into (or stem from, or are predominately installed in) the first domain. These approaches focus on what can be observed and measured. Neuroscience will look at brain activity, for instance, but will not occupy itself with aspects such as the purpose or meaning of the thoughts, dreams, or other brain activity–related processes. Within the field of psychology, the approach that falls into this category is cognitive behavioral therapy. With its origins in B. F. Skinner's radical behaviorism, cognitive behavioral therapy focuses on what can be measured and observed. Although it does go as far as to study human cognitive processes rather than behavior only, it does not occupy itself with answering questions related to the "invisible realm," such as the meaning or purpose of the thought process itself.

Nonquantifiable expressions of the individual—the inner processes, the intrapsychic—have occupied the attention of the approaches within the second domain. These approaches focus their attention on "invisible" aspects that can be expressed and explained through words but cannot be directly observed or measured—aspects such as personality structure, moral development, and the attribution of meaning or purpose to human emotion, cognition, and behavior. Psychoanalysis, psychodynamics, and humanistic approaches belong in this category. Transpersonal psychology also stems from this domain. It could be argued that philosophy, religion, and the arts in general have their roots here as well.

The third domain studies the individual in relation to its context, most often another individual. The focus is the *interaction* between the elements rather than the elements themselves. All natural sciences and disciplines, such chemistry, physics, and biology, are fundamentally relational too, but human individuals are not generally contemplated in relational, interactive terms. It is true that in certain areas of medicine, such as epidemiology, the interaction of the human being with its context is core to the field, but it is quite exceptional. Sociology may be the only field that studies the human being primarily in relational terms, yet sociology's primary focus is not the individual. There are very few theoretical approaches that focus on the interaction between individuals, how human units impact one another, or how they shape one another's behavior or personality. The most important contribution within this category, in my view, comes from attachment theory (Bowlby), which stems from (and includes) the previous category. It was actually the intrapsychic, psychoanalytical approaches (e.g., object relations theory) that were the first to "open up" and introduce the relational domain, mainly focusing on the mother-infant relationship. The other most important contribution in this area comes from the communication-related theories (e.g., Shannon and Weaver's model of communication[2]) and cybernetics (Wiener[3]), which were further developed by theorists such as Gregory Bateson (*Steps to an Ecology of Mind*) and Paul Watzlawick, Janet Helmick Beavin, and Don Jackson (*Pragmatics of Human Communication*). Unlike attachment theory, the study of human communication is greatly linked to the fourth domain and forms part of the epistemology of systemic relational therapy (or family therapy).

Within the fourth and last domain, the individual is no longer contemplated as an individual but instead as a part of a greater unit (e.g., family, community, nation, etc.). Individual behavior is understood as an expression of a working and evolving system. Emotions, cognitions, and behaviors do not just arise from the individuals themselves; rather, they correspond to the needs and functions of the system the individuals form part of, in the way that a body organs' functioning can only be understood as they link to the rest of the body. Within this framework, the individual ceases to "exist" as a separate entity. This is the factor that distinguishes systemic theory from any other theory—and makes it so important. It provides a different and broader scope for understanding the human being.

And so the wise blind men who approach the elephant of the individual human come from these four different domains. Sadly, this particular "elephant" has been the trigger of the greatest levels of fighting and disagreement ever recorded. Other groups of wise blind men (e.g., those seeking to figure out physical phenomena, viruses, animals, rocks, and plants) have managed to find ways to work together and collaborate. Yet the "human factor" seems to activate the wise blind men in ways that no other entity does. At the same time, slowly but surely, more and more bridges are being built and more understanding is being achieved between some of them with the passing of time. The author of this book stands with the bridge builders.

In terms of theory, this work seeks to embrace and connect all four domains. The fourth blind wise man—the one coming from the systemic standpoint—is considered here to be in possession of "key" conceptual elements able to provide a possible link across domains, as was originally suggested by the "father" of systems theory, Ludwig von Bertalanffy.

It should probably be noted that the blind wise men who apply systems theory in the mental health realm—namely, those from the systemic family therapy field—have shown little interest in the cross-disciplinary potential of the theory. They have largely ignored or opposed the blind men of the first two domains, especially those coming from the individual, external, and visible (e.g., cognitive behavioral therapists and "medically oriented" psychiatrists), who are considered to be the blindest among the blind. Systemic family theorists (who move almost indistinguishably between the third an fourth domain) did not make that much of an effort to approach the second domain either, which is held in higher esteem overall but nevertheless has generally been considered to be quite ineffective in its postulations and practices.*At the same time, the systemic folk have been practically invisible to the rest. They seem to exist in a separate universe in terms of journals, conferences, and scientific literature in general. There are exceptions, of course—gradually more. And, siding with those exceptions, this work proposes ways for the wise blind men to come together.

What follows is a summary of how the theories that have sustained the ideas of this work have been integrated. It is important, however, to underline

---

*This stance is wonderfully reflected in most essays included in the book
The Power Tactics of Jesus Christ by Jay Haley.

that this is just a brief summary. Entire disciplines and schools of thought, rich in knowledge and history, have been summed up here in just a few words or paragraphs. In the author's (self) defense, it should be emphasized that the aim of this brief intellectual exercise is not to inform the reader on the theories per se, but rather to provide an overview of the main theoretical premises that have nurtured the ideas in this book.

Systems Theory

As mentioned before, the axis that sustains all the theory discussed in this book is systems theory. General systems theory was introduced by Karl Ludwig von Bertalanffy in 1928 with the publication of his seminal book *Kritische Theorie der Formbildung* (*Modern Theories of Development*). In his most well-known work, *General System Theory: Foundations, Development, Applications,* he writes:

> [T]here exist models, principles, and laws that apply to generalized systems or their subclasses, irrespective of their particular kind, the nature of their component elements, and the relationships or "forces" between them. It seems legitimate to ask for a theory, not of systems of a more or less special kind, but of universal principles applying to systems in general. In this way we postulate a new discipline called *General Systems Theory*. Its subject matter is the formulation and derivation of those principles which are valid for "systems" in general.[4]

Such universal principles are the basis of the theoretical argument proposed in this work. In line with Bertalanffy's ideas, everything, every entity—from the human body (organs, cells, molecules, atoms) all the way to human social structures (couples, families, societies)—is contemplated as a system, subject to the same universal principles. Consequently, systems theory provides us with a method and a framework that allows us to theoretically cover an extremely broad area and the ability to move within great levels of complexity.

Most principles have already been mentioned in the main body of the book, but we will go over some of the main concepts again here in order to further explain the reasoning. First of all, a *system,* in order to be defined as such, needs to be composed of two or more interrelated components, forming a coherent unit. The interaction between the components will bring about properties that are different than the properties of the components themselves. If we randomly bring together all the components that make up a car, for example, we will not get a car; instead, we will get a conglomeration of random, disconnected parts. The car is not just a sum of its parts; neither is an individual or a couple. Rather, the organization and interconnection between the parts of every system bring about *emergent* properties.

Some key concepts of systems theory that have also been referred to in this book are:

- *Homeostasis,* or the tendency of the system to "resist" change, maintaining its key properties.

- *Morphogenesis,* or the tendency of the system to change in order to adapt to and interact with its environment more effectively.

Homeostasis and morphogenesis have been more commonly defined in systems theory and cybernetics as *negative and positive feedback loops.* Again, they refer to the process of the system adapting internally or externally in relation to its environment and other systems' influences.

Other concepts which have provided a conceptual basis to the arguments built in this work and are central to systemic thinking are:

- *Circularity or circular causality,* or the activity observed within and between systems being circular and interdependent, which means that, when it comes to communication, we are talking about "loops" of interaction and circular rather than linear causality.

- *Open and closed systems,* which refer to the structure of systems, in terms of whether they are connected or not to their context. According to Bertalanffy, a *closed* system is the one that is in no way connected to its medium and does not interact with other systems. The opposite is true for *open* systems. All of the systems discussed in this book, and all living systems in general, are "open" systems.

- *Cybernetics,* an approach intimately connected to the systemic approach, seeks to understand and define system processes and functions. Core concepts such as *circular causality, circularity,* and *feedback* are central in this broad, cross-disciplinary field.

Finally, systems also have boundaries and, as mentioned before, are organized hierarchically, as they include and are made up other subsystems (atoms, molecules, cells, organs, etc.). A system can be complex (e.g., the world's human community) or simple (e.g., an amoeba), as Napier and Whitaker explain in their book *The Family Crucible*:

> Look at a very simple system: the amoeba. It is a system, but a system with clear boundaries. Within these boundaries there is an organization of sorts. This organization is active, and it "works" to maintain its structure. If the amoeba encounters a hostile chemical or organism, it may dodge or attempt to elude the intruder in order to protect the integrity of its life. This is an interesting characteristic of living systems (…): they make changes in their own behavior based on information about the environment. This mechanism, called feedback, permits the system to alter its activity, its structure, its direction, in order to further its own goals. (…) The systems concept allows one to compare the simple organism like the amoeba with the more complex system like the family. And indeed, there are similarities: the family has boundaries and within the boundaries it has an organization which its members work very actively to maintain.[5]

And so does the couple, the system that has been explored throughout this book. The couple also has boundaries, and within its boundaries it has an organization that its members work actively to maintain so that the system can preserve its integrity and further its goals.

The theory proposed in this book has its roots in systemic theory and cybernetics, so it is very much in line with all the concepts that stem from these approaches. The main difference within the present conceptualization of a system is to be found in the idea of the forces of *connection* and *autonomy*. The novel claim is that for any system to be operational and function, the parts that make it up need to be both connected and separate at all times. The system would lose its emergent properties if the parts that composed it either totally merged or completely disconnected.

Given that every open system is contemplated as connected to other systems (the broader context) as well as an entity operating autonomously, maintaining its properties, it is further argued that connection and autonomy are fundamental aspects to the constitution of any system, both for its internal operativity and for its interaction with its context. This pair of forces therefore constitute a binary code of interaction within or between any system.

In other words, systems theory has been changed here to include the autonomy-connection pulls. These pulls, despite forming part of the very definition of a system as a "regularly interacting or interdependent group of items forming a unified whole" (understanding that if there were no autonomy there would be no items, and if there were no connection there would be no unified whole), are not part of systems theory.

The fundamental premises (the "universals") of the theory proposed here are outlined in the diagrams on the following page. As shown in Figure A on the following page, a system requires inner and outer connection and autonomy, pushes to evolve (morphogenesis) and remain the same (homeostasis), and involves emergent properties that "belong" to the system as a whole but not to the elements that compose it. These new properties represent the pull of *emergence*. As shown in Figure B on the following page, this process occurs within all systems and subsystems, ad infinitum.

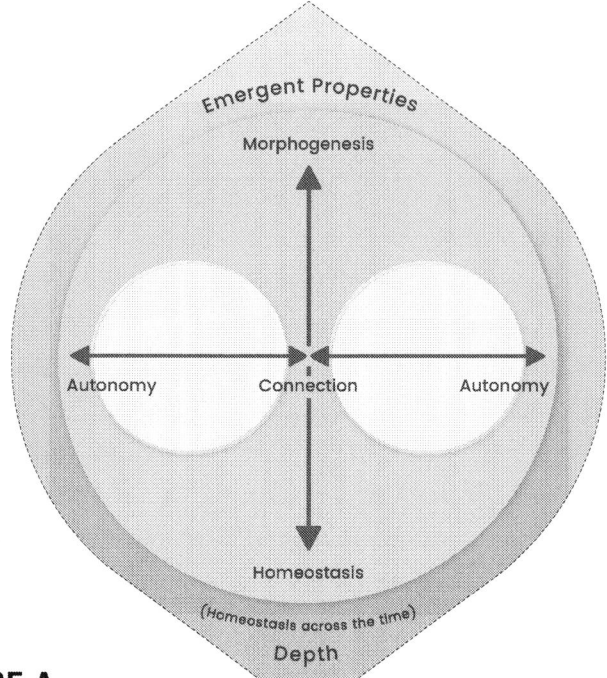

FIGURE A.

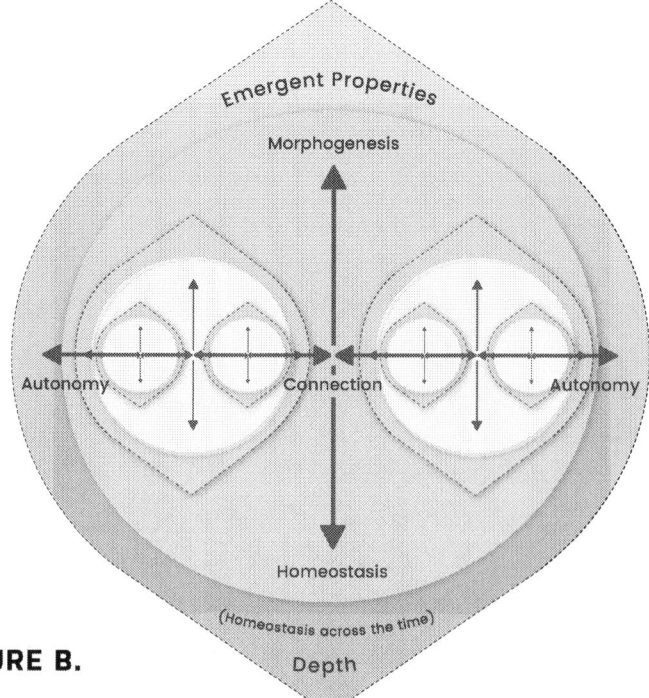

FIGURE B.

The fact that cells, the body, the brain, the individual, the couple, etc., are all understood and approached as systems in themselves is another element that distinguishes this theory from systems theory as it is applied in systemic family therapy. The latter has studied the family as a system but has not contemplated the individual in these terms, and even less so the brain or the inner organization of the human being.

Here, it is argued that there is a strong correlation to the way we will relate to ourselves and the way we will relate to others, especially our partner. Our relationship to ourselves, our parents, and our partners is then replicated in the ways we approach and form systems in the world. It is suggested that these patterns of relationship may also be reflected in brain processes, functions, and structure. Consequently, it is understood that external systems (such as the couple, the family, and society), as well as internal systems (such as the body and the brain), should all be taken into consideration when it comes to understanding the human being.

All theory put forward in this book is based on the diagram on page 188, which could be defined as the representation of a primal system. In order to understand the dynamics at play within the system, the brain has been used as a metaphor, being viewed from two main perspectives: a horizontal and a vertical axis. The horizontal axis distinguishes the right from the left hemisphere, which correspond to connection and autonomy functions. The vertical axis distinguishes the subcortical "primitive" brain from the cortical "higher" brain, which in turn correspond to homeostatic and morphogenetic functions. The "mind" is considered to be an emergent property of the brain.

The synthesis of theory that follows is also largely organized according to this framework.

The Horizontal Axis

Attachment Theory

The binary code of connection and autonomy is proposed to be a fundamental component of every system. Within psychological theory, the connection-autonomy interplay is best accounted for in attachment theory. It should be noted that John Bowlby, who developed the theory of attachment, did not talk about connection and autonomy as they have been defined here, nor would he have contemplated them as forces. He actually considered his model a departure from these kinds of conceptualizations: "There are therefore no propositions concerning psychological energy or psychological forces; concepts such as conservation of energy, entropy, direction, and magnitude of force are all missing."[6] This postulation moved him away from Freud's theoretical premises. According to Freud, human behavior, cognition, and emotion are a manifestation of a complex interplay of psychological forces. According to the present theoretical framework, Bowlby succeeded in tapping into a different part of "the elephant" by moving, as I would define it, from the vertical to the horizontal axis. From this perspective, these two extraordinarily brilliant minds both revealed central and fundamental aspects of human nature, but like most other wise men, they were also partially blind and biased in their interpretations.

Though Bowlby discarded the ideas of psychological energy and psychological forces, central to the psychodynamic approach, he did embrace systems theory, which is key to the systemic family therapy approach. Nevertheless, he did not embrace the approach itself. Attachment theory and systemic family therapy have been developing separately over the past decades. Thus, for Bowlby, parent-child interaction was not viewed as part of the family system's dynamic, as it is understood in systemic-family therapy. He continued to view the individual as an individual only—the focus being the dyadic interaction between child and caregiver. Nevertheless, he did talk about systems in biological and evolutionary terms, introducing notions such as *adaptedness,* and he viewed the child's need for proximity to the caregiver as a homeostatic counterpart to the need for exploration.

So, despite its limitations, attachment theory tapped into all four domains of knowledge. It stemmed from the second (individual internal, qualitative) domain, incorporated the third (relational) domain, created important connections to the first (individual external, quantitative, biological) domain, and acknowledged aspects of the fourth (systemic) domain. From this book's perspective, attachment theory is important, not only for being one of the best supported and broadest psychological theories there is, but also because it taps into a universal principle that goes far beyond attachment theory itself. From this book's perspective, it has the potential to provide a connection point across all four domains in relation to the horizontal axis: the connection-autonomy pull.

Attachment, as described by Bowlby,

> is regarded as a class of social behaviour of an importance equivalent to that of mating behaviour and parental behaviour. It is held to have a biological function specific to itself and one that has hitherto been little considered. … In this formulation, it will be noticed, there is no reference to "needs" or "drives". Instead, attachment behaviour is regarded as what occurs when certain behavioural systems are activated. The behavioural systems themselves are believed to develop within the infant as a result of his interaction with his environment of evolutionary adaptedness, and especially his interaction with the principal figure in that environment, namely his mother.[7]

Attachment theory focuses on proximity-maintaining and caregiving behaviors between offspring and caregivers, and it is considered to be a common yet extremely important phenomenon in nature—especially among mammals, where it is universal. Harry Harlow's studies on rhesus monkeys provided us with some of the most important insights on attachment behaviors of nonhuman primates, which are closely linked to those observed in humans. Like Bowlby, Harlow maintained that caregiving and caregiver-offspring proximity were determining factors for the young's development.

Within the human realm, attachment theory focuses on a child's long-lasting psychological connection with a caregiver, who soothes in times of stress and serves as a safe base—a source of safety and pleasure—in times of play. The quality of the bond has been found to have a critical effect on the child's cognitive, emotional, and social development, and it has been linked to various aspects of positive functioning and psychological well-being in later life.

American-Canadian developmental psychologist Mary Ainsworth, whose work is directly linked to Bowlby's, introduced the concept of *secure base,* and, with it, a model of parenting that would adequately respond to a child's developmental needs. She defined four attachment patterns in infants: secure attachment (the kind of attachment derived from "secure base" conditions), anxious-avoidant (insecure) attachment, anxious-ambivalent (insecure) attachment, and disorganized (insecure) attachment. In the 1980s, the theory was further developed and expanded to include adult attachment styles. Ainsworth's research is widely known for the "strange situation" experiment, a study that was designed to evoke attachment behavior in individuals under situations of stress. Such behaviors were evoked by briefly separating the mother from the child within an unfamiliar environment. Children's responses and behavior before, during, and after their separation from their mothers set the foundation for the subsequent definition of the four different attachment styles.

- *Secure attachment* describes an infant-caregiver relationship and interaction that is functional. The child is likely to show explorative behaviors before the separation occurs. When the caregiver leaves the room, the child gets distressed but then greets the caregiver and is content to be with them again. The child will seek comfort and will resume their exploration a little while afterward. The child shows trust in the caregiver, and the latter is consistent and attentive to the needs of the child.

- *Anxious-avoidant insecure attachment* describes a relationship between child and caregiver in which children act indifferent to their caregiver's presence or absence, showing no marked distress when they leave or return. Children appear to be emotionally distant, as do their caregivers, whose behavior appears to be disengaged.

- *Anxious-ambivalent insecure attachment* describes a relationship in which children show distress, anger, or helplessness toward their caregiver. They get upset when their caregiver leaves their side but are not comforted upon their return. The caregiver's behavior in these cases is usually inconsistent.

- *Disorganized/disoriented attachment* describes a pattern of behavior between child and caregiver that is inconsistent and confusing. Children do not show attachment behaviors and may appear to be confused or act depressed, angry, passive, or apathetic in the presence of the caregiver. Caregivers tend to act in varying extremes, such as attacking, yelling at, or neglecting the child when the child approaches to seek comfort.

Now, how does the above theory connect to the postulations of this book? As mentioned before, Bowlby did not talk in terms of connection and autonomy, yet it could be argued that it is implied in his work. Connection, for example, is reflected in the concept of proximity, while autonomy is implied in the importance attributed to play and exploration.

The *Circle of Security Intervention* authors, frequently cited in this work, state:

> Interestingly, while attachment theory has always acknowledged both attachment behaviours (careseeking) and exploratory behaviours (building mastery), when we originally created the Circle of Security, we did not depict exploration in terms of a "need"—until Jude Cassidy stated that children need a secure base for exploration as much as they need a safe haven for comfort. Meeting both needs is critical to secure attachment and to the child's emotional regulation skills. The Circle of Security shows that little children can be viewed as constantly "going out and coming in."[8]

Within the framework put forward in this book, carer and child are seen as two entities working to establish a system: a WE. Revisiting Ainsworth's "strange situation" study and the four different styles of attachment, it is understood that the caregiver who has been able to establish secure attachment has provided adequate connection and autonomy to the child during the child's development. When the connection is momentarily "broken," with the caregiver leaving the scene, the child shows discomfort, which is the normal reaction in the face of a lost component of a system that is essential to its functioning and durability. The caregiver's return is met with the child welcoming and seeking comfort in them, a reflection that connection is—and can be—(re)established in the system. The child resuming play is an indicator that the caregiver can and has served as a provider of autonomy.

When autonomy is achieved, but there is discomfort in connection, we are in "avoidant" territory. The two components of the system (child and caregiver) can share space in an operational manner, but they fail to connect and engage affectively. When connection is achieved but there is discomfort in autonomy, we have an anxious-ambivalent attachment. In this case, the caregiver has been able to establish connection but has been inconsistent in providing autonomy, sometimes giving too little (patterns of neglect), sometimes giving too much (controlling, overbearing behaviors).

Finally, when both autonomy and connection are provided inconsistently, we have the conditions for what has been defined as disorganized attachment, which inevitably entails a disorganized system. In this case, caregivers behave in ways that connect to the survival of the caregiver only, rendering their behavior in relation to the child incomprehensible or inappropriate. All severe mental health disorders, ranging from personality disorders to schizophrenia, involve individuals raised within such disorganized systems.

Within the present framework, part of what has been defined as attachment behavior has been interpreted to describe the fundamental interpersonal dynamics involved in the establishment and operability of any human system. Although, admittedly, attachment is a necessary developmental process during the early stages of life, the behaviors that have been defined as attachment behaviors are described here as necessary components to all human systems and interaction—at all times. Attachment behaviors may be most visible and important when the system is in construction mode, as it seeks to establish itself, but the dynamics at play will continue to be present as long as the system exists. Therefore, where there is a system, there is attachment behavior. And attachment behavior is all about the interplay of connection and autonomy.

Any given system requires both the connection of its parts and their autonomy in order to operate. Patterns of interaction between individuals are therefore not predefined or fixed. They depend, instead, on the nature and needs of the system as a whole. From this perspective, individuals are not secure, avoidant, anxious-ambivalent, or disorganized per se. Although their behavior is heavily influenced by the initial learning acquired within the primary systems they belonged to, their patterns of behavior also always respond to the particular characteristics of any given interpersonal context.

Systemic Family Therapy and the Differentiation of Self

Systemic family therapy also focuses on aspects related to connection and autonomy. Bowen's theory on the differentiation of self could serve as an example: He devised a scale (0–10) to determine the level of an individual's differentiation in relation to their context (family). The lesser the degree of differentiation, the more enmeshed the individual within the family system—and, consequently, the less their ability to function independently and the more their emotional dependence in relation to their context. Conversely, the greater the differentiation of the individual within the family system, the greater their freedom and emotional flexibility in times of stress and the more relaxed and capable they are within the interpersonal sphere.

Systemic family therapy has, in many different ways, underlined the importance of the ambivalence individuals experience between preserving their bond and loyalty to the family system and their need to function as individuals, differentiated from the rest of the family. Although it can easily be argued that this is a reflection of the horizontal axis—the struggle between connection and autonomy—it has not been conceptualized or defined as such. Connection and autonomy become visible within the systemic therapy theoretical framework mostly within a certain "stage" in the family's development, where the main task is differentiation—and then, indeed, autonomy is almost always conceived as the goal to be achieved.

The fact that most family therapy takes place when symptoms appear (i.e., around adolescence) has, in my view, created a bias in favor of autonomy. The differentiation of the individual in relation to the system he or she belongs to occupies a more important role than a secure and quality connection between those composing the system. Furthermore, as the therapeutic intervention usually involves a developmental task for the whole family system to move from one stage of the life cycle to another (e.g., a family with dependent children to a family with emancipated children), the interplay of these two forces is understood to be more about the vertical rather than the horizontal axis.

Also, although the interplay of autonomy and connection is almost always implied in the theory and practice of systemic family therapy, it has not been explicitly defined as an ongoing, necessary, and ever-changing dynamic within all systems at all stages throughout their life span. Such notions have not been clearly defined on a theoretical level. Neither has there been a theory in this field that has defined the parts of the system in terms of poles—e.g., masculine and feminine—that might in some way correspond to the horizontal axis. In fact, gender differences have been largely ignored in almost all domains and by almost all approaches, despite the existence of research and data that indicate important distinctions (e.g., men being significantly more prone to suffer certain mental disorders and women, others). The psychoanalytical approaches are probably the only exception to the rule, having at least explicitly acknowledged in their theories the existence of different genders.

Jungian Analysis

Jungian analysis postulates the existence of a layered psyche, both personal and collective, and an inner organization related to archetypes, the main ones being the self, shadow, anima, and animus. Animus would be the unconscious masculine side of a woman, and anima, the unconscious feminine side of a man.

This is the only piece of existing theory that somehow approaches the conceptualization of the present framework in terms of the inner organization of the masculine and the feminine. It suggests that the masculine and the feminine are present in every person and that the aspect that is not visible or expressed still forms part of the individual. The current framework coincides with this view in that it conceives the two poles existing in every individual (and, in a way, in every system composing an individual). It also shares the idea of one of the poles being more dominant but the other one continuing to exist (e.g., we are left- or right-handed but we still have two hands).

Apart from the above, there is not much more common ground between the two theories. The masculine and the feminine are understood here as expressions of the need for connection and autonomy, which also means that they are neither static nor necessarily gender related.

In general terms, the horizontal axis has not been much accounted for in psychological theory. It could be argued that the division between the schools of thought is itself a reflection of the divide, with cognitive-behavioral and medicalized approaches being more representative of autonomy (and left hemisphere functions) and those approaches that stress the importance of integration, emotion, or the client-therapist bond being more representative of connection (and the right hemisphere functions). But this is just a metaphor of the state of affairs, one of many reflecting our general bias toward the autonomy side of things, sometimes treating it as if it were the only existing pole (which may also explain why there is such little acknowledgment of the horizontal axis itself). It may also explain why we are so much more prone to argue and dissect rather than to come together and integrate.

The Vertical Axis

Psychodynamic Approaches

The individual's inner organization has been defined, described, and interpreted in numerous ways by different schools of thought within the second domain. The focus of what is defined here as the vertical axis involves the interplay between complementary, hierarchical levels, such as conscious-unconscious, cortical-subcortical, parent-child, and superego-id.

Within psychoanalysis—the first theoretical approach to design a map of inner processes—the inner organization of the individual is defined by the interaction of three agents: the id, the ego, and the superego. According to this view, the individual interacts with the world while primarily responding to inner forces or drives. Object relations theorists, coming from the psychoanalytic movement, placed greater importance on the external factor "objects" (e.g., the mother), claiming that the individual's inner organization is related to the internalization of primary objects or its representations, rather than the inner drives—a view that was also developed by Bowlby and his work on attachment. Attachment-based theories define inner processes in terms of "internal working models"—i.e., mental models or schemas derived and established from experience.

Transactional Analysis

In this work, the vertical divide has been defined to represent the subcortical and cortical parts of the brain, and, in order to describe the main corresponding dynamics at play within it, the metaphor of child and parent (or grown-up) has been used, as well as that of a horse and a rider. A working, balanced, and constructive interaction between the two has been described as adulthood. These metaphors echo the premises of transactional analysis (TA), as they were described by Eric Berne. According to Berne, the personality of the individual is structured around three constructs that are called ego states:

- *Parent* ("exteropsyche"): Contains what has been absorbed by our caregivers. Actions, emotions, thoughts, and behavior derived from this state are learned and involve the individual's unconscious mimicking of the caregivers on all of these levels.

- *Adult* ("neopsyche"): A state of the ego that is reflective. It processes internal and external information and can adjust its behavior, decisions, and predictions accordingly. The adult state involves reasoning, and its behavior is less predictable than that of the parent or the child. (A main goal of transactional analysis is to strengthen this ego state. The individual is guided toward an objective appreciation of reality.)

- *Child* ("archaeopsyche"): Berne defined this as the archaic state of the ego, which is also quite close to the definition given here as "primitive." According to Berne, this state is comprised of the ways the individual behaved, felt, and thought during the early years of childhood. In this state we find emotion, creativity, selfishness, fantasy, exploration, manipulation, tantrums, fascination, magical thinking, and any other expression that related to the way we behaved or perceived the world as children.

It could be argued that what Berne defines as child, parent, and adult states quite neatly correspond to what has been defined here as child (primitive, subcortical, or "horse"), grown-up (cortical or "rider"), and adult (a balanced relationship between the parent-child, cortical-primitive, or "rider-horse" parts). Berne's idea of "crossed transactions" (in which the ego state that responds to a stimulus is different than the one that was invited to respond) also echoes the ideas presented here on the main challenges regarding partners' communication. Thomas Harris's summary of the child being a felt concept, the parent being a taught concept, and the adult being a learned concept could also serve as a summary of the ideas presented here in relation to what has been defined as child, grown-up, and adult. Despite the parallels between these concepts and definitions, I was not aware of them until recently, having arrived at them from very different pathways (in what could be defined as another blind person landing on that one indivisible yet multi-interpreted "elephant").

TA stems from the second domain; it can be defined as relational, as its name suggests, but it is not systemic. In regard to the first domain, there has been some interest in linking TA theory to the brain, but these attempts have not yet been reflected on a more comprehensive, epistemological level. In my view, one of the main issues with TA is that—like many other theories—it has been construed as if it were to be a closed system, comprehensive and apparently complete in itself but not in a way that it can easily connect with other theories from its own or other domains.

In terms of the mind's inner workings and organization, one could argue that there is also a correspondence between Freud's id, ego, and superego and Berne's child, adult, and parent ego states. Nevertheless, Eric Berne is known to have broken with psychoanalysis due to unbridgeable differences between these concepts. Berne, for example, claimed that it would be "demonstrated that Parent, Adult, and Child are not concepts, like Superego, Ego, and Id, or the Jungian constructs, but phenomenological realities."[9] According to Berne, unlike the id and superego that reside in the preconscious and the unconscious, all three ego states (child, parent, and adult) remain in the conscious or preconscious areas. He also claims that each ego state has its own ego, superego, and id.[10]

Such seemingly abstract concepts tend to be perceived both as very close as well as distant to (or even competing with) one another. Close because, at least as I understand it, they describe the same territory; distant because they have often developed in apparent opposition to one another. The most brilliant among the theorists, after having approached "the elephant" from the standpoint of their mentors, would then become aware of other parts of it that were not accounted for and would move toward them. This movement involves a process of differentiation and probably a conflict of "loyalty," often leading to the creation of new theoretical schools (systems) that have been unable to "integrate" previous and new knowledge. Ironically, they have been unable to do as academics what they invite patients to do as clinicians: facilitate integration.

Interpersonal Reconstructive Therapy

Going back to the way inner organization has been conceived here in relation to the vertical division, the model that has served as a baseline to explain the interaction between the child and the parent, the primitive and the higher, the subcortical and the cortical brain, is to be found in the postulations of interpersonal reconstructive therapy (IRT), which introduced the concept of "the family in the head" or important person's internal representation (IPIR). This approach is also consistent with object relations theory, as well as attachment and internal working models theory.

Lorna Smith Benjamin's interpersonal reconstructive therapy framework is based on the understanding that interiorized early attachment patterns continue to inform an individual's affects, thinking, and behavior during adulthood. As explained in Benjamin's book *Interpersonal Reconstructive Therapy for Anger, Anxiety and Depression,*

> IRT is an integrative, interpersonal, and intrapsychic psychotherapy that is organized by the IRT case formulation that assesses each of a patient's presenting symptoms (one or more disorders) in relation to interactions between inherited proclivities (e.g. startle responses) and early lessons from caregivers about what to be afraid of (threat) and how to be safe (safety). Very briefly, the argument is that affective psychiatric symptoms represent miscued and maladaptive attempts to adapt to perceived stress. The method is copying automatically (be like him or her) <identification>, act as you

did with him or her <recapitulation>, and/or treat yourself as you were treated <introjection>. Such copying of messages about safety and threat is sustained by love for and loyalty to the copied loved ones. In IRT the focus is on these environmental contributions to what develops within the "envelope of potential" determined by the genome.[11]

The infant therefore internalizes the interactions that will then influence and inform the way she relates to the world later on in life. During childhood, the infant develops external relationships with her caregivers and the world. Simultaneously, the child develops an internal model based upon her experience or understanding (attributed meaning or fantasy) of these experiences.

According to this theory, if someone was abused as a child, she will then be likely to be abusive as an adult or form relationships in which she is abused and/or relate to herself in an abusive way. Internalizations will continue to inform the individual's affects, thoughts, and behavior during adulthood, even if the caregivers are not present anymore. The individual will continue to follow these patterns in an attempt to feel safe and achieve a sense of connection to the caregivers (who now exist as inner representations), seeking their approval and love.

According to Benjamin, every psychopathology is a gift of love, and the ideas presented in this book draw heavily from her conceptualizations. There are other unique features to her model that, as she states, "result from the appeal to the rules of evolution."[12] A great deal of my determination to link psychological theory to biology and evolution I owe to Benjamin. She was the first to point me in this direction. "According to natural biology," she says,

negative affective symptoms (e.g. anger, anxiety, depression) are not decontextualized "bad" internal energies that must be suppressed, expressed, controlled or redirected. Viewed as attempts to adapt, they are understood to be embedded in a sequence: perceived threat (C1), elicited affect (A) and predisposed behavior (B). An individual's C1AB sequences reflect modeling by early caregivers of what to fear and how to be safe. Such copying of behavioral information quintessentially relevant to survival is generally comparable to RNA copying DNA to pass along information about how to build bodily structures that have worked for the previous generations. The relatively new science of epigenetics explains how such copied information can be stored in ways that are inheritable. It adds to descriptions of expression and silencing, yet another way of understanding how information about the environment can be recorded by genes in order to support life in this and following generations.[13]

IRT's theoretical framework stems from the second domain and heavily focuses on the intrapsychic and individual inner organization, but it also includes the first and third domains. Within my own theoretical journey, IRT constituted one of my most important "eureka" moments (after the systemic one, many years ago), providing me with a key "piece" to this most fascinating and complex jigsaw puzzle of connecting the systemic and relational to the intrapsychic and the biological.

The "Primal System" and Other Perspectives

Transpersonal Psychology

Another important contribution to the ideas presented in this book comes from transpersonal psychology—specifically Ken Wilber's theoretical postulations, which involve both the vertical and the horizontal axes (and beyond). To start with, the ideas of *autonomy* and *connection* (originally drawn from attachment theory) also correspond to Wilber's ideas of *agency* and *communion* in relation to systems (or holons, as he has defined them).

The very definition of the term holon has been adopted here, as it is considered to be a more accurate term than that of a "system." A holon is a whole that is simultaneously a part of another whole. The term expresses both the wholeness and the partness of an entity, and therefore it indirectly accounts for the constant "struggle" of all elements to simultaneously connect (form wholes) and be autonomous (maintain their integrity as parts). The term *system* does not express this peculiarity of the way the world and nature are structured. In fact, I believe the word *system* may be preventing us from having a more accurate perception of the world and therefore develop theory further. The main reason I have opted to use the term *system* more than the term *holon* is because that the former is more familiar to the reader.

Wilber has also categorized all knowledge on holons in fours quadrants that corresponded to four different combinations of the "interior-exterior" of a holon or the holon in "individual-collective" (singular-plural) form:

1. interior-individual

2. exterior-individual

3. interior-collective (cultural)

4. exterior-collective (social)

At first, I was very excited about the apparent correspondence with the four domains I had devised to classify the existing approaches and knowledge on the human being, but I did manage to go too far with it after all. There is definitely a correspondence between first two domains, individual exterior and interior. I also toyed with the idea of the relational domain corresponding to "interior collective" and systemic to "exterior collective," but such correspondences are not that clear. It remains to be explored and studied further.

Wilber defines four drives of all holons: a pair of drives (agency and communion) described as operating horizontally, and a pair of forces (dissolution and transcendence) described as operating vertically. About dissolution, he writes:

> If a holon fails to maintain its agency and its communion, then it can break down completely. When it does break down, it decomposes to its subholons: cells decompose into molecules, which break down into atoms, which can be "smashed" infinitely under intense pressure. The fascinating thing about holon decomposition is that holons tend to dissolve in the reverse direction that they were built up. And this decomposition is "self-dissolution" or simply decomposing into subholons, which themselves can decompose into their subholons, and so on.[14]

It is interesting how Wilber links dissolution to a holon's failure to establish communion and agency, which in this book (defined as connection and autonomy) are both considered necessary for an organism's survival. It could be further argued that transcendence (understood here as "emergence" or emergent properties) can only take place when both pairs of forces (connection-autonomy and morphogenesis-homeostasis) are present and at play in a system.

Dissolution is a pull that has not been defined as such in this work. What is present instead is the pull of homeostasis (i.e., the pull to conserve). However, what is here defined as positive and negative feedback—that is, homeostasis and morphogenesis—could be conceived as the result of the combination of the two forces of dissolution and transcendence, as defined by Wilber, or even Freud's opposing life instinct "eros" and the death drive "thanatos." In other words, homeostasis could be defined as thanatos-within-eros, dissolution-within-transcendence, or death-within-life, while morphogenesis could be defined as eros-within-thanatos, transcendence-within-dissolution, or life-within-death. Similar to this book's connection and autonomy, the complementarity of the forces related to the vertical axis in both Wilber's and Freud's theories maintains and keeps the system alive and active. Under this light, a force without its counterbalance would be deadly for the system.

Here, the term *transcendence* is applied differently than it is by Wilber. The fourth pull (defined as transcendence by Wilber) is defined in this work as the pull of morphogenesis or evolution. If we were to define the four pulls in Wilber's terms, we would be talking about agency-communion and evolution-dissolution. *Transcendence* is a term that has been applied here to define a different phenomenon: that of emergence, the creation of something entirely new and original. In sum, combining systems theory with this revised version of Wilber's theory, homeostasis would then translate into "dissolution within evolution," morphogenesis to "evolution within dissolution," and transcendence, as stated before, to emergence.

Another part of the present theory that is very much in line with Wilber's postulations is that the process of evolution—in this case referring to the standard notion of evolution—always involves the past (previous structures and information) being included and setting the foundation (and an imperative) for the new to emerge. He claims that there is a directionality in evolution and that the drive of evolution is to increase *depth,* "to go beyond what went before, and yet to include what went before, and thus increase its own depth (. . .) its very nature is to transcend and include, and thus it has an inherent directionality."[15]

He describes evolution as a process of transcendence, the reverse process of dissolution:

> . . . the building-up process, the process of new holons emerging. How did inert molecules come together to form living cells in the first place? The standard, glib, neo-Darwinian explanation of *natural selection*— absolutely nobody believes this anymore. Evolution clearly operates in part by Darwinian natural selection, but this process simply selects those transformations that have *already* occurred by mechanisms that absolutely nobody understands.
>
> Take the standard notion that wings simply evolved from forelegs. It takes perhaps a hundred mutations to produce a functional wing from a leg—a half wing will not do. A half wing is no good as a leg and no good as a wing—you can't run and you can't fly. It has no adaptive value what-soever. In other words, with half wing you are dinner. The wing will only work if these hundred mutations happen *all at once,* in one animal—and also the same mutations must occur *simultaneously* in another animal of the opposite sex, and then they have to somehow find each other, have dinner, a few drinks, mate, and have offspring with real functional wings.
>
> Talk about mind-boggling. This is infinitely, absolutely, utterly mind-boggling. Random mutations cannot even begin to explain this. The vast, vast majority of mutations are lethal anyway; how can we get a hundred non-lethal mutations happening simultaneously? Or even, four or five for that matter? But once this incredible transformation has occurred, then natural selection will indeed select the better wings from the less workable wings—but the wings themselves? Nobody has a clue.[16]

I may not be able to accept Wilber's last statement, as I trust there are a lot of academics who do feel they have a clue and would probably build quite an argument against Wilber's stance. Yet I do agree with his theoretical posi-tion regarding evolution, distinguishing the drive to adapt from the drive to transcend. In systemic terms, adaptation would correspond to the positive feedback loop, while transcendence, as mentioned before, would correspond to emergence and emergent properties.

The Theory of Evolution

The theory of evolution has been used in this book as a fundamental theoretical framework. It connects to the biological aspects of human nature that are considered essential for the development of any psychological theory and for our understanding of humans in general. Evolution is generally defined as a process of descent via modification, responsible for the practically infinite variations of life-forms that exist on the planet.

What has been humbly suggested here is the existence of two more pulls:

1. *The pull "back"* (conservation): This pull, which preserves the organism's lineage, would account for the negative-feedback processes (or homeostasis, in systems terms). Homeostasis is already accounted for in regard to living organisms; the difference here is its purpose across time, as happens with positive feedback (adaptation) in the theory of evolution. Such "negative feedback" across time would provide a possible explanation for the human need to preserve heritage and identity in evolutionary terms too. The pull to conserve, as defined in this book, could be the counterpart of transcendence and emergent properties, since it "looks backward." It could be said that it is about keeping past information and structures ("conserved properties") across space and time. It may correspond to what Wilber has defined as "depth."

2. *The pull "up"* (transcendence): As described above by Wilber, adaptation and natural selection within the same species are considered to differ from transcendence and the emergence of new species. Here, the idea of transcendence is understood as an expression of evolution itself, as new species propel nature beyond what seemed to be its limits at innumerable stages in its evolution.

Psychological Theory and the Brain

One of the most important conceptual pillars of the new theory presented here is the idea that all theory related to human interaction, development, and behavior should ultimately be linked to the brain. Despite the complexity of such an enterprise, it is understood that scientific advances within the last decades have allowed us to have a more thorough view and understanding of the brain, to the point that such a bridge is now possible.

Nobel Prize winner neurobiologist and psychiatrist Eric Kandel provides five principles that enable such a bridge:

1. All mental processes are neural.

2. Genes and their protein products determine neural connections.

3. Experience alters gene expression.

4. Learning changes neural connections.

5. Psychotherapy changes gene expression.[17]

According to Kandel,

> A renewed involvement of psychiatry with biology and with neurology, therefore, not only is scientifically important but also emphasizes the scientific competence that, I would argue, should be the basis for the clinical specialty of psychiatry in the twenty-first century.[18]

It is further advocated here that all theory should converge in this way, not only within the field of psychiatry but also within all fields that study the human mind and behavior. No theory should exist in a vacuum, autonomously, without science backing it up, as religions do. Endorsement of psychology, psychiatry, and theory in general should not be a matter of faith. In order to achieve this, we would need to find a place to meet. The meeting point suggested here is the brain.

It is understood that at first clinicians had practically no access to the workings of the brain. They therefore developed theories of the human mind and behavior based on meticulous observations that, now that we do have more access to the brain, can finally be linked to neuroscientific knowledge and findings. Interpersonal neurobiology proposes such a conceptual framework.

Interpersonal Neurobiology

Also known as relational neurobiology, interpersonal neurobiology (IPNB) presents an interdisciplinary framework for the understanding of the human being. Its founder, Daniel J. Siegel, sought to bridge divisions such as nature versus nurture. He also attempted to bridge divisions between different scientific fields by exploring the interplay among the brain, the mind, and relationships.

The conceptual framework of IPNB is organized around the following ideas:

1. A core aspect of the human mind is an embodied and relational process that regulates the flow of energy and information within the brain and between brains.

2. The mind as an emergent property of the body and relationships is created within internal neurophysiological processes and relational experiences. In other words, the mind is a process that emerges from the distributed nervous system extending throughout the entire body, and also from the communication patterns that occur within relationships.

3. The structure and function of the developing brain are determined by how experiences, especially within interpersonal relationships, shape the genetically programmed maturation of the nervous system.[19]

Siegel goes on to say, "To put it simply, human connections shape neural connections, and each contributes to the mind."[20]

The theoretical stance of this book coincides with the premises of interpersonal neurobiology. It is understood that relationships have an impact on the brain and that the mind, as a regulator of inner processes and information, is conditioned by external (relationship) and internal (brain) factors, in an interplay that is continuous and circular. Mind, brain, and relationships form part of a continuum, influencing and giving shape to one another.

What is not present in this approach, which is nevertheless informed by systemic theory, is the view of the human system (e.g., couple or family) as a determining factor of individual behavior and relationships as a *system*— in other words, the impact the whole has on the parts, or how the whole conditions the parts that it is made up of. We could say that IPNB is an approach that takes into account the first and second domains, fully endorses the relational, but does not quite fully embrace the systemic approach—at least not as far as systemic family theory goes, according to which individuals cannot be understood if they are not (also) observed as parts of the main systems they belong to.

The relational, on the other hand, is thoroughly, efficiently, and skillfully accounted for. First of all, as attachment theory, systemic family therapy and other important approaches that include the relational domain do, IPNB stresses the importance of interpersonal experiences during early developmental years. IPNB claims that early interpersonal experiences with caregivers have a significant impact on brain development, linking the "attachment system" to the brain—and thus bridging the third domain to the first, as well as connecting them both to the second domain, the intrapsychic, through the proposition of relational experiences being encoded in implicit memory as mental models. As Siegel writes in *The Developing Mind*,

> "Attachment" is an inborn system in the brain that evolves in ways that influence and organize motivational, emotional, and memory processes with respect to significant caregiving figures. The attachment system motivates an infant to seek proximity to parents (and other primary caregivers) and to establish communication with them. At the most basic evolutionary level, this behavioral system improves the chances of the infant's survival (Main (1999),[21] Simpson and Belsky (2008)).[22] At the level of the mind, attachment establishes an interpersonal relationship that helps the immature brain use mature functions of the parent's brain to organize its own processes (Hofer 2006).[23] (. . .) Repeated experiences become encoded in implicit memory as expectations and then as mental models or schemata

of attachment, which serve to help a child feel an internal sense of what John Bowlby called a "secure base" in the world (Bowlby, 1969, 1988a).[24, 25]

The relevance of childhood experience has been underlined by all the main approaches to psychotherapy that have focused and explored individuals' subjective experience. Within the framework of interpersonal neurobiology, which encompasses and integrates attachment, it is assumed that dysfunctional early experiences, in which the caregiver has not been established as a "secure base," will result in attachment disorders that will, in turn, manifest in neural structures in the brain, which in turn influence individuals' perception of the world and people, and how they relate to them. This view coincides in all its main points with this book's theoretical framework. The main difference, as stated earlier in relation to attachment theory, is that attachment patterns are viewed as related to both internal and external factors, which implies that individual attachment styles and behaviors—though greatly conditioned by early childhood—are also understood to depend (and therefore potentially shift and change) in accordance with the needs, organization, functions, and conditions present within a given system at a given moment in time.

Conclusion

There is a common denominator in practically every approach cited here—namely, the importance of the notion and experience of integration as a therapeutic goal. Borrowing again the voice of Siegel, whose approach has been heavily cited here, due to its integrative demeanor: "A number of scientific disciplines support the proposal that integration is the core mechanism in well-being and optimal living."[26] Siegel uses as example Olaf Sporns' (2010) neural system approach[27] to illustrate his statement:

> The notion underlying this approach is that differentiation comes from segregation and specialization. Linkage is the resultant integration of these segregated, differentiated elements. In these terms, the movement toward

complexity is achieved by balancing differentiation and linkage. The most adaptive flow of a system arises when it moves toward maximizing complexity.[28]

In other words, evolution—"the movement toward complexity"—requires a balance between "differentiation and linkage" (autonomy and connection) and the elements that compose a system. Different approaches describe it in different ways. Still, integration is a notion that is widely shared as a desired, therapeutic—or evolutionary—goal. Discrepancies immediately arise in terms of *how* it can be achieved.

This book's stance is that what is therapeutic about psychotherapy is the experience of a functioning relationship within a well-functioning system, within the framework of sound theory. If the relationship with the therapist—and, consequently, other significant relationships—is not experienced as positive, constructive, and functional (promoting both connection and autonomy within and outside the therapeutic relationship), therapy does not take place. If theory fails, therapy does not take place either. The narrative that sustains the integrity and potential growth of everyone involved in the process—the story of WE—is essential. The changes in one's inner organization will therefore depend on a) the relationship between the client (individual, couple, or family) and the therapist, and b) the theory, "the story" that sustains the therapeutic process. This means that, clinically speaking, *what* professionals know is at least as important as how they put it into practice and how they relate to the client.

There are vast amounts of research that show that the effectiveness of therapy is immensely dependent on the quality of the relationship established with the professional. As Jeremy D. Safran and J. Christopher Muran put it, "After approximately a half century of psychotherapy research, one of the most consistent findings is that the quality of the therapeutic alliance is the most robust predictor of treatment success."[29] A good therapist, therefore—like any other human being that will have a positive impact and constructive effect on another—is, not only an expert in terms of academic, theoretical knowledge, but is also interpersonally skilled and has mastered the art of relating. This is also backed up by evidence. According to the same authors,

Another related finding is that some therapists are consistently more helpful than others; differences in therapist ability seem to be more important than therapeutic modality, and the more helpful therapists appear better able to facilitate the development of a therapeutic alliance.[30]

Or, as Bonnie Badenoch puts it, "Many years of research tell us that the single most important ingredient in effective therapy, regardless of paradigm, is the empathic capacity of the therapist."[31] With so much evidence available, one would expect that in order to achieve professional excellence schools of therapy would heavily focus on developing psychotherapy trainees' interpersonal skills, which is not the case. In the best of cases, there will be an emphasis on personal development, which is also extremely important (and may indirectly lead to building interpersonal skill too). But, interpersonally speaking, we are still too far behind. How many therapists have been specifically trained with the objective of building interpersonal competence, for instance? How many psychiatrists? The percentage is low. Extremely—and dangerously—low, in my view. I am only aware of one or two programs worldwide that stress the importance of such skills, that invite their trainees to actively work on and constructively change their most significant relationships, while also building interpersonal skills within the clinical setting. Such programs are the exception. The rule is for these aspects to be ignored, especially by the more mainstream clinical training programs. In Spain, for instance, a professional can get to work as a clinical psychologist in the public or private sector without having had a single hour developing their relational abilities in their training, or even developing themselves personally or interpersonally in any structured way. Psychotherapy or clinical psychology training (and even less so, psychiatric) does not focus on the mastery of this kind of competence, despite all the accumulated evidence pointing to the therapeutic relationship being precisely the one universal, top determining factor of a therapy's effectiveness.

Further, most approaches still predominantly focus on the client–therapist relationship and the inner maps and workings of an individual. This is, understandably, important. Yet, how can it be more important than helping people be more confident, comfortable, and competent within their most

significant relationships? If the therapist-client bond—being a p
artificial, conditional relationship, based on money exchange and ‿‿ ‿
place just a few hours per month—is considered to be so significant and
important to the point of having the power to reshape our brains, then what
could the impact be of the "real" relationships that matter to us the most and
take place closer to 24/7? What kind of impact could individuals who learn
to be skillful, constructive, and competent within their own relationships
have? In my view and experience, such impact is massive, and it is far more
important than that of a therapist. Just imagine, for example, a professional
psychotherapist telling you everything you have ever wished to hear about
yourself. Take a moment to feel the impact of those words on you. And
then do the same, thinking instead that it is your mother, father, partner,
sister, brother, or even mother-in-law pronouncing the same words. Whose
impact is greater? Therapists tend to go all the way to back of the list after
such a formulation.

So this work advocates that everyone should aim to be interpersonally
competent—and above all, mental health professionals whose entire work
and professional prowess is dependent upon their interpersonal skills. But
the interpersonal undoubtedly concerns the entire human species. Everyone
should be competent in these terms, capable of construing functional relationships with their partners, parents, friends, adversaries, and, above all,
their children. In an ideal world, psychotherapists would not be so gravely
needed. We could all help each other to feel loved and acknowledged, to
heal and grow.

NOTES

PART I

1.   I. Newton, *The Mathematical Principles of Natural Philosophy* (Oxford: B. Motte, 1729), 88. https://archive.org/details/newtonspmathema00newtrich/page/n87/mode/2up.

2.   H. Harlow, "The Nature of Love," *American Psychologist* 13, no. 12 (1958): 673–685; S. J. Suomi and H. A. Leroy, "In Memoriam: Harry F. Harlow (1905–1981)," *American Journal of Primatolology* 2 (1982): 319–342.

3.   M. Bowen, *Toward the Differentiation of Self in One's Family of Origin* (Northvale, NJ: Jason Aronson Inc., 1978), 529–547.

4.   L. S. Benjamin, *Interpersonal Reconstructive Therapy for Anger, Anxiety, and Depression* (Washington, DC: American Psychological Association, 2018), 20-21.

5.   L. Hoffman, *Foundations of Family Therapy: A Conceptual Framework for Systems Change* (New York: Basic Books, 1981); J. Lebow, A. Chambers, and D. Breunlin (eds), *Encyclopedia of Couple and Family Therapy* (Cham: Springer, 2019). https://doi.org/10.1007/978-3-319-15877-8_288.

6.   M. Smith and E. Karam, "Morphogenesis in Family Systems Theory" in J. Lebow, A. Chambers, and D. Breunlin (eds), *Encyclopedia of Couple and Family Therapy* (Cham: Springer, 2019). https://doi.org/10.1007/978-3-319-15877-8_288.

7.   H. Bergson, *Creative Evolution* (New York; Henry Holt and Company, 1911).

8.   G. G. Simpson, *Tempo and Mode in Evolution* (New York: Columbia Univ. Press, 1944).

9.   C. Lloyd Morgan, Emergent evolution : the Gifford lectures, delivered in the University of St. Andrews in the year 1922 (New York: Henry Holt and Company; London: William and Norgate, 1923). https://archive.org/details/emergentevolutio00morg_0/.

10.   K. Wilber, *A Brief History of Everything* (Dublin: Gill & Macmillan Ltd., 1969), 23.

11.   Ibid., 24.

12.   J. Bolte Taylor, *My Stroke of Insight* (New York: Penguin, 2009), 32.

13. Ibid., 33.
14. Ibid., 30-31.
15. Ibid., 28.
16. Ibid., 29.

PART II

1. J. Bolte Taylor, *My Stroke of Insight* (New York: Penguin, 2009), 18.
2. Ibid., 19.
3. B. Powell, G. Cooper, K. Hoffman, and B. Marvin, *Circle of Security Intervention: Enhancing Attachment in Early Parent-Child Relationships* (New York: Guilford Press, 2014), 52.
4. Ibid.
5. Ibid., 51–52.
6. Ibid., 53–54.
7. Ibid., 51.
8. Ibid., 55.
9. Ibid., 54–56.
10. Ibid., 26.
11. Ibid.
12. Ibid., 24.
13. B. Cyrulnik, *Psychoterápie de Dieu* (Paris: Odile Jacob, 2017).
14. See bibliography entries for Luigi Cancrini (2012, 2017).
15. H. Hurt, *Lost Tycoon: The Many Lives of Donald J. Trump* (Brattleboro, VT: Echo Point Books & Media, 2016).
16. J. L. Sampedro, *La Vieja Sirena* (Barcelona: Destino, 1991).
17. K. M. Hertlein, N. Gambescia, and G. R. Weeks, eds., *Systemic Sex Therapy* (New York: Routledge, 2019), 222.

PART III

1. "Omnia vincit amor" (Latin translation): Virgil, *Eclogae* 10.69.
2. P. Blumstein and P. Schwartz, *American Couples: Money, Work, Sex* (New York: William Morrow, 1983).

PART V

1. P. Watzlawick, J. Beavin Bavelas, and D. D. Jackson, *Pragmatics of Human Communication* (New York: W. W. Norton, 2011), 40.

2. Ibid., 37-38.

3. I. Sanchís, interview with Carmine Saccu, *La Vanguardia,* April 10, 2015. https://www.lavanguardia.com/lacontra/20150410/54429782744/la-contra-carmine-saccu.html.

4. A. Y. Napier and C. Whitaker, *The Family Crucible: The Intense Experience of Family Therapy* (New York: Harper Perennial, 1977), 117.

PART VI

1. D. Noriega, interview with Jorge Barudy, *El Diario,* November 11, 2019. https://www.eldiario.es/nidos/modelo-economico-actual-infanticida-psicologico_128_1268653.html.

2. A. de Saint-Exupéry, *The Little Prince* (New York: Mariner, 2000).

3. A. Y. Napier and C. Whitaker, *The Family Crucible: The Intense Experience of Family Therapy* (New York: Harper Perennial, 1977), 160–161.

4. Ibid., 154.

5. Ibid., 155.

6. Ibid., 88-89.

7. P. Watzlawick, J. Beavin Bavelas, and D. D. Jackson, *Pragmatics of Human Communication* (New York: W. W. Norton, 2011), 32-33.

8. R. Haim, "Narrative of the Allegory," as told by M. Kranc, "Heaven or Hell: A Corporate Fable," *Hodu,* February 4, 2011. https://web.archive.org/web/20110204060500/http:/hodu.com/parable.shtml.

9. B. Badenoch, *Being a Brain-Wise Therapist* (New York: W. W. Norton, 2008), 11.

10. Ibid., 33.

11. P. Cozolino, *The Neuroscience of Human Relationships: Attachment and the Developing Brain* (New York: Norton, 2006).

12. A. N. Schore, "The Science of the Art of Psychotherapy" (paper presented at a conference in Los Angeles, CA, 2007).

13. B. Badenoch, *Being a Brain-Wise Therapist* (New York: W. W. Norton, 2008), 23.

14. D. J. Siegel, foreword to B. Badenoch, *Being a Brain-Wise Therapist*, xiii.

15. A. Y. Napier and C. Whitaker, *The Family Crucible: The Intense Experience of Family Therapy*

(New York: Harper Perennial, 1977), 225.

16. Ibid.

17. W. Blake, "Auguries of Innocence" in D.V. Erdman (ed.), *The Complete Poetry and Prose of William Blake* (New York: Anchor Books, 1982), 490. https://archive.org/details/complete-poetrypr00blak/page/490/mode/2up.

18. N. Kazantakis, *The Greek Passion,* translated by J. Griffin (New York: Simon & Schuster, 1954).

PART VII

1. E. R. Kandel, *Psychiatry, Psychoanalysis, and the New Biology of Mind* (Washington, DC: American Psychiatric Publishing, Inc., 2005).

2. A. Einstein, quoted in W. Sullivan, "The Einstein Papers. A Man of Many Parts," *The New York Times,* March 29, 1972. https://www.nytimes.com/1972/03/29/archives/the-einstein-papers-a-man-of-many-parts-the-einstein-papers-man-of.html.

3. K. Wilber, *A Brief History of Everything* (Dublin: Gill & Macmillan Ltd., 1969), 52.

4. 4.B. Cyrulnik, "The Social Brain" (online seminar organized by Hestia: International Psycho-therapy Centre, September 2020).

5. L. Mineo, "Good Genes Are Nice, but Joy Is Better," *The Harvard Gazette,* April 11, 2017. https://news.harvard.edu/gazette/story/2017/04/over-nearly-80-years-harvard-study-has-been-showing-how-to-live-a-healthy-and-happy-life/.

APPENDIX

1. C. R. Snyder and C. E. Ford, *Coping with Negative Life Events: Clinical and Social Psychological Perspectives* (Medford, MA: Springer Science, 2013), 12.

2. C. E. Shannon and W. Weaver, *The Mathematical Theory of Communication* (Champaign, IL: University of Illinois Press, 1949).

3. N. Wiener, *Cybernetics; or, Control and Communication in the Animal and the Machine* (Paris: Technology Press, 1948).

4. L. von Bertalanffy, *General System Theory: Foundations, Development, Applications* (New York: George Braziller, Inc., 1968), 32. https://monoskop.org/images/7/77/Von_Berta-lanffy_Ludwig_General_System_Theory_1968.pdf.

5. A. Y. Napier and C. Whitaker, *The Family Crucible: The Intense Experience of Family Therapy* (New York: Harper Perennial, 1977), 48–49.

6. J. Bowlby, Attachment and Loss, Vol. 1 (New York: Random House, 1997), 14.

7. Ibid.

8. K. Hoffman, G. Cooper, and B. Powell, *Raising a Secure Child* (New York: Guilford Press, 2017), 63.

9. E. Berne, *Transactional Analysis in Psychotherapy* (New York: Grove Press, 1961), 4.

10. T. White, "Freud and Berne: Theoretical Models of Personality," *Australasian Journal of Transactional Analysis* 2, no. 1 (March 1980): 18-19. https://admin99.files.wordpress.com/2011/12/freud-and-berne.pdf.

11. L. S. Benjamin, *Interpersonal Reconstructive Therapy for Anger, Anxiety and Depression* (Washington, DC: American Psychological Association, 2018), 4-5.

12. Ibid., x.

13. Ibid.

14. K. Wilber, *A Brief History of Everything* (Dublin: Gill & Macmillan Ltd., 1969), 22.

15. Ibid., 41.

16. Ibid., 23.

17. T. R. Insel, "A New Intellectual Framework for Psychiatry," in E. R. Kandel, ed., *Psychiatry, Psychoanalysis, and the New Biology of Mind* (Washington, DC: American Psychiatric Publishing, Inc., 2005), 27.

18. E. R. Kandel "A New Intellectual Framework for Psychiatry" in E. R. Kandel, ed., *Psychiatry, Psychoanalysis, and the New Biology of Mind* (Washington, DC: American Psychiatric Publishing, Inc., 2005), 54.

19. D. J. Siegel, *The Developing Mind* (New York: Guilford Press, 2012), 3.

20. Ibid.

21. M. Main, "Mary D. Salter Ainsworth: Tribute and Portrait," *Psychoanalytic Inquiry* 19, no. 5 (1999): 682–736.

22. J. A. Simpson and J. Belsky, "Attachment Theory within a Modern Evolutionary Framework," in J. Cassidy and P. R. Shaver, eds., *Handbook of Attachment: Theory, Research, and Clinical Applications*, 2nd ed. (New York: Guilford Press, 2008), 131–157.

23. M. A. Hofer, "Psychobiological Roots of Early Attachment," *Current Directions of Psychological Science* 15, no. 2 (2006): 84–88.

24. J. Bowlby, Attachment and Loss: Vol. (New York: Basic Books, 1969); J. Bowlby, *A Secure Base: Parent-Child Attachment and Healthy Human Development* (New York: Basic Books,

1988).

25. D. J. Siegel, *The Developing Mind,* 91.

26. Ibid., 337.

27. O. Sporns, "Brain Networks and Embodiment," in B. Mesquita, L. F. Barret, and E. R. Smith, eds., *The Mind in Context* (New York: Guilford Press, 2010), 42–64.

28. D. J. Siegel, *The Developing Mind,* 337.

29. J. D. Safran and J. C. Muran, *Negotiating the Therapeutic Alliance: A Relational Treatment Guide* (New York: Guilford Press, 2012), 1.

30. Ibid.

31. B. Badenoch, *Being a Brain-Wise Therapist* (New York: W. W. Norton, 2008), 5.

BIBLIOGRAPHY

Badenoch, B. *Being a Brain-Wise Therapist: A Practical Guide to Interpersonal Neurobiology.*
New York: W. W. Norton, 2008.

Bateson, G. *Mind and Nature: A Necessary Unity (Advances in Systems Theory, Complexity, and the Human Sciences).* New York: Hampton Press, 1979.

———. *Steps to an Ecology of Mind: Collected Essays in Anthropology, Psychiatry, Evolution, and Epistemology.* Chicago: University of Chicago Press, 1972.

Bateson, G., D. Jackson, J. Haley, and J. Weakland. "Toward a Theory of Schizophrenia." Behavioral Science 1, no. 4 (1956): 251–264.

Benjamin, L. S. *Interpersonal Diagnosis and Treatment of Personality Disorders.* 2nd ed. New York: Guilford Press, 1996.

———. *Interpersonal Reconstructive Therapy: An Integrative, Personality-Based Treatment for Complex Cases.* New York: Guilford Press, 2003.

———. *Interpersonal Reconstructive Therapy for Anger, Anxiety, and Depression: Healing Broken Hearts, Not Broken Minds.* Washington, DC: American Psychological Association, 2018.

Berne, E. *Games People Play.* New York: Grove Press Inc., 1964.

———. *Transactional Analysis in Psychotherapy.* New York: Grove Press Inc., 1961.

Bolte Taylor, J. *My Stroke of Insight.* New York: Penguin, 2009.

Bowen, M. *Family Therapy in Clinical Practice.* Northvale, NJ: Jason Aronson Inc., 1978.

Bowlby, J. *Attachment and Loss.* Vol. 1, *Attachment.* New York: Appleton-Century-Crofts, 1969.

Caillé, P. *Uno más uno son tres: La pareja revelada a sí mísma.* (Paidós Terapia Familiar.) Barcelona: Ediciones Paidós, 1992.

Cancrini, L. *Ascoltare i bambini: Psicoterapia delle infanzie negate.* Milan: Cortina Raffaello, 2017.

———. *La cura delle inanzie infelici: Viaggio nell'origine dell'oceano borderline.* Milan: Cortina

Rafaello, 2012.

———. *L'oceano borderline: Racconti di viaggio*. Milan: Cortina Rafaello, 2006.

Cyrulnik, B. *Psyhothérapie de Dieu*. Paris: Odile Jacob, 2017.

———. *Sous le signe du lien*. New York: Hachette, 1989.

Ecker, B. *Unlocking the Emotional Brain: Eliminating Symptoms at Their Roots Using Memory Reconsolidation*. New York: Routledge, 2012.

Haley, J. *The Power Tactics of Jesus Christ and Other Essays*. New York: Crown, 1986.

———. *Uncommon Therapy: The Psychiatric Techniques of Milton H. Erickson, M.D.* New York: W. W. Norton, 1972.

Harris, T. A. *I'm OK—You're OK*. New York: HarperCollins, 1967.

Hertlein, K. M., G. R. Weeks, and N. Gambescia. *Systemic Sex Therapy*. 2nd ed. New York: Routledge, 2015.

Hill, D. *Affect Regulation Theory: A Clinical Model*. New York: W. W. Norton, 2015.

Hoffman, K., G. Cooper, and B. Powell. *Raising a Secure Child*. New York: Guilford Press, 2017.

Jackson, D. Communication, *Family and Marriage*. Vol. 1, Human Communication. Palo Alto, CA: *Science & Behavior Books,* 1968.

Kandel, E. R. Psychiatry, *Psychoanalysis, and the New Biology of Mind*. Washington, DC: American Psychiatric Publishing, Inc., 2005.

Koestler, A. *The Ghost in the Machine*. 1990 reprint ed. New York: Penguin, 1967.

LeDoux, J. *The Emotional Brain*. London: Orion Publishing Group, 1998.

Levine, A., and R. S. F. Heller. Attached: *The New Science of Adult Attachment and How It Can Help You Find—and Keep—Love*. London: Penguin, 2011.

Minuchin, S. *Families and Family Therapy*. Cambridge, MA: Harvard University Press, 1974.

Napier, A. Y., and C. Whitaker. *The Family Crucible: The Intense Experience of Family Therapy*. New York: Harper Perennial, 1977.

Porges., S. W. *The Pocket Guide to the Polyvagal Theory: The Transformative Power of Feeling Safe*. New York: W. W. Norton, 2017.

Powell, B., G. Cooper, K. Hoffman, and B. Marvin. *Circle of Security Intervention: Enhancing Attachment in Early Parent-Child Relationships*. New York: Guilford Press, 2014.

Safran, J. D., and J. C. Muran. *Negotiating the Therapeutic Alliance: A Relational Treatment Guide*. New York: Guilford Press, 2000.

Siegel, D. J. *The Developing Mind: How Relationships and the Brain Interact to Shape Who We Are*. New York: Guilford Press, 2012.

————. *Pocket Guide to Interpersonal Neurobiology*. New York: W. W. Norton, 2012.

Vaillant, G. E. *Aging Well: Surprising Guideposts to a Happier Life from the Landmark Harvard Study of Adult Development*. New York: Little, Brown and Company, 2003.

Watzlawick, P., J. Beavin Bavelas, and D. D. Jackson. *Pragmatics of Human Communication*. New York: W. W. Norton, 1967.

Whitaker, C. A. *Midnight Musings of a Family Therapist*. New York: W. W. Norton, 1989.

Wilber, K. *A Brief History of Everything*. Dublin: Gill & Macmillan Ltd., 1969.

Willi, J. *Couples in Collusion*. Lanham, MD: Rowman & Littlefield, 1996.

ACKNOWLEDGMENTS

I am deeply grateful to all the people who have contributed, in one way or another, to this book: those who shared with me the life experiences to base it upon; those who inspired me with the ideas that sustain it; those who believed in me and motivated me to take them further; those who stood by my side during the whole process; those who helped me with the actual process; and those who patiently had to "suffer" through the process.

First of all, thank you to my husband, "the man of the future," as I like to call him. He believed in this project from the very beginning (even before I did) and has given me immense amounts of unconditional support every step of the way over the past years. His interpersonal mastery has also pushed me to grow and learn in real-life terrain. Thank you, Greg, for everything—for being the best partner and father to our children I could have ever wished for.

A big thanks also to our children, Danae and Alex, for all the beauty and learning they have brought into our lives; for reminding us, above all, that in favorable conditions, every human expression can be simply divine. I would also like to thank them for their patience. This book has been another "baby" in the family that has needed extreme amounts of time and attention. Thank you for having welcomed it and turned it into another member of the clan and a common project.

Thanks to my parents, Kathy and Apostolos, for being the first to show me, in the most unforgettable, experiential way, how relationships can work and, also, how exquisitely dysfunctional they can get. Thank you for all your teachings on autonomy and connection, on love and independence, on the most beautiful aspects of the human being and, at the same time, on the great pain relationships can entail. Thank you for being there at all times, for giving me the strongest roots and wings I could possibly have, and for managed to base your relationship on love, care, and respect for one other. Special thanks also to my other set of "parents"—my godparents, Maria Mavrou and Eudoxos Petridis—who have always provided me with immense amounts of love and support, an alternative safe base, and the opportunity to experience a very different kind of relationship.

Another very special thanks to Ana Checo for being one of the most remarkable mothers-in-law one could have; she is an extraordinary, wise woman who has been both an inspiration and an invaluable support to me. Thanks also to Marites Aguito Dela Cruz, another member of what is now our extended family, who took care of everything we could not. Women such as these two may remain behind the scenes, but nothing could happen without their extraordinary contribution. They are the roots that nurture. They may be invisible, but it is thanks to them that the visible is sustained.

Talking about extraordinary women: my sister, Christina Doumpioti. Thank you for your insight and invaluable support; for making me feel so great when you have always really been the great one; for always being there to celebrate every big and small success; and for your unfathomable beauty, inside and out.

To my troop of dearest friends (and another set of extraordinary women): Christina Barpaki, Hari Volioti, Anna Printezi, Tina Kamma-Lorger, Rena Psifidou, Stella Grimpa, Cristina Llagostera, Bet Font, Elena Luaces, Ana Garcia, Marina Martínez, and Erika García. Thank you for being there, for the greatness of your spirit and hearts; for cheering me on along the way. I am so fortunate to be your friend and have you in my life.

My beloved colleague, Gaudalupe Fernández: you are one of a kind, and one of the first to know about this project, to believe in it, to push me to get it done. Thank you for your invaluable help in making this book—and so much else!—happen.

I am also deeply grateful to three very important pillars in my life, the mentors who have been there to show me the way and guide me through some of the most difficult moments in my life. Thank you, Pamela Corin, Gemma Baulenas, and Josep Checa: for your strength, integrity, and wisdom; for showing me the way back to myself; and for being models to follow on how to be of service. There have been more people who have provided me with invaluable support and wings to "fly": Aleksandar "Sasha" Pavlicevic, Joy Fernández, Steve Potter, Juan Luis Linares, Carlos Lamas, Myriam Guttiérez, Susana Vega, Jaci Molins and, most recently and especially, Alberto Gimeno. You have all been there at the right time, having contributed to important turning points in my life.

I want to also thank the authors cited in this book (and so many more who are not), all the pioneers and brilliant minds who have opened the way and have pushed the field of mental health forward, including Sigmund Freud, Melanie Klein, John Bowlby, Harry Harlow, Gregory Bateson, Jay Haley, and Carl Whitaker. Within this practically infinite list, I would underline the contribution of Boris Cyrulnik, for the impact his work and epistemological framework have had on mine in recent years.

This project would have not been possible without my professional "parents": Luigi Cancrini and Lorna Smith Benjamin, who would have been mentioned in the previous paragraph were they not so extremely special to me. Their contribution in the past decade has been immense. Thank you, Lorna, for providing me with an exquisite theoretical framework that helped me bring my own knowledge and theory together. A master in seeing patterns, in discerning the simple within the complex, you helped me rework my thinking. You also reactivated in me the love for science, for rigor, for investigation. Thank you, Luigi—a.k.a. "Prof."—for helping me reacclimate my heart as a professional; for reminding me that we are not problems that need solving, but loving human beings who hurt; for showing me how to see with the heart or "la panza"; for challenging my ideas, giving me food for thought, and generously sharing your infinite knowledge and wisdom; for helping me and the whole team at Hestía grow—and glow. You are the wisest and most exceptional professional father I could have ever had.

My professional team: for being the best possible crowd to learn and grow with, to be challenged and also supported by; for believing in projects even when there was nothing there to believe in; for being a group of beautiful people, both personally and professionally; for providing learning, inspiration, questioning, fun, joy, and a safe haven to the people we attend (and to each other); and for setting an amazing example of real-life integration, clinically and culturally speaking. The richness of this experience is the very fabric of this book.

From within the team, special thanks to Amy Bramley for having put vast amounts of her time—without any to spare!—into reading the text, sharing ideas, and supporting me in the final stages of this process. Thank you for your generosity, first-class intellect, and invaluable support! Another special thanks to Nina Frerich, Adelaide Margiotta, and Carol Bastides, for teaming up with me to further study, organize, and explore the ideas in this book and further our work with couples in general. Thank you to Emilia Lecaro, for providing me with her exquisite care and support; and Marga Ulrich and Marcos Silfa, for their ideas and designs, and for supporting and nurturing this project both directly and indirectly.

A very special thank you to my editor, Melanie Madden, who has been the best partner I could have ever wished for—my "other half"—during this process. She saw the book's potential, suggested how to "take it apart," and showed me the way to put it back together again, to its best possible version. Good editors and good therapists work in very similar ways, I have come to realize. Thank you for your vision, insight, and pushing toward excellence—even if that meant so much more work for both of us. Thank you for accompanying me in such a meaningful way along this path. There have been more professionals involved in this long, long process who I am also grateful to: David Ter-Avanesyan, for the interior layout; Matt Davies, for the cover design; and Karen Levy, for the final edits.

Finally, thank you to everyone I have had a relationship with, "good" or bad"—the most challenging having been my most important schools in life. Thanks to friends and partners with whom I have had the chance to share a common project, for all the learning our spontaneous emotional laboratories provided—very often despite ourselves.

And above and beyond everything, thank you to all the people who invited me to accompany them for a while in their life paths as a professional—students and clients alike. Thank you for letting me travel with you. Thank you for showing me the way, for pushing me to be a better version of myself, a better therapist, a better teacher, and a better human being. Thank you for being such great teachers.

A very final thanks to our beautiful world and its resources, which sustains us and keeps all alive. There is nothing if there is no context.

INDEX

ABOUT THE AUTHOR

Dimitra Doumpioti was born in Thessaloniki and raised in Volos, Greece. The daughter of a civil engineer and a biologist, she chose to study psychology when she was sixteen, after her experience as an exchange student in the United States. She obtained her bachelor's degree (honors) in psychology from the University of Manchester and was hired as a research assistant at the Department of Developmental Psychology, in conjunction with the Max Planck Institute (Leipzig, Germany), under professors Elena Lieven and Michael Tomasello. Simultaneous to this, she completed postgraduate studies in transpersonal psychology at Liverpool's John Moores University.

Dimitra's decision to return to the Mediterranean rather than pursue an academic career in her mid-twenties marked an important turning point in her life. She relocated to Barcelona and rebuilt her life from scratch, learning a new language to fluency and initiating four years of study in systemic relational therapy. In 2005, she founded Hestía, an international psychotherapy center offering services in multiple languages. It soon became a reference point in the city of Barcelona. Over the years, Hestía has grown to become a psychotherapy training center with strong links to the Centro Studi in Rome, overseen by Professor Luigi Cancrini.

Since 2015, Dimitra has commuted to Rome monthly (online during the pandemic) as part of her training as a psychotherapy supervisor. Since 2016, she has also been an academic collaborator at ESADE, a prestigious business school in Barcelona. Her work and thinking have been significantly influenced by her varied life experiences and endeavors—which include sports at a competitive level; traveling; and studies in music, dance, painting, and language—as well as those of her clients. A mother of two, she has been happily married for fifteen years.

Printed in Great Britain
by Amazon

60787920R00151